MORE THAN JUST A JOB

Worker Cooperatives in Canada

by **Constance Mungall**

Steel Rail

Canadian Cataloguing in Publication Data

Mungall, Constance
   More than just a job: worker cooperatives
in Canada

ISBN 0-88791-034-3

1. Cooperative societies — Canada
I. Title

HD3448.M96 1986   334'.0971   C86-090328-1

Typeset and printed in Canada by a unionized worker co-op, Our Times
Cover by Emerging Design

ISBN 0-88791-034-3

Steel Rail Publishing
P.O. Box 4357, Stn. E.
Ottawa, Canada
K1S 5B3

CONTENTS

FOREWORD

I come from B.C. When the Socreds introduced cutbacks in government services there three years ago, my family and friends felt hit by a ton of bricks: jobs threatened, seniority wiped out, young families fearing the loss of homes they'd built themselves. Forget the government, I told them. Your jobs still need doing. Your services are still needed. Offer them directly. Easy for me to say, maybe, with years of conducting my own business as a freelance writer under my belt. Hard for a young ferry boat crewman to do, or a social worker or a nurse used to working in a big social services system. But not impossible.

At the same time, back in Ottawa, I myself was feeling hampered by the bureaucracy I was then part of, my creativity stifled by my lack of choice about when, where and how I worked. In February 1984, I joined a small group of idealistic people. Like me, most of them them felt over-employed and under-productive. Some, like my B.C. friends, were un-employed.

The group had come out of the Unemployment Committee of the Ottawa District Labour Council, which had asked me for a meeting about worker co-ops in late 1983. The participants broke into two groups, one to dis-cuss the theory and philosophy of employment co-ops. The other, which later became Cooperative Enterprises, wanted to actually found and oper-ate one or more worker co-ops.

We met every two weeks, pooled a list of possible projects, and discussed the pros and cons of each. We considered manufacturing devices for the disabled, taking over a campground from the government and operating it, and producing, packaging and distributing gourmet health foods, among other ideas.

Then my son got multiple sclerosis. This major family crisis tended to sharpen my values and the feeling that I must go for the best in every aspect of my life, including work. My government job paid well and was not actively destructive, but I knew from earlier experience as a journalist and radio documentary maker that it was not the most gratifying and use-ful work I could do. I took a year's leave of absence to do peace work for the Quakers across the country. My fellow cooperators suggested that during my travels I could collect the experiences of other groups like ours. That would help us know what might work and what wouldn't work. Moreover, it would be a good complement to my peace work: a challenge to the hierarchy that makes both inner peace and the outer man-ifestation of it difficult.

My colleagues helped me develop a list of questions, and they contribut-ed $25 each to help with extra expenses. At first the idea was to gather the information for our group only. But early on my instincts as a communicator emerged. The stories I was recording were so fresh, so real, so practical, so touching — so relevant to what every group with our ideas had to sort out — that I could see the broader use of them. Other Canadians should know what was going on in approximately 350 small groups in all cities and some isolated valleys across the country. We could gain ideas and comfort from the courage and initiative of these pioneer worker cooperators.

I came back from my sojourn anxious to pass on what I'd learned. A grant from the Canada Council, and help from the Ontario Arts Council and Communityworks, an Ottawa resource group, paid for the travel and expenses of transcribing the taped interviews. Terry Binnersley, a member of Steel Rail Publishing, itself a cooperative, game me good if sometimes harried support. Susan O'Leary, a summer student at Steel Rail, gave me research back-up. Skip McCarthy, back in Ottawa from the University of Saskatchewan Centre for the Study of Co-operatives, vetted the manuscript. And finally, my own group, Cooperative Enterprises, continued to encourage me and more important, to evolve. I would like to thank them all. And I would like to dedicate this book to my father and mother, Denis and Joyce Taylor, who were both workers.

— Constance Mungall
Ottawa, October 1986

PART I
The Stories We Tell Ourselves

CHAPTER ONE
The What, Why and Where of Worker Cooperatives

This book is about working together. Working in groups of people who cooperatively own and control the enterprise they work in. Not new to Canadians. In fact, working together has been so much a part of the development and settlement of this country that we've taken it for granted. This often happens — the people or the ideas that are the most important to us are the ones we are least aware of until for some reason they jolt into our consciousness. But ignoring them, for whatever reason, can be dangerous, because the stories we tell ourselves — the myths our society creates — deeply affect the ways we act and the institutions we develop for ourselves to live within.

Recognizing and being proud of our ability to compete, we've made laws to facilitate and regulate competition. We've overlooked that other major drive of people in general and Canadians in particular — to cooperate. So when we industrialized, we forgot to institutionalize cooperation, to make laws and give grants to stimulate it. This despite our long history of cooperation, and the fact that we still work together to rebuild after a storm, or to help a sick or injured neighbour with the harvest.

This book tells some of the stories we've neglected — how people are joining together to make a living cooperatively.

What is a worker co-op? The simple answer: a business enterprise that's owned and controlled by the people who work in it. The workers hold the basic ownership or membership rights in the company. There are two paramount membership rights. First, the right to vote equally: one-person/one-vote. Second, the right to share any profits the company makes.

Today in Canada there are about 350 operating worker co-ops. Their numbers have nearly doubled in just the past five years.

I myself am eager to leave behind the theorizing and to get into the rest of the book, where some of these real people talk about their real problems and their solutions. My goal is to help all of us who want to evolve better working lives make decisions with some knowledge of what has and has not worked. But worker co-ops are rare enough in Canada so that many people still ask, "What are they?" and only then consider how the concept might be useful at some point in their own working lives. Much of this chapter is therefore about what worker cooperatives are, how they compare to other enterprises, and where they can be found.

The worker cooperative movement is world-wide. The International Committee of Workers and Artisans counted the number of worker or artisanal cooperatives in the world as around 91,000 in 1983, with more than 23 million members. While membership in other types of cooperatives increased at the rate of 30 percent, worker co-ops took off. The number more than doubled between 1975 and 1983. And the number of members quadrupled. These international statistics indicate that what's happening today in Canada is part of a strong and vital world-wide movement.

Why this international trend? The reason is need: people need work. And in this time of economic, social, political change, job patterns are shifting. Whole industries are disappearing, others emerging. Government cutbacks and talk of privatization strike fear into people over 50, fear that they'll never work again. New technology changes everything. Young people with years of professional training are repairing bicycles and washing dishes for a living, if they're lucky.

As a response to this need, worker co-ops create jobs more cheaply than any other job creation activity. And the jobs have a far better survival rate. In the U.S., eight in ten employee-owned companies survive five years — a reversal of the usual statistics for small businesses.

Add to the virtues of job creation and stability another advantage: worker co-ops give a community more control over its own economic development. More than one community has been saved by its cooperatives. Fogo Island, Newfoundland is one. The cooperative there began in 1968, after the Newfoundland government started to move people from small communities considered difficult to service into larger "growth centres." The privately run fish companies closed up business on Fogo Island. But the people decided to stay. They started a combination fishery producer and worker cooperative, and rebuilt and enlarged the abandoned fish landing facilities.

From 1967 to 1985, the population rose by 20 percent to more than 5,000. The number of fishermen went to 620 from 374. Their annual earnings from fishing, in stable dollars, stayed about the same. The number of fish plant workers increased even more, to 475 from 60, and their earnings went up. Sales volume went to $5.9 million from $657,000; even with inflation that is a significant increase. Only one figure declined: the number of welfare recipients, to 75 from 257.

This success story covers all the bases. It models an effective way to respond to economic and social change while keeping families and community together. However, today, most workers are in cities, and that's where most worker cooperatives are too. Here, there's another push beside the basic desperate need for survival. People are demanding more quality in their working lives these days. Despite unemployment, they're changing jobs voluntarily more often, asking for part time work, flexible work options and a freedom to define their own working life and environment.

My own life is a constant push and shove between a passion to be responsible for myself and what I produce and a need to share, to live and work with other people, and to somehow make a compromise between their needs and mine, or better still, to integrate them.

Guy Donsey, a British writer who has published several books on unemployment and is now working in local employment development in Winnipeg, calls this attitude "a hidden revolution . . . very different to the expectations that we were reared with . . . that you get a job in your early 20s or when you leave school, and you work at that job until you retire . . . told when to have a holiday . . . told when to go off for training . . . told when to retire, and it's all looked after by someone else."

Not so in a worker cooperative. Here, you are responsible for your own enterprise. You are extending democracy to your workplace. The trend towards cooperation in the workplace is only part of a larger, older movement. A 1983 study done by the Canadian Unity Information Office showed that 43 percent of Canadians 18 years and over were members of at least one cooperative organization. That means between eight and ten million people have organized to control and own the enterprises they use. They share this drive with worker co-ops, and they cover a wide variety of economic and social activities, from grain handling and fish processing to financial services, from providing housing to running taxi companies and day-care centres.

Most of these cooperative enterprises are financial services — credit unions, caisses populaires. In Quebec, the oldest caisse populaire, the Desjardins system, founded in 1900, has over five million members and more branches than all the chartered banks in the province put together. In addition, more than a million Canadians belong to retail co-ops, with annual sales of $7 million. A smaller but still significant number, 100,000, live in non-profit housing cooperatives. Producer and marketing co-ops, vital to farmers' survival, can be big business. United Grain Growers, along with the three western wheat pools, annually make the "Financial Post 500" of Canada's largest corporations. So does Agropur in Quebec, the biggest dairy enterprise in the country — most of us don't know it, but cooperative dairies market 80 percent of Canada's dairy products. Next to the government, cooperatives in the Arctic employ more native people than any other type of business. Membership, which often includes a whole community, represents 85 percent of the Inuit and 25 percent of the Dene population.

These producer, financial, consumer and housing cooperatives account for nearly all the close to 9,000 cooperatives in Canada, and they themselves altogether employ over 70,000 people. But those 70,000 often have no more control over their work conditions than any other hourly paid or salaried employee. It is the 350 worker co-ops which are experimenting with new structures and new relationships in the work place, where control is in the hands of the workers. Their goal is not return on money investment, but work: maintenance of a good job in good working conditions, and a product or service the worker can be proud of.

Worker cooperatives are functioning in almost all economic sectors: service, sales, manufacturing, forestry, fish processing . . . you name it. The details of their operations are as diverse. Among the 16 employee-owned companies I visited, some are incorporated as cooperatives, and others as corporations with internal by-laws that protect their cooperative status. In some the financial equity held by each worker was the same; in others it varied widely; in some non-members had equity too. In all but one, each member-worker had one vote.

Some of the companies I explored had government funding — and periodically rued the fact. All were under-capitalized. All were working out new ways and dealing with new relationships — and some personality conflicts — as a result. Some were in danger of burning out. All could have done with and lacked professional advice — legal and management, financial and marketing, and conflict resolution — from their point of view as cooperatives, not from the established, hierarchical point of view. "Pack up the co-op and become a regular business," advised more than one unsympathetic accountant, bewildered by the different values, the emphasis on product and work satisfaction rather than on financial profit.

Of the 13 companies I interviewed on my first, 1984, sojourn (I added three later, to balance the coverage), one, the sealers' cooperative, was still being planned, and the rest were between one and 17 years old when I visited. One had converted to a partnership before our interview. In my updating, I discovered that all are surviving now, two years after our original interviews, although another has converted to a private ownership. Compare that to the statistics of 50 percent failure in the first two years for small businesses in Canada.

When we define a worker cooperative in Canada we obviously have to take account of all this diversity. The basic definition remains: worker-owned and -controlled equals one-person/one-vote, and workers share the profits.

In a worker co-op the membership rights to vote and profit are *personal rights* which are assigned to the workers in a company because they work there, not because they bought stock in it. David P. Ellerman, of the Industrial Cooperative Association, a Boston-based resource group that gives services for a fee, makes this more precise definition. He compares a worker cooperative to a municipality where voting rights are not property rights which may be auctioned to the highest bidder, but are non-transferable personal rights attached to the functional role of living in that community. You may sell your house, but unless you move out of town, you still have a vote. Similarly, in a worker co-op, the membership rights are not for sale, are attached to the functional role of working in the company, and apply to everyone working there, blue- or white-collar, manager or office boy. If you leave your job, you relinquish membership in the co-op.

Ellerman distinguishes between worker co-ops and employee-owned corporations. In the second, voting is based on the number of shares owned, or the vote is held by a trust, as in the U.S. Employee Share Ownership Plans. Voting is not democratic: one person does not necessarily have one vote. Moreover the profits are shared, not according to the work contributed, but according to the value of the shares held.

Small worker co-ops, except for their longevity, are in economic terms no different from any partnership where equal partners work in the business and share the profits. But a further difference is that, theoretically at least, they espouse the "Rochdale principles," set up in Britain around the worker-formed cooperatives in 1844:

— open membership, regardless of social, political or religious beliefs
— democratic control: one-person/one-vote regardless of money invested
— limited return on capital: co-ops are for the benefit of those who use them, not to yield a return on investment
— outreach by education of members and public in co-op principles
— cooperation with other co-ops.

To sharpen our sense of what a worker cooperative is, let's look at the 16 presented in this book, keeping in mind the two basic membership rights: the right to vote equally, and the right to share the profits of the company. Let's exclude Fiddlehead Restaurant in Thunder Bay and Wheat Song Bakery in Winnipeg, both of which have left the cooperative mode. Almost all the rest require a share purchase from a worker who has been accepted for membership. The only exceptions are two graphic arts companies, Dreadnaught in Toronto and Dumont in Waterloo. In both of those, workers may help capitalize the company, but a share purchase is not required. At the others, the share goes along with the job; it's turned in when a worker leaves, and not before. In almost all, any profits have so far been shovelled back into the company. Where dividends have been declared, they have been calculated according to work done.

We have no trouble defining the small enterprises I visited as co-ops. Their members participate directly in just about every decision made, and their votes have equal weight. It's the big ones, where operating decisions are made by a board of directors, where doubt creeps in. Northern Breweries, with plants in four northern Ontario cities, has 155 employees, 85 percent of whom own shares. Richmond Plywood Corporation (Richply), near Vancouver, B.C., has 283 workers who own shares, plus 150 non-member workers. Comparing these two enterprises helps us distinguish between employee-owned corporations and worker co-ops.

At both Northern Breweries and Richply, shares can be sold by an owner-member, and they have increased dramatically as the market value of the company has gone up. This can be a drawback for plant workers who want to buy in, but at both places the shares can be bought over time. At Richply, it is still one-member/one-vote, and there is a sense of true worker democracy. There are several reasons. The board of directors and the revolving committees are elected directly from the work force. The directors continue to work in the plant, continuing close contact with the other workers. And members all get the same hourly wage, with only slight allowances for the chief executive officer, foremen and supervisors. The democratic spirit pervades the mill, despite the high number of non-member workers, many of them relatives or friends of members.

Richply people call themselves a worker-owned company. Despite some variations from the Ellerman definition, I would call it a worker cooperative.

Northern Breweries is 85 percent employee-owned. Management holds half the stock, and elects half the board members. Both votes and dividends (when they are declared) are distributed according to stock held. Although the workers do *feel* they own Northern Breweries, I would not call it a co-op. They themselves call it an employee-owned company and skirt the issue of cooperative control. The president calls it a hybrid. I kept their story for the sake of comparison.

My selection of co-ops to visit had as much to do with the cities I happened to be in as anything, but in fact their geographic distribution does pretty nearly show where the trend is most advanced. Except that I did not visit any co-ops in Quebec. And before I'm roundly denounced, let me say that I do know that is where the action is. To write a book about worker cooperatives in Canada without celebrating what's going on in Quebec would be ludicrous.

The Quebec Assistant Deputy Minister for Cooperatives reported 234 worker co-ops in the province at the beginning of 1985. The oldest and largest single manufacturing co-op under workers' control is the Harpell printing cooperative in Quebec. It was a successful printing and bookbinding business when the employees bought it from the estate of the previous owner in 1945. By 1983, it had built up annual sales of nearly $10 million, and 97 percent of its 183 workers were co-op members. The Quebec forest industry is another area with a long history of worker cooperatives. Today, 30 years after the first woodcutters organized, there are 3,000 worker-owners, with about $50 million in annual sales.

Since 1970, the movement has become more and more popular, accelerating in the last few years with government support in financing, tax benefits and managerial advice. The enterprises range from the most sophisticated electronic and data processing systems, to diesel truck repair, sewing factories and greenhouse operations.

"You appreciate the achievement when you understand the economic and social culture of Quebec," says Alain Roy, the Agriculture Canada expert on worker co-ops who is computerizing statistics on them across the country. He points out that their place in the Quebec economy means their contribution has been recognized; their success is proven; more people know about them. University people are interested and are studying them. Moreover, politicians have been sensitive to the new demands for control and flexibility in work environment — and to the unacceptable unemployment rate. Finally, Quebec's affiliation with France, where worker cooperatives are encouraged and helped by the state and are growing fast, is a stimulus.

Why hasn't this outlook spread to other provinces? Roy raises his shoulders. "It's the same with everything. We don't have the day-to-day habit of working together. Anglophones have to go to Quebec if they want to benefit from our experiments."

I did not go to Quebec. That will have to be another book and maybe another language. I have, in Chapter Nineteen, summarized some of the ways the Quebec government has helped its burgeoning movement. And the news is seeping out. Government of Manitoba bureaucrats, revising their Co-operative Act to encourage worker cooperatives, explored the Quebec system and borrowed from it. The Conseil canadien de la coopération joined with the Co-operative Union of Canada to present *A Cooperative Development Strategy for Canada*, the 1984 Report of the National Task Force on Co-operative Development to the federal government.

And a Quebec government representative joined 1986 discussions with resource groups at the national level about educational programs to familiarize the public with the worker co-op option.

Only three provinces beside Quebec encourage worker cooperatives: They are Saskatchewan, Manitoba and Newfoundland. In Saskatchewan, famous for the turn-of-the century cooperatives the farmers organized to store and transport their grain, almost four in every five adults belong to some cooperative today. The sector was consulted in the design of a new Cooperatives Act, which came into effect in 1983. Field staff in the Saskatchewan Cooperation and Cooperative Development Department give advice and guidance in financing, management and organization of employment co-ops, but there were only eight operating in 1985.

Manitoba's new Employment Co-operative Initiatives Program, incorporating ideas from Quebec, Britain and the U.S., has given worker co-ops a big push in that province. Both new starts and employees of firms about to go out of business are taking advantage of guaranteed government loans and other support.

The two new worker co-ops I went to investigate in Winnipeg had a different character from the longer-established ones. The older groups had been set up, almost every one of them, for ideological as well as economic reasons. "Cooperation is best," any one of them would say, and it would be a moral judgement as well as a preference. At VentAir and Accu-Graphics in Winnipeg, the workers had nothing *against* cooperation to start with, but the dominant push was to find a way — perhaps the only way — to save their jobs. Ironically, in doing that, they began to experience some of the other benefits, including increased productivity, increased profits, and a glow of satisfaction.

Newfoundland-Labrador is the remaining Canadian province with a stated government policy of supporting worker co-ops. Cooperation is a way of life there — but so is colonial domination in one form or another, and marginal economic conditions. "Worker cooperatives are not seriously considered as alternatives in large-scale industry in Newfoundland," said Robert Thompson, the Director of Research and Analysis of the Department of Rural, Agricultural and Northern Development at the 1985 Saskatoon conference on the subject, ". . . there exists no overall plan for worker co-op development." However, he did see worker co-ops as "reducing the external leakage of capital, enhancing local control, encouraging import substitution, and cushioning the horrendous shock of de-industrialization."

The Newfoundland government has funded planning studies and given information and organizational help to new groups. It lists two workers co-ops, incorporated as such, both in building trades and household services in the St. John's area. One is Atlantic Employees' Co-op, which

I visited. However, there are also community development cooperatives, formed to bring back employment to fishing villages and pulp mill towns reeling under economic cutbacks, and often they include everyone in the community. Like Fogo Island Community Co-op, they may develop worker co-ops as part of their strategy. Another six Newfoundland fishing cooperatives include not only the fishermen, but plant workers, collector boat workers, office staff as well as families and community residents among their members. Some of these would fit our criteria for worker co-ops.

The remaining provinces — the Maritimes, Ontario, Alberta and B.C. — maintain only small offices to register cooperatives when they incorporate, and officially they offer no other help. In fact, except in Nova Scotia, where the registrar is a one-man support system, you're more likely to be discouraged than helped. "What do you want to do that for?" the clerk in the Alberta registry asked Evergreen Tree Planting when they tried to incorporate as a cooperative there.

Ontario differs from other provinces in that it has more employee takeovers of big, long-established companies. Often the sellout by the private parent company is for political or strictly bookkeeping motives, and a group aiming for jobs and good working conditions rather than high profits can often succeed. Sometimes profits increase when top-heavy management is scrapped, or when a subsidiary cuts loose from a parent company. The success rate is remarkable: of 50 Canadian firms that would otherwise have closed during the 1970s, all but four were still in business in 1979.

Some have been so successful that employees have taken their gains and sold out. For example, the employees of Byers Transport, a medium-sized Canadian trucking company, bought it in 1975. Five years later, they sold their shares for about 50 times what they had paid, and the company reverted to conventional ownership.

Some of these enterprises are large, with most of their employees among the owners — like Northern Breweries. Others are mostly management-owned, like Epton Industries of Kitchener, an engineering division of Goodyear Tire bought by 80 of the 500 employees in 1983. The financial arrangements with employees are often complicated and imaginative, and they often have a say in management through committees and board representation, certainly more than in most business enterprises. They feel like part-owners, as indeed they are, but the voice of each individual worker is not equal. Usually, control of the company and therefore of the working conditions depends on the amount of capital invested. They don't maintain the one-person/one-vote rule.

It's helpful to look again at the distinction between worker co-ops and employee-owned corporations. As David Ellerman of the U.S. Industrial Cooperative Association points out, "After an initial period of enthusiasm, the 'employee-owners' realize that they are only the beneficial owners, and that the bank officials and managers are their trustees." (Beneficial owners ultimately receive the monetary benefits of ownership, but do not exercise other ownership rights such as voting.) "The company is run like any corporation owned by outside investors and the 'employee-owners' are treated like 'just employees'," Ellerman concludes.

An Employee Share Ownership Plan proposed in the 1986 Ontario budget and now being written into law could encourage the kind of employee-owned corporation Ellerman talks about. Employees of small- and medium-sized firms could buy up to $2,000 annually of "newly issued shares of their employers' corporations" and get a tax rebate of $300. What hits me about that quote from the budget statement is the definition of the corporation as *belonging* to the employer. Working there isn't enough to make it the *employees'* corporation. The employer would get access to more capital — the purpose of the legislation — and compensation from the government for a third of the cost of setting up the plan, up to $10,000.

As envisioned now, the plan *might* be used by some true worker co-ops — but since the purchase is limited to less than five percent of the total stock in the company, that means only groups with more than 20 members could take advantage of it. In a smaller group with equal equity, each member would necessarily own more than five percent. Of the Ontario co-ops I visited, only The Big Carrot health food store in Toronto, with 25 members soon to increase to 40, could qualify. Northern Breweries is also an employee-owned company that is looking for ways to take advantage of this scheme.

Given the size of the work force, we might expect to find more worker cooperatives in Ontario than in other English-speaking provinces. But we don't. One reason: incorporating in Ontario can be a legal nightmare. The present Co-operative Corporations Act of Ontario was set up for producer (that is farmer) and consumer co-ops. The Act defines a co-op in terms of the services it provides. If a worker co-op wants to register, it sometimes has to suggest that the service supplied to its members is employment — as if it were selling employment like milk or eggs. Minor changes as have been brought about in Quebec and Saskatchewan would make it vastly simpler for worker co-ops to incorporate, be registered, and attract investment and get loans.

The present Ontario Co-operative Corporations Act limits the return to workers on investment they make in their co-ops to 10 percent. There are no tax incentives to the general public to invest in shares in cooperatives. And since few people have ever heard of a worker co-op, they evaluate the risk as unknown.

"The banks are not familiar with alternative forms of management structure," says Paul Jones, a Toronto lawyer who has worked with cooperatives. "The more alternative it is, the more problems a bank is going to have with it." They will apply tougher lending procedures to worker co-ops, and they may be more likely to "pull the plug" on the business at any sign of trouble.

"Unless the large credit unions and cooperatives become interested in developing third sector worker co-ops and start providing some funding, there is little chance that a serious worker co-op sector will develop in Ontario," says Steve Schildroth, who has worked with Paul Jones in advising new enterprises through a Toronto resource group called Co-operative Work. There are some signs — which we will look at more closely later — that some credit unions at least are looking in this direction.

Despite the disinterest of B.C.'s Social Credit government, that province has one of the biggest, oldest, most stable and best known worker co-ops. Collective Resources and Services Workers' Co-op (CRS) grew out of the consumer co-op movement in the late 1960s, and now has 23 workers selling natural and bulk food wholesale, and making and selling bakery goods. Annual sales are about $3 million a year.

Another well established company, Richmond Plywood Corporation (Richply), was incorporated in B.C. in 1956. With projected sales of $50 million for 1986, and a total of 430 workers, it was the biggest worker co-op I visited. Unlike most of the other plywood mills, and 49 percent of the labour force in B.C., this 30-year-old plywood company is not unionized, and there has been no move to unionize.

This fact points us to another sector of Canadian life that might legitimately offer support, the trade union movement. When I began searching for worker cooperatives in 1984, they were as new to the labour movement as they were to most Canadians. Since then, unions have had to take notice. Of all the companies I went to originally, only Northern Breweries was fully unionized, "And that's only because we're selling beer," said Eric Holm, manager of the Thunder Bay brewery and soft drink bottling plants. He felt that with plant committees to cover employee grievances and the fact that hourly rated workers could elect two directors, their rights were protected.

Perhaps significantly, the two most recently organized worker cooperatives in the book, and the last two I visited, are both unionized. Evergreen Tree Planting, also in B.C., has also had recent experience with a union, the International Woodworkers of America (IWA), which requires any workers on Vancouver Island to join.

At around the time I visited Richply, the spring of 1986, the powerful IWA was instrumental in the purchase by workers of another plywood company, with plants at New Westminster and Sooke on Vancouver Island. Lamford Cedar Products went into bankruptcy in July 1984, and the union helped form a worker cooperative to save the jobs.

The IWA had earlier refused to support the employee take-over of Victoria Plywood, a former Canadian Pacific Industries subsidiary. Terry Smith, the president of the New Westminster IWA local, explained the different union action by comparing the different circumstances of the two recently formed cooperatives. The buy-in for each worker at Lamford Cedar Products is $12,500, and the workers can pay for their shares with a 25 percent deduction from their union wages. Unlike at Richply, that share will not fluctuate in value, so membership will always be reasonably affordable. From the beginning, Lamford was a modern plant, whereas Victoria Plywood was outmoded and expensive to run, according to Smith. The workers at Lamford are covered by an IWA agreement, and will get the same wages and benefits as other IWA members in the province.

Victoria Plywood Co-op reopened their 36-year-old mill in the summer of 1985. Two hundred workers paid $2,500 each to bring together enough working capital to lease the plant and get underway. The workers accepted a cut in pay, to a base rate of $8.70 an hour compared to the IWA base rate when the plant opened of $13.48. To make this possible, the union had to be decertified as an IWA bargaining unit. Victoria Plywood hopes to make up the pay cut with bonus payments in good years, and there will be medical insurance and a dental plan.

The union did not actively oppose the decertification, and spokesmen are careful now not to be critical. Terry Smith says, "As far as support for worker cooperatives and employee ownership, I think we would have to look at each case separately." He added, probably thinking of Richply, "We would not look favourably, for example, on a 'two-class' co-op where there was one wage for shareholders and another for non-shareholders. Nor would we be very happy with a co-op that set itself in direct competition with unionized firms by undercutting union wages . . . . "

The story of the two plywood plants indicates the union stance on worker cooperatives at this moment: in transition. Traditionally, unions have been wary of cooperatives in the production area, and not without reason: fights between fishing co-ops and fishing unions on both coasts, a rather niggardly reputation among big producer and consumer co-ops in dealing with their own employees. Used to the adversarial stance, unions have been suspicious of the tendency among people who own their own business to make concessions. For instance, to be willing to capitalize their business by taking less disposable income, as did the organizers of CRS food wholesalers in Vancouver and Dreadnaught Publishing in Toronto and Accu-Graphics in Winnipeg. Or to volunteer weekends without pay as they do at Northern Breweries. These concessions could, in the union view, lead to abuses if applied to the big firms where union organization is focussed. Moreover, the labour movement has been traditionally slow to explore innovative solutions, having trouble also with other demands for flexibility.

Nevertheless, it's moving. The Canadian Labour Congress (CLC) is looking at the ability of worker cooperative conversions to save jobs, and of new starts to create them. Guy Adam, who himself with his wife has organized worker cooperatives in Quebec, is the recently appointed National Representative for Social and Community Programs at the CLC. He sees a role for unions within worker cooperatives, as liaison between the worker-owners and their management, to watchdog health and safety measures, and during wage negotiations to give independent information about current job classification, rates of pay and benefits.

Adam also sees more unions taking the lead, as did the IWA with Lamford Cedar Products in B.C. and the United Food and Commercial Workers with the famous supermarket take-over in Philadelphia, and as the Aluminum, Brick and Glass Workers in Hamilton tried to do with the Canadian Porcelain take-over in 1985.

On the other hand, the bosses can't impose cooperation, points out Adam, indicating the attempt of the Quebec government to privatize their liquor outlets by making them available as co-ops to the employees. The government agency which helps worker co-op formation in Quebec, the Société de développement des coopératives, established 60 worker co-ops to bid on some of the first 129 liquor stores offered for sale, in Montreal. But the Union of Store and Office Employees of the Quebec Liquor Board demanded and got an injunction from the Quebec Supreme Court to block the process. When the Parti Québecois government was ousted, the Liberals quietly dropped the project.

The government learned a lesson: organization from the top down, without worker consultation, can be risky. And maybe the unions learned something too. The option was presented to them, and some union leaders now seem to be reconsidering the cooperative movement as a compatible, not a contradictory, direction.

After all they, like the rest of us, are engaged in redefining goals, in creating a society — a way of life — uniquely appropriate to the geographic, economic and social circumstances we have to play with. We all need information — concepts — stories to tell — that help us do this. That is what the stories that follow are all about.

PART II
Our Daily Bread

CHAPTER TWO
The Big Carrot
Toronto, Ontario

"It's a natural complement to the peace movement."

The Big Carrot is a success, a model of how a worker co-op can be organized and what it can be, celebrated in magazine, newspaper and TV. It's successful as a business — over $1 million sales in its first year of operation; salaries doubled. It's successful in the service it offers — a health food store and delicatessen in a big corner store with gleaming windows in a district east of mainline Toronto, once predominantly Greek, now attracting young upwardly mobile families. Its produce is fresh, its bulk food bins efficient. And whoever does the buying keeps an eye open not only for specials but for exotic treats. The day in May that I visited, the store was decorated in Japanese style: cherry blossoms and paper parasols hanging from the ceiling, Japanese products like seaweed and canned fish featured. And it's successful as a worker co-op. Not of course without problems. When I visited, the general manager, Mary Lou Morgan, was on the edge of burnout.

Mary Lou said later I hit her on a bad day. She was preoccupied with the injustice of the fact that five of the original employees, the ones that had personal assets, mortgaged everything they owned to get the initial financing. Philosophically, she was committed to the one-person/one-vote ideal. But she had mortgaged her home; it was on the line if someone made a mistake. Moreover, despite the time the co-op took to prepare for opening — nine months — and despite the careful market studies and hours of meetings, it was she alone who had educated herself about worker co-ops, and she who, along with one other member, drafted by-laws and tried to involve other members. She had just finished reading *Future Bread*, the story of the union-initiated conversion of two A & P grocery stores in Philadelphia into worker co-ops. She was green with envy at their preparation and the amount of organizational support they had had, and just beginning her own participation in a Toronto resource group. (Now incorporated as the Worker Ownership Development Foundation, the group includes lawyer Brian Iler, who helped The Big Carrot and a number of other Ontario cooperatives incorporate).

Structures permitting worker participation don't necessarily result in meaningful worker participation, according to Sherman Kreiner, Executive Director of PACE, the Philadelphia Association of Cooperative Enterprises that helped the A & P chain stores convert.

"They only create the potential for that participation," he says. "We put a tremendous priority on educational programs prior to the opening . . . . " In a process still continuing, workers learn about financial statements and balance sheets, as well as corporate law. The training program also includes democratic process training, so people know how to make decisions in groups. Only then do the workers themselves define the details of their enterprise, forming committees to look at issues such as by-laws, division of responsibility between shareholders and board of directors, and management selection.

Nine Big Carrot workers have gone through the whole process in the past two years, but they had to do it all on an ad hoc basis, learning as they groped their way along. They would have benefitted enormously from the advice and guidance of an agency like PACE.

"You have to figure out a way to finance creatively."
— Mary Lou Morgan, May 1984

Mary Lou Morgan: Five of us had worked together for two years in a natural food store. The owner encouraged us to buy into the business, but he owned 56 percent of the shares and the rest of us only owned 44 percent. So when there was a real crunch we lost. We eventually had to hire a lawyer to get our money back . . . very messy, with a lot of bad feelings. But the five of us really worked well together; it did unify us . . . we all left on the same day in February and we thought we could get a second store opened in about six weeks — it took nine months because of raising the money.

We didn't even know at that point that we *wanted* a worker co-op; it just seemed like a possible way of avoiding more power problems. And so we asked everyone to invest an equal amount of money to cover one share. We have three classes of shares: Class "A" which are outside friends and investors who put up a total of $30,000; Class "B" which is ourselves, the workers — each of us has to buy $5,000 worth of Class "B" shares — and for that we each get one common, Class "C" share which is worth one dollar and entitles you to a vote. Nobody has a vote if they don't work in the store, so that the control is totally within the store.

At the beginning we were all unemployed, so we had to go out and borrow $5,000 each, or get it from friends and relatives. It took a lot of guts, you know, to do that. Some of us were accepted at the bank, and some of us weren't. The people that weren't eventually found the Bread and Roses Credit Union, which listened to a submission and was willing to invest in us and loan us the money personally. They had a limit for personal loans of $3,000 a person, so we could only borrow three times five, which is $15,000, and we needed $50,000. But I used that money to go to the bank to borrow more money. You have to figure out a way to creatively finance. My goal was $120,000 to get the store started. Most small businesses fail because of lack of capitalization.

It turned out to be exactly enough. I even had some left over, mostly because of the good will of my suppliers; they all gave me credit to start with, and that was because we had experience in the business, we had a track record. That's how I got the loan from the bank, too, on the strength of my previous experience. I don't think they would have given it to me without that.

We met twice a week. We looked for jobs during the day, and would meet in the evenings and divide off in groups to try to figure out what the rules of the co-op would be, the business strategy, looking for locations, thinking about the name.

The only person we paid then was the carpenter for six weeks. We didn't get paid and we'll never recover that. You can't expect to.

But on the other hand you see you've started something. It was really interesting for me; I had never had to go to the bank manager before, never dealt with a lawyer. And when you're unemployed you don't have the same confidence as if you had your feet on the ground. My first submission to the bank projected sales of about $600,000 a year, and as I became unemployed longer and longer the predictions kept dropping and finally I submitted a plan that we would do $400,000 the first year!

In fact, the store has done incredibly well financially. We have only been open seven months, and we'll do $1,000,000 business if we keep going at this rate.

We got help with the legal structure from the lawyer. First of all, we chose to be incorporated as a share corporation rather than as a cooperative. If you're a cooperative you have to follow the co-op rules, which only allow 10 percent return on investment, and you have to be more flexible than that if you are really serious about getting money from outside sources. Also, when we go to the bank they are not frightened off by this worker-collective image. We have another set of by-laws, our more private by-laws, protecting us as a worker collective, but the bank doesn't see us that way. We haven't really advertised ourselves as a worker collective so far. We're just a business, basically; we're weak on the co-op side just now, because we're not altogether sure that it is going to work. We're not sure if it's even important in the running of our business in a day-to-day way. I think we're setting a good example, but only if our business is successful. If we fail as a business, then the fact that we are a worker collective doesn't really matter.

We give investors 10 percent on their investment and a 10 percent food discount. We wouldn't be able to do that under the co-op rules. And also, as a cooperative, when you go to look for investors, you have to be very careful because legally you can only approach family and friends and very close customers without going to the trouble of getting a prospectus, and that's much too expensive. You have to have a financial analysis done. It's all pretend anyway because you don't know what your sales are going to be; you don't know how many people you are going to employ. We wanted to get going. We didn't want any government handouts — you have to follow their rules for doing things, and applying for them takes too much time — it would probably take nine months or a year. Other co-ops have done that and then when the money ended, they have failed. We want to be responsible for our own money.

I think we're secure enough now that if the bank pulled out we can go out and get it somewhere else.

I knew as soon as we had been open a month we were going to be OK. At first I didn't think there'd be work for nine people, but within seven months we were all working full time. We have more work than we can handle.

Constance Mungall: You sell natural health foods and macrobiotic foods and you have a small delicatessen. How did you define your product and your market?

MLM: Our main parts are the delicatessen, the bulk and the produce. Our strength is our organic produce. We fly that in once a week from California. We've been trying to present ourselves as a very modern up-to-date food store, not that old health food hippy image. We offer cooking classes, education classes, demos on Saturday, and try to be more than a store, to fit in to this community.

We defined our market before we opened. This wasn't the first location we considered, it was about the fifth. We went door to door, did a survey: "Did people think it would go in this neighbourhood?" It is a very heavy Greek shopping area here, although that is deceiving because the houses are a little cheaper and a lot of young married couples are moving in, so the market was here. We got in on the bottom end of it, so our rent's good.

Nothing we did was an accident; it was all planned thoroughly from the beginning, part of our nine month's preparation. I don't feel that anyone could have done it better. Every time someone came to us and suggested that they could spend our money for us — they could go to the bank and hold our hands; they could do a survey for us — we just did it ourselves. There are lots of people at a hundred dollars an hour who will do that, but you have to do everything yourself, I think, because you understand it better, and it costs too much to let other people do it for you.

I had done a survey where I had worked before, and I also have all the American data. I know that the natural food shopper is a woman aged 35 to 45, university educated, usually has one child or no children. I know the percentage they spend on food per week and what they would spend in a natural food store. So then you go to the census data and just try to match up the area you've chosen with that kind of person. You give products that that kind of person is going to buy.

CM: Is that how you chose the Broadview area? On that kind of theoretical basis?

MLM: Yes, you have to be ruthless in terms of your business sense. Some of our suppliers didn't think it would work, because they didn't feel comfortable with the neighbourhood; they felt it was too Greek. But they had not done the survey. And there are three other health food stores within three blocks. They all do very poorly, but they aren't presenting the merchandise in the right way for this customer. Competition isn't a problem.

I basically designed the store; I had seen that in California. I have been to New Orleans to look at stores and have just taken all the best things I've seen and tried to put them into the store without spending any money. One of our members is a carpenter, so he was able to take my idea and translate it into wooden bins, and I think they're really stunning. They're top loading bins, but they're so beautiful in themselves that it contributes to the store as well.

CM: Do you have any formal training? Can you send people to courses in market strategy, in how to work together as a co-op?

MLM: I wish we'd had more help in how to work together. If there's too much tension, not enough money, if you can't afford to eat properly, it's asking too much of people to be able to work cooperatively. But I feel in terms of the cooperative style we're not unified, so that now we have to go backwards, almost, and pick up all those pieces. Hopefully we'll resolve all those things and be able to stick together.

There are two ways to start. We did it one way — focussing on the business — and the co-op was beside the point. We have been successful in the business sense. In the co-op sense, we have a lot to learn. I just finished reading a book called *Future Bread*, published by a union in Philadelphia which transferred a supermarket into a worker co-op. It was a huge thing, and they studied the co-op model seven hours a day, six days a week for six weeks before they opened. We were so weak in that. We didn't know enough about it, there wasn't anyone to teach us, not everyone was interested in reading. There must be a better way.

CM: How did you choose the co-op model, then?

MLM: I just read and read, and that seemed the most logical, the most comfortable, the most business-like. I wanted to be successful on a business level as well as on a co-op level. There wasn't anyone else who was really interested at the time. I sort of dragged them all to see The Mondragon Experiment videotape; several people read one or two books here and there, but there wasn't really any interest except, "Let's just get on with opening the store!" Now, other people are becoming interested.

CM: Are the salaries competitive?

MLM: At the beginning we just took the amount set aside for salaries, 12 percent of sales, and divided it by the number of us working. Right now we're paying each of us $16,500 a year. It's gone up considerably, more than double. In Toronto, a single person does need a fairly good salary to live on, and there's no reason why you should suffer just to be part of a worker co-op. But there won't be any dividends this year, I'm sure.

We also give ourselves 20 percent discount on our food. While we were starting, and there wasn't enough money to live on, we had charge accounts for food, but now the charge accounts have to be paid off.

Another benefit is being able to go on vacation when you would like. Even if it is unpaid, it's still better than most jobs. People want different things from the business too. They want different hours; they want flexibility if they have children. It seems to me that's an important thing that the co-op can do. It can respect your lifestyle and give you other things besides money.

CM: You're really operating as the business manager. But you don't get paid any more than the other workers.

MLM: Yes, I am the manager. That was voted by the board of directors, and I am responsible to the board for the decisions. I feel responsible for the profit margin and the success, in a way, of the business.

It has been agreed to pay me more, but it's causing a lot of problems. We're tightly split down the middle — people who want us all paid equally, and those who don't. We've hired someone to come and lead us through discussion of group dynamics, conflict resolution, and to help us solve this problem. We've had two meetings so far with her and we're going to meet once a week until it's settled.

We met her through the co-op resource group; she's a woman who has worked with unions. She's had a lot of experience, and we could afford her fee. We've met twice with her but we have meetings once a week anyway. It's very difficult to come to decisions as it is. That's what we're finding most difficult at the moment.

I can see the next big decision could be, should we have two stores? Or should we spend $10,000 on a new kitchen? That kind of money decision will always be difficult. Do people want to expand, stay the same, rest on our laurels, forge ahead? Do you want to hire more people, do you want worker co-ops to spread? These things are going to be very difficult, I think.

CM: Aren't these challenges that any group would have to meet anyway?

MLM: There is a special problem that I foresaw, but I didn't know how to resolve. That is that the people that start a co-op are put in a very risky position. Can people who come into the group after that point ever understand what was given by the initial people? The core group of five people has been joined by four new people who basically don't have the experience in the business, and yet they are hard workers and contribute. Should they make as much without having had the responsibility or the experience of the old people?

CM: They buy their Class "B" shares, and they get their one share for voting, but they haven't suffered as you have.

MLM: After we've been going for a year, there won't be any risk to joining this group. It'll just be easy to come in and earn a salary. Should the new people earn the same as the people who signed their houses away on the dotted line?

CM: So this is your problem, not so much the type of work that you're doing as the kind of investment that the first risk-takers took.

MLM: I think so. It seems to me from my reading that most worker co-ops do best in very labour-intensive businesses, like stores. The grocery business is a fairly low skill job; every job is perfectly within everyone's capability. It's flexibility, not level of skill the job needs.

Our goal is to share around all the jobs. We've already switched once and we'll keep switching and I think eventually we will be rotating managership as well. That seems to be very important to the feeling of equality.

CM: How do you recruit new people when you need them?

MLM: We haven't had that problem yet. We just keep working harder (laughter). We've been open seven days a week from the start because we wanted to make sure that everyone could work. One of our by-laws states that everyone shall have an equal opportunity for work, so we went for broke on the hours. That was a risk in itself.

CM: Have you any inkling of what you may be evolving as a decision-making process?

MLM: I feel we're just at a crux right now. I don't really know how it is going to turn out. We use consensus as a technique, but it doesn't work.

It's asking too much. For instance, it took us weeks and weeks to come up with our name. Finally two of us came up with The Big Carrot. We must have talked about it for another four weeks after that, always reluctant to make that final decision. One particular person really didn't care for it, but he was really graceful in that he said that he'd have to give in on this one. Since then, I think he has grown quite attached to it; people don't forget it.

CM: But in fact, that is a consensus decision.

MLM: Yes, but it isn't as easy to come to a decision. Perhaps in a co-op, you have to have more than a simple majority, but somewhere in between. If we are all working 50 hours a week, and we have to meet once a week and the meeting goes from 8:00 to 12:00 at night, and you still haven't resolved it, it's too much. It's asking too much of people to hash around things, and we haven't learned how to do it faster.

I do most of the day-to-day decision-making, and also cash flow. I keep track of how much money is coming in, what cheques are being written, is there a problem, are we spending too much, keep track of the inventory — but everyone feels this as their responsibility too. The decisions that have to be shared basically are the ones that involve spending a lot of money. We set a ceiling of $2,000. Over that, or decisions that involve a lot of people, have to be discussed with the group.

CM: Is there any way to change a management decision?

MLM: Oh yes. Just go to the next meeting, object to it and I would have to defend myself. If it wasn't defensible I would have to change. At the beginning, I made a decision to buy a yogurt machine that I didn't discuss with the group. It was brought up at the next meeting. That's the kind of thing I wouldn't do again.

CM: Have you had any problems with prima donnas?

MLM: It seems to me, now that I've had a bit more experience, that there is a type of person who works best in a co-op. A person can be very bright, very hard working, good with money, but really not work well in a group. I feel it takes an even temperament, a hard worker, someone who's willing to take responsibility. Prima donnas . . . it's just not worth it for the group. There have been a few problems, it seems that there's always one person who's the source of friction.

We do have in our by-laws a six-month waiting period for people to join, but at the beginning when we were looking for new people, we were desperate for money, and we took people in that could help in that way. It was very difficult, working out their personalities with the original five, and I suppose that's always going to be true, whoever we bring in.

CM: I notice in your by-laws a reference to how you get out if necessary, and there is a possibility of being fired.

MLM: Yes, there's always a possibility of being fired. We have also in our by-laws a discipline policy which we stole from a place called Gentle Strength in Arkansas. It's basically getting everything out on the table, keeping track of problems and trying to deal with them as you go along, not letting them build up.

You try to resolve small things like swearing, you try to put things in a perspective. Firing on the spot would probably happen for something like stealing, or drug abuse. Any other firings certainly wouldn't be up to the manager; it would be up to the board of directors to come to a conclusion. It's not a one-person decision.

Age doesn't seem to be a problem. We're all similar ages, 30 to 40; I think it would be nicer if we were more spread out. We have four men and five women, and we're very lucky because the men are very gentle. There doesn't seem to be any problems with men and women working together or division of labour. I have to give the men credit for that. They don't seem to be chauvinistic at all.

We have a board of directors. We started off with seven — we got two extra people after that, but basically, all the decisions are made by everybody, meeting once a week. If we got much larger the bigger decisions would be made by a seven-person board. I think the manager would not be on the board, but would report to it.

CM: What were the goals and objectives you began with?

MLM: OK. The first one was to provide meaningful employment for ourselves, work in an atmosphere that was good for health and that was cooperative. The second goal was to supply to the community and to our consumers good food at reasonable prices — basically the best food we could find. The third goal was to support the co-op movement.

CM: And you obviously feel that you have fulfilled the first two.

MLM: Yes. And we don't know how the cooperative movement needs help. We don't know where it is. We've been so overwhelmed with our own narrow vision . . . . I'm beginning to feel like part of a network in my association with the resource group, but for the other people, I think it is on a more intellectual level. They feel part of a difference, a change, an alternative, but I think there's just not enough energy to go around.

CM: Is there any input, any nourishment in the interest of other groups that care about what you're trying to do?

MLM: They're watching us, perhaps to see how we are going to resolve our problems, but there doesn't seem to be any support. I'm not sure what we want from them. Also, within the co-op movement there's so much diversity. There are people who believe in the Mondragon example, people who would prefer the English, the French. When you start writing your by-laws you go to the American experience, or to the Spanish. There's no good Canadian example. There just isn't enough background in Canada.

CM: This is something that the resource group might help with?
MLM: They're beginning to. In Toronto I figure they're not as far ahead as we are ourselves. What I am learning at the resource group is that people are coming from many different places . . . there are those huge enormous factories that go bust up and the workers try to revive them through union and co-op working together.

Last week, I read something from Quebec. And there were conferences in South Carolina, in Newfoundland and in Alberta. It is really quite excit-·ing, isn't it?

These connections are so vital, and then meeting Brian Iler — having a lawyer that knew what you were trying to do. It is such a relief . . . you can't even go to a normal accountant and try to explain what you are doing because he doesn't really understand or agree.

There are networks. Bread and Roses Credit Union has been very suppor-tive. For instance, while we were opening, they let us pay the interest on the loan and not the principal. That kind of financial easing of the strain is good. And those Federal Business Development Bank seminars in Ottawa are very good, too. We send people to them all the time. People in a co-op have to understand the financial aspects.

The only thing I really found very, very difficult was that when we went to the bank to borrow the money, we all submitted our names as guaran-tors of the loan, but the banker was only interested in the people who had something to back up the guarantee. So it ended up with five of us signing the guarantee and the other four not. That is very unequal. Some people have the risk hanging over their head, and others don't. I feel that the government could have helped in that way, could have guaranteed the loan. That would take a lot of stress off us. But there isn't any provision for that.

CM: Have you been able to pay off any of your loan?
MLM: Oh yes. We make payments every month. It's an eight-year loan, a Small Business Development Bank loan for $50,000 at one percent above prime. I figure the longer we take to pay it off the better, because then the people who come later will also be paying it off; it won't all be the core group. And we want to get rid of our Class "A" investors because payments to them sucks money from the company. We hope to pay back two of our investors this year. The sooner we can stand on our own the better.

In this business, it's sales that are the bottom line — are you making money off your sales? Your profit margin should be 30 percent to be successful. In the food business, your salaries can be 14 to 15 percent of sales and no more, so we just have to get sales up.

I feel we have been successful in the visual presentation of the store, and the atmosphere. People feel comfortable in the store; we know a lot of our customers' first names. We had that atmosphere when we worked together in the other store, so I did expect it again, and I would say that we were exactly on target.

CM: What do you see in the immediate future?

MLM: I don't see staying at this level. People will get bored with it. The store is running well, it has to go somewhere or people aren't going to stay. We might do a little wholesaling of vegetables, organic produce, but our strength is in retail. The wholesale business is a totally different ball game; you need different kinds of money . . . we should stick with what we do well when we expand.

In some ways, I feel kind of low energy. We have a meeting tonight, and I'm thinking about that and I'm wondering will it be another four-hour meeting and not get anywhere? And I am interested in the resource group tomorrow night, but is it just energy flowing out?

I feel wilted actually, because I don't have the answers; I don't know how it's going to work out. I've risked everything to set it up, signed my life away for the loan, and now it's that feeling of . . . is it going to work out the way I want? I wish I'd done things differently. In the beginning, it was just simpler to read the books myself, and develop the model myself. There was one other person who did it with me. But I should have spent more time insisting that the other people understood what we were getting into, that we all agree.

My position of manager, I find a little isolating, too. You almost have to separate yourself in a sense to keep making the right decisions and keep things going.

CM: That is a good reason for rotating the managership.

MLM: Yes, it is, but it's not simple. It's all tied up. If I'm not manager, and if my house is signed away on the loan, am I going to stand there and let someone else make a mistake on it? And yet, it is totally necessary for people to learn. It's hard to know; I feel that we're going to work things out with this resource person, but it's just so time consuming. It is almost like we now need a meeting to do that every week, and a meeting to run the store every week, and if you have a family, it is really a lot.

CM: You are on the edge of burnout.

MLM: Possibly, although I can get very, very excited about it still on many different levels — the business level, the co-op level. For instance last week we decided we couldn't manage any more without an office. We couldn't manage anymore without a bulk room. They were luxuries, and yet not having them causes such disorganization that we push ahead to get them. Besides running it from day to day, you have to be thinking ahead — I am trying to think into next fall, I'm only interested in the growth of the business; I'm not interested in sitting still on it, even though it might be safer.

CM: I guess I'm surprised that it isn't enough for you. To me, in terms of growth, that process is your success.
MLM: I guess it should be. I suppose that will be the basis of our expansion, too. I see that as important because I know that we can't satisfy people's requirements for salaries without that. We can talk about what we want to make, but we can't get it until our sales hit a certain amount. Everyone is quite aware that salaries are going to grow only through the expansion of sales. All the personal growth isn't making up . . . . No, it can't because it causes too much stress in the other parts of your life, I think. This age, 30 to 40, is the time when people are having families and they want to be able to support them and have a decent job. It is quite important.

I do feel that this is a wave, the co-op movement, from the middle class. People are looking for value in their working life, that is why it's so important. It's giving employment to young people who are not going to find work on their own. It's such a fair way of working, working for yourself, getting the return for yourself, able to have small children and work three days a week, be home when they get home; when you need to have a month's holiday, you can have it. It's so humane; it's so right that people will take on the responsibility for giving it to themselves. I think it's important because we do all feel it's *ours*.

Actually, we put an ad in the peace calendar. I was trying to think of how to advertise, and I thought, the fact that it is a worker cooperative is the key. Here we have nine people who are going to live together peacefully. It is like a family. We are not going to dump any of those people; we are going to work through our problems with them, and it seems to me a natural complement, too, to the peace movement. We're all looking for alternatives in the way we eat, in the way we live. One of our members, Jane, has just had a baby and we're going to have it here, as part of the working of the store. We do have things in common. So there are a lot of really positive things.

"There's going to be a huge change."
— Mary Lou Morgan, July 1986

I heard rumours of big changes at The Big Carrot just before this book went to press, so I went back to Toronto to check them out. They were true. The Big Carrot members had formed a consortium with the owner of a real estate company and backer of innovative projects including small businesses. Together they had bought the building across Danforth Street from The Big Carrot for $1.8 million. It was a former automobile showroom and the plan is to convert it into a mall, with space for The Big Carrot and another 15 retail stores. There will be 20,000 square feet for stores on the street level, and another 10,000 square feet for offices on the second floor.

The Big Carrot will be the major lessee, with first say about who the other occupants will be. Mary Lou Morgan, who's been given the job of coordinating the mall and the move to it, is already looking for businesses and stores that complement The Big Carrot: a restaurant, a bakery, a fish store, a cotton clothing store, perhaps a credit union and a Co-operators insurance outlet. She would like to find other worker cooperatives, but doesn't see them in Toronto at present. She visualizes eventually a co-op mall, shared by the groups established there.

"It's possible," says Ethan Phillips, of Co-operative Work, the co-op consulting group which did a business plan and prospectus for The Big Carrot expansion. "It could be an incubator, a stimulus for the whole co-op movement in the area."

Another major step for The Big Carrot since our original interview in 1984: the Bank of Montreal has granted the worker co-op "joint and limited liability" for its bank loan. This means that each co-op member shares equally in possible liabilities. Before, the bank would only accept members with personal assets as guarantors of the loan, and each could be held responsible for the total. Mary Lou Morgan and one other member had mortgaged their homes. This was no longer necessary.

Sales in the second year were nearly $2 million, profit nearly $200,000. And The Big Carrot had bought a five percent share in the 150-acre Kawartha Hills Organic Farms, to ensure fresh produce for the store.

On my second visit, Mary Lou Morgan wanted to tell me about the expansion, and about other progress. She also had something to say about how she came through in the transcript of our original talk.

Mary Lou Morgan: We all had this vision of a store that we wanted. We had to compromise, because we didn't have the money. So this time we're trying to do what we originally wanted to do. It could be fantastic. We've been given an incredible chance. It's going to be about three or four times as large as this, with a staff of 40. It's working quite well now although I can see there's going to be a huge change when we go across the street, because we're going to go from 25 employees, where we're at now, to 40, and we won't be able to work the way we've been working, because everyone's been coming to all the meetings, and helping with all the decisions. We're going to have to streamline that, and go to a board of directors, who the management reports to.

Constance Mungall: And how much funding do you need for the store expansion?

MLM: I think we need about $400,000. Although it's three times as big, I've been conservative; I've estimated less than twice as much business. Raising the money is a killer — it's just very, very hard to do. We're trying to raise $100,000 from our customers with a deadline of July 27th. It's July 10th now and I'm up to $35,000, and I have some promises, but until you have it, you can't count on it.

The investors are getting Class "A" shares which have no vote. That gives them 10 percent dividend on their money, and 10 percent off their food. We're trying to keep the investments to five or ten thousand, keeping them very small. It's actually a very, very good deal because they're also taxed at a different rate on the interest since we're a taxable Canadian corporation. I'm trying to get $100,000 from our customers, and $300,000 from a bank or trust company. It doesn't seem like an overwhelming amount, but it's just that it's slow, and people need time to think about it, and you don't always approach the right people . . . . We need the $100,000 by July 27th and then the rest can come in October, November — we hope to open in November, but the payments wouldn't have to be made until then.

We need more money this time than Bread and Roses can lend so we went directly to Credit Union Central. To be turned down is so frustrating. They told us there wasn't enough hard security for the loan, something they could take back. Well, I mean the store as it is, is incredibly successful . . . .

In some ways the worker co-op movement is still being developed, and financial people don't know what it is. They loan for housing co-ops, because that's old hat . . . . "No hard security for the loan" — I can't really understand that, since our liability is limited on the property. It's a separate company. If the mall failed, The Big Carrot *might* fail too but it's highly unlikely, and we still have the land that we can resell. I feel confident of The Big Carrot's success. I don't feel as confident of the mall's success. It's so new. I don't know if we'll come up with the right mix . . . I'm pretty confident that we will.

CM: Have you done the same sort of careful market evaluation that you did before opening?

MLM: Yes, we did a really detailed survey of our customers and basically they say we want more products, more variety, more service, but we don't want you to change! So, in a way that's what we're trying to do — sort of move over there without changing — try to emphasize the goods and not the cabinetry.

Things are changing quite rapidly and now we're meeting and discussing the new store and how that's going to change the internal workings. We're trying to think ahead this time . . . .

We've already come through quite a few problems and solved them. One thing, remember we had a very difficult time deciding how we were going to be paid, whether it was going to be equal or variable rates? After meeting twice a week for four hours a night with the consultant we hired to help us, we finally decided that we had to do it ourselves. We set up a committee with two people from either side, and they came up with a solution in two hours. Probably the group was so sick of meeting that they accepted it right off!

What we did was, we have four categories of work. The first category is part time people like our bookkeeper who comes one day a week, or people that are on contract. The second category is people who just start training, and learning about co-ops — that is part of their training now, they really have to do some reading and researching. The third group is the department heads, and the fourth is the management team.

The rates for the categories range. The managers decide on the pay-scale for the first group, and it can vary. I think the second one starts at $15,000, the third one at $17,000, and the fourth at $20,000.

In addition, every six months, which I think is 1,040 hours, we get a $500 increment, after an evaluation across the board. People that work a four-day week don't gather their hours together as fast, and counting the hours is important because the labour dividends are given out in addition to the $500. It has worked well but we're now wondering whether it's going to work in the new store again.

One thing I've learned about a group is that you have to be very patient because if you wait long enough and the idea that you have is right, everyone will come around to it, but you can't force things, you can't . . . you have to give people lots of time to think about issues, you can't bring something up at a meeting and expect it to be decided. It almost has to get discussed before and then be formalized at the meetings, but it never gets dealt with at the same time.

For us the committee structure works very well; if you care enough about something you go onto the committee — for instance getting a computer or buying a new truck — you do all the research, you bring it to the board for approval, and other people have to trust that you've done the research properly.

CM: And the board is still all the members?

MLM: Not as of last night. We had our annual meeting, and we've changed the structure so that now the board is seven people. I'm president, so I see myself in the year coming trying to set up a better relationship between board and manager, trying to work out who's responsible for particular things, and to encourage the management to report to the board and to be more responsible for the staff. Then the board will be responsible for more general areas. I'm not sure who's going to lead, the manager or the board, yet.

I haven't been general manager for 18 months now. I've stepped out of it, and I know that it was very difficult for me to keep my mouth shut, and not to interfere, but it was really worth it because I saw the development of the other people being given responsibility and almost taking on the pride of it.

Last night we had the second person who was general manager for 18 months come off, so now we're onto our third management. We're going to go into the expansion with a really strong background. I think that's the strength of the co-op — the development from the bottom, starting at the bottom and working up, it's the only way.

There's a management team of three people now, and they each serve 18 months, elected at six-month intervals. There's a management training program, and the general manager is responsible for everything for the six-month period. It's not really long enough, that's the only thing — you really need a year almost, as a general manager.

The staff is 25 now. There are 14 members, and the rest are on probation. We've debated about shortening the probation time, because we need their share capital, and we did that last time, but we feel very nervous about that.

We've had cases where people have been on probation, and at the end of the time we want them but they don't want to become a member. Or they want to become a member and we don't want them. We've decided to go to a system of contracts, so that a person who comes on signs a contract for a specific six-month period. Otherwise we were allowing too many outside people to come and work with indefinite decisions whether they would stay or go. At the end of the year when we divide the profits there's a nice chunk for each of the members but there's nothing for the people who did a lot of the labour and so we have to be stricter about it. If you're not a member you have to leave, basically.

CM: How much is a nice chunk?

MLM: Well, this year there was 10 percent return on the $5,000 share, and there was a labour dividend of about $4,000 each. Now that money we had to turn back into the store because of expansion. That was by consensus, but we had a lot of pain and laughter about it because people feel they've really given a lot and they would've liked to have some reward this year. Whereas going into the expansion, there probably won't be anything now for another couple of years. So in a way the original members again are the ones who are taking the risk. It's kind of odd the way it's happening. The new people haven't anything to lose yet except their original investment whereas now the original people have their labour, as well as their investment.

Three of the original members have left and that's a very interesting juncture in a co-op. We had a very rough situation with one of our original members; finally both parties decided that it would be better for them to leave. But it's not easy when people have spent a lot of their energies in making the store grow. One woman stayed home to raise her family so that was a very positive leaving, and another member left to start a new business. After it's happened a couple of times it's not as upsetting. It seems that you get a real sense that the group is more important, it will be stable.

I also think the management is becoming much more sophisticated in their hiring. We've had so many examples of people who were good workers but difficult to get along with, or who were wonderful-hearted but poor workers, and so you change your hiring practices, looking for the co-op strengths as well as the good work. And the management is getting used to firing — with the consent of the board — but doing it . . . not letting it drag on.

CM: At the time I interviewed you one of the members — I think it was Jane — was going to have a baby, and you were going to experiment with having the baby here.

MLM: Well, it worked really well. We had a play-pen for Jake and customers used to come and see how he was doing. Jane really pulled her weight and did all the work she was expected to do and felt good about him being here. Now he's in day-care and in a way he has a very special . . . we always celebrate his birthday.

Jane's with us still, she's now one of the managers. She works a four-day week, because she still finds that's all she can manage, but she really pulls her weight. We consider you're full time if you work a four-day week, and salary is paid on the basis of a 40-hour work week. We do find it's better to have the five-day people because when you're away three days you miss a fair bit; it's hard to know what's going on.

I think I learned from *not* being manager that a lot of decisions that I made weren't necessarily right. It was just one way of doing things; other people choose other ways; it doesn't really matter, it works or it doesn't work. In a way our systems now are pretty firm, so that we don't do too many things that would cause a big monetary loss. I don't recall that we've made any decisions that have lost more than a couple of hundred dollars over the last two years, so really nothing can affect the real stability of the business. Now maybe this mall will but I don't really think so either.

CM: Where do you foresee getting another 15 workers for your expansion?

MLM: Well it's interesting, because now that the expansion gossip is out we get really good people applying. It's the first time we've ever had a choice of good people. They recognize that there's a chance here for more than a bare salary, and to be part of something that's quite exciting. But I think the commitment to the co-op scares off people. Some just get overwhelmed with the idea that they're going to stay with this job for two years.

CM: And that's what you look for, that kind of commitment?

MLM: Yes, because I'd say it's six months before you figure out how the store works and probably at least two or three years before you can be a manager.

CM: Has the mix changed? You had about equal men and women and I think the average age was in the thirties.

MLM: It's about the same. We went through a period where we despaired of men applying but we just took on four new members and they're all men. I think it's harder to get men, because women seem to be used to working in day-care cooperatives and a different style of work. So I think the men we have are very unusual.

I found the transcript of our first talk quite helpful because — going through a period again of getting started on a new track, and wondering if we're doing the right thing, I felt I could basically stand behind everything I'd said there. I didn't feel comfortable with the introduction, though. I felt embarrassed by some of the phrasing, like "green with envy," the resentments that I had. I think it's very negative. I don't mind that you said I was on the edge of a burnout; I was, that day, and actually shortly after that I resigned from the management, and developed an idea where there would be three managers . . . the emphasis on myself . . . it was true I read the co-op material first . . . I'm not saying that it wasn't true, but I think that it would be offensive to our people who now do understand what the co-op is about.

Actually I've started going out to schools on my days off and speaking on worker co-ops and recently I've suggested sharing this with other people and in a way they've all had to think through the co-op thing. I would say all the original people now are really committed to the worker co-op thing. Now I think they would never let anyone look at them differently than a very special kind of business. So I wouldn't mind you pointing that out, that there has been a development.

CHAPTER THREE
CRS Workers' Co-op
Vancouver, British Columbia

"If we fail as a business, we fail as a co-op."

I felt I'd hit the big time when I visited CRS — Collective Resource and Services Workers' Co-op. And in fact, CRS is a leader in the Canadian worker co-op "establishment," with substantial plant, staff and history. Managing Director Ron Hanson himself adds to the feeling of stability about the place, combining, according to the quarterly publication *Worker Co-ops,* a "fairly conventional approach to management with overall democratic control by the membership."

I found a large and well organized wholesale food warehouse with business offices, a boardroom and an employees' lounge. The plant is in the east end of Vancouver, in a district with mixed small manufacturing plants and residences, many co-op or low-income housing. The bakery and retail outlet are a few blocks north.

CRS started as a group of volunteers in 1971. Its original funding was from the federal government, but since the first three years it has been self-supporting. The structure is interesting and unique among Canadian co-ops; it is divided into sub-groups called collectives. At present there are three separate collectives — the warehouse, the bakery, and the administrative unit. In the past there have been more.

CRS has a firm, idealistic philosophical base. Its Statement of Purpose is defined as: "To contribute to the creation of a society where personal, economic and social relationships are based on cooperation." It carries out that purpose by, as Ron Hanson says, "competing in the North American market" — successfully — and by encouraging the establishment of other worker co-ops. It publishes a handout, "So what's a workers' co-op anyway?" describing co-ops and worker control in general as well as CRS and its functioning. Members counsel and lend their boardroom to beginning groups.

CRS is in good shape to give advice. The cooperative has survived the growth cycle many newer, smaller groups are still working through: the first enthusiasm, the initial push with long working hours at low pay topped off by interminable meetings, philosophical differences, often a challenge to the original founders, finally the evolution of a workable system of decision-making and administration, stabilization, and the experience of pulling back a little to weather challenges like the recent recession.

CRS is an integral part of the cooperative network in B.C., selling to cooperative food outlets (and to worker co-ops like Evergreen Tree Planting), dealing with and influencing the policies of B.C. credit unions (powerful enough to refuse to give personal guarantees on loans — its own credit is enough), affiliated with the B.C. Co-op Council, the Alliance of Warehouses and Federations, and the North American Students of Cooperation.

Since our interview, CRS has continued to grow. At the end of 1985, the wholesale collective merged warehousing operations with Fed-Up Cooperative Wholesale, which was previously owned by small retail consumer co-ops and buying clubs. Later, the bakery expanded to include a full delicatessen. And CRS computerized its invoicing and data-entry systems. Sales of the wholesale food and bakery collectives rose to $3 million in 1985. Worker-members increased to 25. Moreover, the equity system proposed by Ron Hanson in our interview has now been put into place. After years of only nominal financial investment from members, the co-op now asks them to buy $2,000 worth of shares, usually through payroll deductions.

Ron Hanson is used to telling the CRS story, at conferences in Canada and the U.S., at counselling sessions with new groups starting up, and to the media.

Ron Hanson: The business was incorporated as a worker co-op in 1976, but it began in 1971 as a resource group to start consumer co-ops, and supply them. Initially, the idea was that a warehouse would distribute exclusively to the cooperative movement, but in a year or less it became evident that there wasn't a large enough market in the co-op movement alone, so we now sell to anybody that wants to buy from us. The wholesale food business and the bakery, as well as two other businesses, a cannery and a bee-keeping supply company, were all operating before we actually incorporated.

Now we operate with three collectives within the larger cooperative. CRS Food Wholesale has sales of about $2.5 million a year and employs eight workers. Uprising Breads Bakery is a wholesale and retail bakery with annual sales of about half a million a year and employing 11 member-workers and some part time people who aren't members but get the same pay. The administrative collective is made up of a general manager and three accounting staff. The board of directors of five members from these three collectives meets monthly.

We began with volunteer help, but that was always presumed to be coming to an end as soon as we made enough money. We had people collecting Unemployment Insurance and doing volunteer work, and people collecting government grants as wages and kicking back some of the money to help capitalize the business.

The capital actually came from federal government grants, Local Employment Assistance Program grants, and people who were getting a few hundred in wages through the grant put some of that money back into the co-op. It was supposed to be a one-year program, and it was extended to three years. We had a grant of about $100,000 over that time.

The problem with government grants is, they give you enough for salaries, but they don't give you enough to capitalize the business. To make the business effective we had to have more money, and the way to get more money was to take it out of sweat equity. People lived on very low wages; the people that started were all single I think and pretty frugal — most of them lived in the same houses — and they could manage. People who have come along since then couldn't possibly have managed on that; they have families. But now we pay an adequate wage, $1,300 or $1,400 a month for a single person, and another $200 or $300 a month per dependent, up to two. People with two dependents would make as much as $1,500 or $1,600 a month.

Constance Mungall: Everyone gets paid the same no matter what jobs they do? So as business manager you don't get paid more?

RH: No, I get less. The reality is I get less than some people with dependents, because my kids have grown up and left home.

The people that started the co-op felt their sweat equity was capital contributed for the greater good of the idea of worker co-ops. They were willing to forego the interest. It was by consensus. People who radically disagreed didn't stay, or they wouldn't have come in the first place.

People worked long hours — no hesitation about working nine or ten hours a day. Those were steps you take to get something going, and as soon as it was feasible, the hours would be brought down.

CM: Something like starting your own business?

RH: Yes, except that often people starting their own business never get the hours expected in the labour movement. We now have a 37-hour week, in the middle of the norm today. Some people work overtime, and then take time off. Others work overtime and don't claim for it, but not often now. Longer hours were necessary right on till 1978. The business grew substantially between 1976 and 1980, at the rate of 30 percent a year, so we were able to increase wages and cut hours.

Since then we've been hit by the recession. Our growth hasn't been as great, but generally things are all right. We have a position in a particular market, the health food and co-op market. We have a fair amount of allegiance from our customers because we run a good business, and we have to be competitive, just like any other business that's going to succeed.

People learned the skills they needed by experience and by night school courses and by determination. The co-op always paid for night school courses for anything relevant to the co-op: marketing, typing, computer understanding, some immediately relevant and some might be in the future. We also pay for travel to business conferences. I went recently to a large American health food convention in California and one or two have gone to the NASCO — North American Students of Cooperation — conferences in Michigan, every year now for five years. These are fringe benefits but also very important learning experiences, particularly meeting people involved in the co-op world and in some cases in similar businesses. It's often quite inspirational to see what other people are doing. You both learn and teach in the process.

CM: When new people come in, they have the advantage of all the founders' work. They invested a great deal which was not recorded, but that has meant a firm business now.

RH: That's true. I think most people that were involved and left aren't resentful or regretful; some, maybe, but generally speaking no. They made their contribution and people are now benefitting from it. That's a reality.

CM: What they took when they left was their $100 share?

RH: They were just nominal, almost irrelevant. If our resources are worth in the hundreds of thousands of dollars now, those $100 are irrelevant, I guess I'd say. Actually, nobody has a paid-up share. Our legal formation calls for some shares and on our books they are down as $100 shares, but the important issue is that a group of people are working together and have over a number of years created a pool of capital that can be used — that you must have to run a substantial-sized business. I would guess that it's worth somewhere between three and four hundred thousand dollars now.

Our credit union loans, both operating loan and term loan, probably total about $100,000. We get bank interest rates. We deal with the credit union, which has similar principles — to support cooperative enterprises. I guess if there were no credit unions there might be some difficulty in the fact that we are a worker co-op. In an entrepreneurship or a limited liability company, in theory at least, you can always turn to the principal or owner, who is in theory responsible. Some banks might require the directors or some sub-group or maybe all members personally, to guarantee the debts of the co-op. As it stands now, we don't give any personal guarantees, either to the credit union, which doesn't require it, or to creditors. We just say we don't do it.

CM: But the business itself is worth a lot now, so that you have assets for security.

RH: As long as we run the business well. If we ran it poorly it could deteriorate very quickly. And that, of course, is what banks and lending institutions base their judgement on: "Is the management of the business competent? Do they understand what they are doing?" That's just as important as, "Do they have enough money to pay their bills?" because they won't have it tomorrow if their management is incompetent. The food business tends to be pretty basic; you don't make immense returns on your capital the way you do in some hi-tech business. Your margin of profit is kept down. On the other hand, if you operate in an intelligent way, you're not going to go broke. Everybody eats.

CM: Everybody eats. And what is your margin of profit?

RH: The bakery is a fairly high margin business; the gross margin is about 63 percent. The wholesale food business is fairly low, around 14 percent.

The administration performs the financial functions: advises the others and tells them the realities. You have to distribute the funds in some kind of equitable way between the various competing needs for capital, expansion, labour . . . .

Generally the planning is done by a small group, but input is invited from everyone.

Final approval is by the whole membership, which meets every two months. An elected board of the whole co-op meets weekly.

The bakery collective probably meets every two or three weeks, the warehouse once a month, and the administrative group weekly. It depends on what you're trying to do. Some meetings are short, to do with day-to-day things; others are policy meetings. Generally they're scheduled to last two or three hours. Occasionally there are special meetings called for either an emergency or an opportunity, when you want to make sure everyone knows what's going on. It doesn't always require a meeting — it depends how important it is. All the formal meetings are paid for in business time, but people might meet informally on their own time.

You don't stay away from meetings — if people didn't come there would be — I don't know, something would happen; somebody would yell. It's considered very important. We've tried to cut the number of meetings, but when we do have them, we want them to be efficient, and I think they are. They've got better over the years, changed with the times, become more formal, with motions presented and voted on and discussed in a modified parliamentary system. It's evolved. When there were just five or six people, more informal discussions seemed possible, but when you get to 22 people, you need a certain formality. The main thing is to avoid people feeling they have no opportunity to voice their opinions. People who want to have some kind of creative anarchy with no hierarchy at all would probably find they wouldn't operate very long.

CM: What is the hierarchy that has evolved here?

RH: Well, there's the bakery manager and the warehouse manager, and I'm the general manager. Certain kinds of decisions are my prerogative, and if there are major policy decisions, then the board is called. Similarly with the bakery and the warehouse. The board members are their representatives; and any decision can be questioned. And members can call a general membership meeting; I think two-thirds of the members sign a request. In CRS, I'm both member and general manager. A lot of co-ops, usually that have developed from buy-outs and take-overs, have chosen to hire a general manager from outside. He wouldn't actually be a member at all. That's true in Vancouver Richply for instance. Sometimes it has to do with the knowledge required for a particular job.

CM: What is your background?

RH: I've done all sorts of things. I spent about 12 years as a social worker, but that didn't seem too useful an activity to me, and I sort of fell into working with the co-op, worked at the bakery, drove the truck, did warehouse work, but for a number of years I was a buyer for the warehouse. I actually have quite a good knowledge of the bakery and the wholesale food business.

CM: Plus some knowledge of how people get along together.

RH: I hope so. That's important because I don't see my role as dictator, but as supporter of what other people are doing and overseer of a variety of interconnected activities. Mainly support.

One of the main things we have to keep our eye on is the fact that we are a business. If we fail as a business, then we certainly fail as a co-op. The reverse doesn't necessarily follow. We can fail as a co-op and decide to change our structure and still be quite an effective business. But we're competing in the market, in the capitalist, North American market. We can do it differently and have a different perspective about a lot of things, but we still are competing.

Profit considerations are important but not paramount. We place more emphasis on paying reasonable salaries, having good working conditions, producing and selling quality products, and supporting the cooperative community.

Some of the companies we compete with sell to the health food trade as a whole, not just to co-ops, but we're sort of midway in size in a whole group of relatively small companies. The health food business compared to the straight grocery business is piddly. Compared to chains like Safeway stores or Loblaws, we fit in one little corner. But we have a real presence, no question about that, and we are importing goods from all over the U.S., some from eastern Canada, and doing that fairly effectively.

Most small consumer co-ops are also natural food; most of the ones we deal with are. In the last two or three years, 45 to 50 percent of our business goes to the co-op world and 50 to 55 percent goes to the commerical health food stores, bulk food stores, some restaurants, some manufacturers. The distribution has slowly moved in favour of the health food stores because there are more of them. We've pretty well cornered that market. A lot of buying clubs and co-op stores try to buy most of what they buy from us.

CM: You have the support of the co-op movement, first in financing, and then in selling to consumer co-ops. Other worker co-ops I've talked to said they would have it made if they had support from the big groups like Co-operators insurance and the cooperative stores.

RH: We don't expect it to be automatic. We're offering good service, good products, good prices, good quality, all those things as good as anybody else in the market. If, say, the large Federated Co-operative system wanted to buy from us in any kind of scale, we wouldn't be able to supply them, because we don't have the resources. We may have some day, but you have to go after them and say, "Let us submit a bid and do the work." And of course you have to give evidence you can do it. So those are ticklish questions.

CM: How do you reach your market? Do you advertise? How would a new consumer co-op know that you would be good people to go to?

RH: There is a network, but that's one of the really hard questions, how do you promote people getting together and forming buying groups and starting stores, particularly with limited resources. And often they have serious philosophical questions, the same ones that keep being answered over and over again, to do with volunteer labour, with everybody having a say on every issue. It's a very costly procedure, and at some point you have to say, "We will give the responsibility for certain decisions to a committee, or to one individual," and have the trust that goes with that. That's not always easy.

We had those endless meetings years ago. This structure has constantly evolved; it may evolve some more, but part of that evolution has been to recognize you can't spend $100 in time to make a $10 decision.

We've had people get fed up and leave over this sort of thing. Some haven't been satisfied that the organization has been democratic enough. Some haven't been satisfied that it took enough account of special interest groups. Those sorts of thing. Somebody comes and works for a while and says "This is not for me," for a range of reasons, some of them philosophical.

I don't think we've ever had people who felt that the whole organization would stand or fall on them. Important people who have contributed a lot have left, and sometimes at the time you wonder how you're going to do without them, but generally you find no one is indispensible. Their absence may change the way you do things and turn out to be for the better.

CM: I see by your meeting structure that some motions are passed with a two-thirds majority and others with a straight simple majority.
RH: That partly has to do with the co-op law; it's not our decision. In the very early days, we experimented with consensus, depending on the nature of the decision. Financial decisions often don't lend themselves to consensus. Philosophical decisions do, but if you need a piece of machinery that costs $10,000 and that's hard fact, you either get it or you don't. That's an operational decision. Consensus decision-making is more appropriate if there isn't an urgency.

CM: When you use majority vote, is there any problem among those in the minority?
RH: Not if they've accepted that it's a majority system. Sometimes I wasn't too happy in a minority position, but if I want to block any decision while sticking desperately to my point of view, and it isn't based on some larger philosophical issue, then I'm leading to poor productivity.

CM: When you bring a new person in, would they be coming because they want a job or because they want to work in this kind of environment?
RH: When we post for jobs we get lots of applicants. We see coming here as both membership and work; we want people who have some previous co-op experience, or in associations or groups. You can teach the work easier than you can teach people about how a democratic system might work, especially if their experience has been in a standard business where you have somebody who tells you what to do all the time.

CRS has a formal induction process for new members. Workers are taken on for a three-month probationary period before they're recommended for membership by their enterprise's work collective. If accepted, they get full voting rights in the co-op and may serve on a committee after another three months. During the first week of probation, they work in one of the other enterprises in order to get an overview, and they receive a complete orientation package including a history of the co-op.

We have quite a number of people who have been here more than five years. Only one person was here right at the beginning. I came in relatively early — 1975. Employment has expanded steadily. We haven't cut back at all. We have 22 people, three we took on a few months ago, and hope they'll want to stay.

I want to offer more in the way of incentives to stay. There's no equity right now, and we've been talking about changing the system, so if you stayed a number of years you'd get a greater part of the net profits. That hasn't been worked out, but it seems logical. That of course is incentive to stay, just like wage increases. And it's very important for people to stay, because of the knowledge they accumulate and their whole understanding of the business. Something along that line probably will happen for incentive, but also for capital reasons. If everyone put in $2,000 each, you've got $44,000 which becomes part of your business capital and allows you to expand.

When people leave they would take their share, but presumably someone else would come along to put in, so that's not a problem. It's very important as a stable part of your capital. That's part of the reason Mondragon co-ops have been so successful; from the very first day family or somebody came up with each worker's investment. You start with 400 to 500 people each putting in a couple of thousand, it's amazing what you can do. It's been proved in the capital system with mutual funds, where you can invest and do quite well. In this case, it may allow for the creation of other industries.

I'd like to see a range of interconnected industries supporting each other, each contributing to the other by buying the products or selling them or manufacturing components. The bakery is like that; it buys all its ingredients from the warehouse, and we sell products at the bakery.

We did have both a small cannery and a honey business. The cannery had two or three problems. It tended to be very seasonal, capital intensive — you've got to buy a whole bunch of food, hold it all and then sell it; you need a lot of money to do that. Second, it's labour intensive at a particular time of the year, needing short time labour. So we closed it down quite a few years ago.

A lawyer helped us create our constitution and rules, and we used other peoples' work; we didn't create it all from nothing. I think new groups have it easier because there's more information along that line now: *Worker Co-ops* publication and CODA, the Common Ownership Development Association, in the west here. And there's more in the way of model legislation, model constitutions, that are quite adaptable.

My guess is that the original members chose to incorporate as a cooperative because they wanted the same form as the consumer cooperatives they dealt with. Certainly you could incorporate a limited liability company with partners in some special structure where one person would have one vote rather than based on capital.

I'm told that limited liability companies have both tax and financial advantages; they can borrow money more easily. If you go with a cooperative enterprise, a worker co-op, the banks ask who has the power, who's responsible.

As more worker co-ops are created, the drawbacks become less important. If there were enough worker co-ops, we might have some special legislation under which they could be started. And banks and credit unions would be perhaps more flexible or receptive with a known entity. Of course, if a whole bunch of worker co-ops started, there might be some threats that we haven't even thought about, threats to unions, to people in business; legislators might make them even more difficult to start.

We have no problems with the unions. It isn't like a business that is a take-over from a unionized shop where the union wants to continue to represent the workers. In our particular case the workers *are* the members; that's clearly defined and it always has been, but you can certainly see it might be a problem if people felt they were being exploited. When company owners want to sell shares to the employees, the immediate question is, "Why so benevolent? Is it just another game?" Maybe or maybe not.

CM: Your objectives go a lot further than most worker co-ops, to recreational, educational, leisure time activities, and not only for members, but for their families.

RH: That's part of the whole idea of paying a supplement to people with families. We have talked about buying some kind of recreational land for the use of members, but haven't got around to doing it. I'd say there were pretty excellent benefits now; we have everything legally available. People get a month off, and an extra month without pay if they want it. After they've been here five years they can take six months off without pay and come back to their job — a sabbatical idea — so it's far more beneficial to the employees than in many companies.

We've spent a lot of time advising groups starting up. We've got paid sometimes, have charged a fee that goes to the co-op, quite a low fee, to cover transportation and $50 a day or something. We feel it's important but it happens rarely. But we have a role in the community — and sometimes there's a benefit to us, if we help create another cooperative that's going to be a customer. Also if you feel this is important at all, then you better promote it, and so we do.

We've been involved in some publications and pamphlets on how to start buying co-ops, for example. We've financially supported a study of what was going on in B.C. stores. And we support other co-op enterprises like Co-op Radio. We're available to speak to people if they ask us. I've thought about, but never got around to organizing, a course on co-ops, how and why they work and why they don't. I think it should be ongoing. Somebody has to do it.

There was more community education three or four years ago when we were making more money, and things were a little freer. I don't think we've abandoned the idea, it's just that when you are not making much money, your priority has to be the business.

CM: What would happen if you wound up the business?

RH: The assets would go to some similar cooperative enterprise.

Actually the credit union requires a dissolution clause in any co-op they lend to, saying what happens to the assets in case of termination. If we were to dissolve, there wouldn't be much left, but the clause is there, and the current members would not be able to just distribute the capital among themselves.

CM: Would you have benefitted from somebody giving advice or helping to organize?

RH: It depends where they come from. If a government department hires a lawyer who has no interest in his particular role, then you don't expect much. We've gone to Federal Business Development Bank seminars, but have never asked them for money because we can get it at lower rates from the credit union. We have used their consultants and found that useful because the guy confirmed what we were already doing.

Since we got the initial start-up money, we've had very little relationship with government. We've got a few grants along the way, training grants for people at the bakery, but relatively little and with no strings attached. B.C. doesn't have a strong department of cooperatives that offers support as in Saskatchewan. The superintendent of co-ops here is a watchdog agency — a registrar and a distributor of papers. I've never met the guy. Ours were among the earliest LEAP grants; we had quite a fight with the LEAP coordinators. They changed their project administrator, narrowed the criteria for eligibility, and wanted to discontinue the grants altogether. We said, "Bullshit. Here is our proposal and you have to read it again or we are going to go the MLA or the Prime Minister or whatever." They backed down because they were dealing with people who knew their stuff very thoroughly and had good proposals and briefs that were well written, well thought-out, complete — 30 or 40 pages of information.

The main thing is that if people are going to finance this kind of thing, somebody among them has to see it as having some long-term importance — like 20 years, just as a business plan looks ahead for a number of years. The big corporations have 20- and 50-year plans. The directors know they'll all be dead long before the plans are ever carried out. That doesn't mean you don't make them. It is a function of age too. Here, I'm the oldest. Most people are in their 20s and 30s. The range is from 25 to 51.

CM: You could probably make double the salary somewhere else. Why are you here?

RH: It's fun. It's an opportunity for everybody to be involved, and there has been substantial growth, and that's exciting to see.

CHAPTER FOUR
Fiddlehead Restaurant
Thunder Bay, Ontario

"The workers are going to do it . . . or not."

Della Innenan, started as a waitress at Fiddlehead Restaurant in Thunder Bay. She had worked up to the staff responsibility of business coordinator and membership on the board of directors by the time I visited in mid-July 1984. She came out with me to another restaurant for our interview. It was the only way she could avoid interruptions.

The next day, I met Susan Heald, one of the founders three years earlier, still a board member, and a continuing mainstay for the staff. She was also one whose vision of a worker co-op never wavered, despite unforeseen problems on every level imaginable.

Fiddlehead could never have started without substantial grants, totalling $623,000 over three years, from LEAP — the federal government's Local Employment Assistance Program. And yet satisfying the conflicting requirements of a series of program officers, and the built-in restrictions of the program itself, which seemed to purposely limit any possible long-term success, forced the group to use scarce resources in non-productive ways. All this added to the burnout Susan Heald so graphically displays for the rest of the board of directors. Ironically, it is she, the theoretician, policy-maker and liaison with the government agency, who is exhausted, more than Della Innenan, the worker and actualizer of the principles. Nevertheless, despite fatigue, they both felt Fiddlehead was on the brink of success.

It was not to be. Within three months Fiddlehead was closed and subsequently sold to a man who owns a local health food store — apparently Thunder Bay *was* ready for a health food restaurant, if not for a worker co-op. Della was the only staff member to be re-hired. She was made manager; her intelligence and energy were recognized as an asset in any structure. Susan Heald had left only a few weeks earlier, as she had planned, to become a Ph.D. candidate at the Ontario Institute for Studies in Education in Toronto, focussing on state-volunteer interactions. She was my informant about the evolution of Fiddlehead after our interviews. She could not be more explicit. "Pain and distance keep me from finding out more," she wrote.

It's easy to analyse the sequence of events, to label the negative components: lack of clarity among the founders and in the board of directors, unwieldy structure and unclear interface between board, staff and management, untutored staff consumed with personal problems; erratic and conflicting demands from government authorities; lack of any long-term concept in the government program. Only a sophisticated, educated, cohesive and forceful crew like CRS Workers' Co-op in Vancouver could survive the last two impositions, and they weren't prey to the first three. But despite the apparent failure, there's no way the whole experience can be labelled as such. There were perhaps 70 women engaged at one time or another in the project. Seventy women experimented with the idea that they might have some control over a vital part of their lives — their work environment. To about 60 of these women, this was a new and perhaps astonishing concept. For at least 30 of them, the idea worked for months or years. They had a say in their rates of pay, in what they wore at work, in the decor of their workplace, in how to handle a cook's absence in hospital. All new experiences, new ways of thinking. Powerful learning. The beginnings of powerful change. In them and in society.

"I'd never have a chance like this anywhere else."
— Della Innenan

Della Innenan: A small group of women started it, looking for a natural food restaurant in Thunder Bay where you can get food without a lot of additives.

Two of them worked in it themselves as managers at the beginning. They were both on the board of directors, and they did a lot of research into menu planning and set policy, etc. By the time I came they had already left, so I don't know too much about them.

Now the board of directors acts as an advisory board. They hire managers and set policy, but the staff has a lot to say. In a couple of years the board will be 60 percent staff and 40 percent community members, so staff will hold most of the power in whatever decisions are made. The board usually meets once every second or third week, except in the summer. We talk about legal matters, government funding, any major problems that can't be handled in the restaurant, any drastic changes in the menu, like if we decided to put meat on the menu. As it is right now, of a board of ten there are only three staff members, because there are no other workers in the restaurant who want to be on the board. Still, the staff has a lot to say about everything that goes on.

Constance Mungall: Could the staff decide that they do not want the board?

DI: I'm not really sure. It is like a marriage; you work it out.

We have had some conflict about a manager that we had. Staff said they didn't feel that she was working her 40 hours a week. The board said they hire the manager and they tell her what to do. It was worked out by deciding that the manager would punch the time clock to give us an idea of what was going on.

Decisions about menus, hours, etc. are made by the staff. We set up a management team. We have certain people doing, say, liquor ordering, one person does hiring and firing, another girl scheduling, another kitchen supervision. The people who have been there the longest take on a lot of responsibility. For instance, we have a girl in the kitchen who is a preparation cook; she has taken it on herself to look over new workers and make sure they're doing the right kind of things — making the salads the right way for instance. It works a lot that way. If people call in sick, it's a whole staff involvement to find a replacement.

There are about 19 steady staff. There are three bakers who are not really as involved as the rest of us because they work in the middle of the night and no one ever sees them.

CM: Do they get called into the staff meetings?

DI: Oh yes. Staff meetings don't happen as often when things go smooth, about once every three weeks.

CM: What is the staff background?

DI: Most of the staff came untrained. We get a lot of people from Manpower; one of the terms of our grant is that we hire people who are unemployed, so we end up with a lot of young people. The average age is 23 — all women. Because it's a government-funded program, it's for target-group women, disadvantaged women. At one time that meant unwed mothers, people with drug and alcohol problems, but it has widened so that it's now just women. We still try to take in people with special problems and train them, but at one point there were too many of them and it was hard to run a business. Now we pretty well have a stable staff, and we bring in people from the training programs at the college, take them in for two weeks, train them and give them a report. We have done that twice now and would like to do it more. It's like a work term, just to get them back into the work force and make them feel comfortable working with people. Then they go on to something else.

CM: They are not actually part of the co-op then. Has it been very stable from the beginning?

DI: No. There has been a big turnover, but the key people that take on most of the responsibility have been here a year or longer. Maybe a half dozen have been here more than a year. Our head cook, Rita, has been here six months, and I've been here over a year.

I had a grade ten education in Sault Ste. Marie, and moved here because it's where my husband comes from. I started as a sales clerk, and then I waitressed in many different places before I heard about Fiddlehead in June of '83. I started working as a waitress, took a lot of responsibility — we did have a manager — I gradually got more involved, became a member of the board of directors, and in December of '83 our manager quit. We hired an interim manager who didn't want anything to do with the books, so I was asked if I would take them on. I didn't have any training in bookkeeping, but I managed. By the time our interim manager left, I had the bookkeeping down pat and was taking on most of what was going on anyway, so we just said that the staff would take care of it. At that time we had many staff meetings about what to do and we came up with certain people assigned to certain things and that was that. It seems to be working fine, we've only been doing it since February, six months.

CM: Did you have any training other than on-the-job?

DI: No. I learned from old records how to do financial statements. Little parts of it I didn't know — things like where do the credit cards go — but I got the hang of things and went from there. We were working with a local accounting firm; the information would go to them and we had trouble getting it back. So as of April we have done our own statements, with a professional bookkeeper to go over them once a month. The board of directors wanted that because I had no training in bookkeeping.

When the interim manager left, we looked at our budget and realized that we had to do something, so we decided to revise the schedule and cut hours drastically. We cut to the bone. There are still some changes that we are going to have to make — some cuts. It's hard to change something that's working fine, but we aren't making the kind of money that we should be, so we have to figure out a whole new way of doing things, while not changing the concept of the restaurant.

CM: Do you bring in enough from your cash receipts to pay for the food you use and salaries and overhead on the building?

DI: Right at this moment, no, but we predict increases in revenue. We have to. We have had a deficit, but we just have to get it in our heads that this is not acceptable.

CM: How much are you operating under at present?

DI: It varies — around $3,000 a month. We have to cut, that's our biggest opportunity. The staff will decide what to cut. Whatever it takes, we'll have to do.

CM: How much do you get paid?

DI: We pay the waitresses $4.00 an hour, more than at other restaurants in Thunder Bay. The minimum wage is $3.75. The waitress who orders the liquor and does the scheduling gets $4.10 and so does the women who does the hiring, firing and training. I make $6.50. I wanted to make more, but I see the figures every month and I can't do that to us right now. Our cook gets the highest pay; she makes $7.75. She does all the ordering, cooking and planning meals. She's making a good wage; we couldn't afford to lose her. And the cook trainees are making a good wage, $5.50 an hour. Mind you, they do take responsibility for the kitchen.

My pay is very low for what I'm doing, but I'd never have a chance like this anywhere else, and I think a lot of our staff feel the same way. One woman came to us a year ago as a dishwasher, then started waitressing, became a preparation cook, and now is a cookee, worked right up through the whole thing and feels real good about it.

CM: How are those wages decided?

DI: When I started over a year ago, that was the wage. At one time, anyone coming in new would also start there. Now we have a training wage for four weeks. If a new waitress does very well, I go to a couple of girls and ask if they think she deserves a raise. If you get involved in a little more than what you get paid for, participate in the decision-making, then you work your way up. At one point, we were really disappointed that all the staff were not really into this, but you have to accept that. Some people just want a job, not to have to worry about other things.

CM: They have a right to help with the decision-making, but they do not necessarily take on that right.

DI: Right. But they still come to the staff meetings, even though they don't get paid for coming.

CM: How has the business gone since you first started?

DI: This is really touchy. The business was going really well when we first started, but we had staff who didn't know what they were doing. People who came in for lunch did not get their meal; they would be here for two hours. It really hurt our business. We've also had a rough time with the public because of resentment about our government funding. It's kind of sad. We'd like to say, "Look you guys, we are trying; we are doing this work; look at us, we have pulled up this much." The revenue hasn't gone up as much as we'd like, but people are pleased when they come into the restaurant now. You get served a meal in ten minutes now. We have thought of putting up a big banner saying, UNDER NEW MANAGEMENT, when we get rid of LEAP at the end of the month. We were going to close for a couple of days, just close and then have a grand reopening. We want to put the waitresses in uniforms — long skirts — and have a little more welcome when you come to the door. The staff is still talking this over.

CM: Do you get advice about things like that? After all, that is a kind of market strategy. How do you get that expertise?

DI: We are working right now with a woman who's advertising manager at the radio station. She's set up a marketing plan for us, gone into everything, like the colour of the rug. It was one of her ideas to close. She's taken care of most of our advertising. We paid her for the actual proposal because for our second year funding we had to go through a whole thing with LEAP, and part of our problem was our advertising. Actually, she took her wage in food.

CM: Do you get any other professional advice — legal, accounting?
DI: We have a lawyer. That's about it except for some training that we want to take as a refresher; tomorrow we're going to meet with a man who's setting up a training program for us. He works for the college, training people who are already employed, so there's no charge. We're the only health food restaurant in Thunder Bay.

CM: Aside from the salaries, which I gather stand up well, what about other benefits — holidays, sick leave, medical coverage?
DI: We have the legal requirements, that's all. But we are very flexible with leave of absence. You're not going to lose your job if you have problems and have to leave instantly. A waitress in a standard restaurant would have to leave her job. It's nice. Just the other day, one of the cooks had to go for an operation, and we have to cover her. She's worried about losing her job, but she has nothing to worry about. But if it was someone we were having a problem with, the group might decide to let that person go.

CM: Do you often have interpersonal problems?
DI: No. It works well. We're old friends. We go out together in the evening. I can't think of anybody right now who is having a problem. The thing that does go on is respect for whatever anybody does. I feel respect when the girls come in and have coffee with me and take their things away with them when they leave. And everybody knows what everyone else is making. We have a lot of applications for bakers and such, but not for waitresses; we have a hard time finding waitresses, perhaps the tips are not as good.

CM: Is there any trouble in that you do make different wages, implying that some people are more important than other people?
DI: No, because there is a lot of discussion. People know why this person is making this much. We voted on a committee to hire and fire; we voted on closing times.

CM: And what happens to the people who are voted down? Is there resentment?
DI: Nothing that lasts, because sometimes things they are for will go. I may not agree with what everybody else is saying, but there may be something to it, so you think, let's give it a shot. Not everybody is that reasonable, but we have turned down requests for raises, and there hasn't

been any resentment . . . we just say this is the situation, we can't afford it . . . . This is our goal — to have people making good wages. When things get going well, then we may have to decide whether we're going to buy a new stove or pay everybody an extra 10 cents an hour.

CM: It sounds as if you yourself are going to make a real career out of this. What about somebody that sees herself as a waitress, not able to come up as you have?

DI: My door is open. I will teach office procedures to anyone who wants to learn. All she has to do is come in. Three of our waitresses have learned how to do the payroll. That's not to say that since they have learned all this we are both going to be manager. I call meetings because I get the financial statement and I figure we need a meeting. I don't feel that I should always have to call the meetings, but I seem to be the one who sees a lot of what goes on, because I kind of see it from the outside, although I do waitress regularly in the daytime too.

CM: Do you get paid $6.50 when you waitress, too?

DI: Yes. I'm on a salary which includes my car allowance and meals. I would like to take training in business management — a night course or something like that. The two seminars I did attend, the restaurant paid for them.

CM: How have you found meeting government requirements in working with LEAP? Has it been helpful?

DI: At one point, it was. One LEAP officer was not very helpful, but we have a new one now who is giving us some guidance, like maybe you should close Sunday because it's slow — this kind of thing. We make a monthly report. They were the ones who required us to go to an accounting firm to get our books done, which cost us a lot of money. And trying to employ target group women was hard — we went through a long drawn out thing to change that.

Their supervision goes on for a year after we stop getting money from them. We still have to report, and if anything goes wrong with the restaurant, they still have a say.

CM: How much capital equipment do you have?

DI: Close to $45,000 to $50,000.

If this group had done it on their own and raised the money, they would have had more of an attitude: "This is ours and we've got to do it, and we're going to put in as many hours as it takes until eventually we may be able to live off the earnings." I'm glad that LEAP funding is ending, because it's too easy to accept the deficit. There has got to be a way to make it go. If you get enough people to pull together, it will work.

CM: Are other people on the staff feeling the same way as you?

DI: They aren't really into financial statements. But I say, "Wages are too high and we have got to do something — we're spending too much money on food, how come? Is our menu out of whack? What's going on?" They go from there. That is what I see my job as — to see things and to bring it to the staff.

I really enjoy what I'm doing; it gives me so much more, and I think that a lot of people that work here feel the same way. It works well, and I would be really upset if anything happened, because it's more than a job. And you begin to wonder what will happen to these women if they lose their jobs.

"It is the bane of my existence."
— Susan Heald

Susan Heald: Ten of us formed as a group to apply to LEAP, for money to open a natural food restaurant. LEAP gives you money to start businesses they believe will become self-sufficient. It stands for Local Employment Assistance Program. LEAP will allow you up to a year's research and development time and $90,000. We asked for nine months and $96,000. During the nine months, equipment was found, the site was found, designs were looked at, menus were investigated. We also had to do an initial feasibility report; you have to hire an outside consultant, and they all know the maximum fee is $15,000 so they all charge $15,000. That was one of the worst experiences of our group to date. The consultants we had were absolutely terrible.

We had asked for tenders and decided that we wanted to stick with local people as consultants. But the first thing we got was the results of a survey in which the statistical procedures didn't even begin to be right, but it was all printed up fancy, which we were paying for, and we had to meet in a hotel room to receive this document which really said nothing. There wasn't a single correlation made. It was unbelievable. They were supposed to do pricing for us. Well, they went to a speciality cheese shop, and priced spices in 500 pound bags — completely irrelevant to our needs. Their writing was also so bad that we had to rewrite everything; we had to re-do all the statistics. We ended up paying about $12,000, but in protest, because in the end they said they wouldn't give us the document, and we couldn't apply for our first year's funding without it.

On the basis of this report we got our first year's funding approved in May, to begin in August. Between May and August we had to do all this, turn this building from a warehouse into a restaurant.

Constance Mungall: How did you choose this site?

SH: Downtown is a ten-minute walk away, and we are as close to the university and the college as nearly anywhere else. This area is where a lot of the people who are into health foods live and work and do their business. There's a co-op bookstore down the road, the offices of the Folk Festival, the credit union where we all go. Now that group is too small to support the restaurant and as things happened, it became much more appealing to a middle class crowd. I don't think we really knew that at the beginning, but also it's not like we had a million choices. At one point we were going to locate in the old station down by the waterfront — it would have been wonderful, but it still isn't off the ground — we considered the brand new mall which was going up at that time, but none of us wanted to have to deal in that kind of atmosphere. And this place was cheaper than the mall.

CM: It sounds as if you chose the location by the kind of reasoning you have just been doing rather than as a result of an economic analysis.

SH: You're right because we didn't get one. We discussed with the consultants and with LEAP where we were going to put it, but we weren't getting any advice from them anyway.

CM: So after you bought the report, how much funding was allowed?

SH: To do everything, $227,000, to renovate, build the furniture, build the window, build the kitchen, buy the equipment or rent it — most equipment is rented — then open the restaurant and supplement whatever revenue we were making. We had only up to $30,000 in capital and that is why most of the furniture is built, because that doesn't count as capital. The amounts were based on our projections, which we got from the jerks who had done the study.

The first of November this place still wasn't finished.

CM: What was the hang-up?

SH: A lot of licensing, a lot of rules being changed, a lot of we are not sure.

CM: Who administered that $227,000?

SH: Our board of directors, composed of community volunteers, plus the two women who were coordinators at the time — they were paid out of that money, and they had been paid during that nine-month period as well. So we opened late, we hired too many people, and we were not even close to meeting our expenses. And we also got an enormous amount of bad press before we even opened. The Chamber of Commerce was very angry. Our own Member of Parliament, who was even a Liberal, was hollering about it, just utter nonsense. Letters to the Editor about wasting the taxpayers' money. Two weeks after we opened, the Member of Parliament called on the front page of the newspaper for an investigation into mismanagement of the funds, without even contacting us. That ended up working in our favour because we were in his office the next morning, called a press conference for an hour later and had him running with his tail between his legs. Then he dared to tell the press that everything was all right; the investigation was all done and there was absolutely no mis-management of funds!

CM: What was he basing his criticism on?

SH: On a complaint that he got from a local member of the Chamber of Commerce who resented the competition. Our argument was that none of *them* had opened a natural food restaurant and none of *them* were hiring the kind of women that we were planning to hire. Basically, I think that the problem was that the people of Thunder Bay had never heard of this program before. What they were really objecting to was not us but government policy, and I didn't feel that we should have to be responsible for government policy. All *we* did was follow the rules. So we had all this bad press.

But we finally opened, and we ran out of money and we had to get an amendment. We ended up getting about $350,000 for that year, which was the maximum. Basically, you are monitored by LEAP. You submit financial reports. They are supposed to help areas where things are falling apart. But built into that whole structure are a lot of reasons for failures. In fact optimistically they have a three percent success rate. I don't know if it is done on purpose or if it is stupidity. One of the regulations is that there will be a board of directors made up of community people who are *not* business people and who don't work in that business. So you have board members who don't know anything by design, and you have to hire staff who don't know anything by design — natives, youth and disabled people who are "employment disadvantaged."

Our argument is that any woman is automatically disadvantaged, but their thing is that we are not to hire anyone who leaves another restaurant to come here or in fact leaves any other job to come here. So nobody has any experience. And then you have to have some kind of structure that they call acceptable; it is debatable what that is. Particularly when you're going for something like a worker ownership with a board of directors that is sort of floating around in the middle. And then you have a project officer that is cracking his whip, and every once in a while he decides we should jump in this direction and so we do, and then he decides we should really have jumped over there so we do that too.

One of the requirements that LEAP made was that we hire a so-called restaurant expert in addition to the consultant, which imposed yet another level of authority. We had the LEAP officer, the board, the expert, and the two women who are supposed to be in charge. The expert planned a training program that went on for a month. Two weeks they trained here while the place was still being finished — they practised on each other.

Then for two weeks we had groups in town come in and have their meals for half or cost price for filling out an evaluation. It was a great training program. And within three months they were all gone — every single one of them.

CM: They got their training and went.

SH: They were trained but they still couldn't get to work because of their personal problems. Initially the women we got were employment disadvantaged for very good reasons. Two were too beat up to work. One of them dragged herself to the back anyway, and then I had to come in and do a shift because she got a call that the Children's Aid had come and taken her child. Others were too drugged to work; they were dropping trays. There were women who were afraid to go to the tables.

Then there were the ones who kind of were interested in a co-op because to them that meant they could do what they wanted. So they wanted to leave rather quickly, too. We had a staff of about 30. And as we looked at our finances we realized that we had about three times too many, so we had to start laying people off right away. So we had a great training program, but it has not benefitted most of the people that are here. They are now planning another one, but I'm hoping it will be not just in how to be a good restaurant, but also in getting a sense of pride in something that they are part of — that this is *their* restaurant.

With LEAP, you are eligible for three years of funding after your research and development. We got our first and second year grants. The second was $97,000, but by February we had spent it and we still weren't breaking even, so we applied for an amendment. Then we were going to come back and apply for another year. Instead they gave us the amount of money we'd applied for — the total was $46,000 — and said you're kicked out after July. Don't come to us again.

I have a lot of problems with that. We prepared a proposal, and then they told us that wasn't good enough and we prepared another one and they said they'd decided to do it this way instead, and we don't need your proposal. It's a lot of work to make up a proposal. It leaves our volunteer board members jumping.

So we are on contract with LEAP until the end of this month. They have liens, basically, on the operation for at least another year, so we still have to report to them and keep within their guidelines; if we have to dissolve, they kind of take over. After a year, we could sell it and the workers would get the money.

CM: How do the shares work?

SH: I did some research and came upon a place in Kitchener-Waterloo that makes some kind of steel — it was a LEAP project also. They had a plan that incorporated both community members and workers. It ensured that the shareholders were workers.

We wanted to have a share that was bought for a dollar and sold for a dollar, so that the advantage of holding that share was only in the dividends, and the dividends were paid when you made your share worth something by the work that you did.

We got a whole incorporation done and then they changed the Business Corporations Act last summer to make it much more difficult. We were advised by several people *not* to incorporate under the Co-op Act, because of limits on what you are allowed to do in terms of running a business and government monitoring — apparently it is much more complicated and not suited to a profit-making enterprise. We want to be a successful business and be able to turn profits back to the shareholders, who are the workers. You can't do that anymore, so that means that either you can sell shares at a good high price — so your workers can't afford to buy them — or you can sell them at a low price, but cash them in at their actual value. Because we are still under LEAP we haven't had to worry about this just yet.

There are three kinds of shares: Common, Preferred "A" and Preferred "B". They are all voting; they all entitle you to dividends. Now if you work 400 hours you get a preference share. At 800 hours you can cash that preference share in for one common share which costs a dollar, and is the only share that entitles you to a piece of the assets. You can convert your preference shares up to five shares. In that sense it isn't a co-op; there are people who hold different numbers of shares and have a different number of votes. The range is zero to five.

Community people have a different kind of Preferred Share "B" which will cost some money. To date, only board members own them, and we didn't pay for them except in our time. The number of community shares that are out is intended to never be more than 40 percent of the total number, so that the workers as a group will always have more say.

CM: Does that 40 percent of shares carry with it a monetary value?

SH: Yes. First of all, they will be sold at an arbitrary price, and they are redeemable at that price. But if in the interim any dividends are paid on shares, those shareholders get their dividends. If the restaurant were sold we would give back the money that people paid for the preference shares and the rest of the money would be divided among the common shareholders, who are the employees. Also, when a worker leaves she is entitled to the amount of money that the shares are worth. And this is where we are going to have problems. We have a maximum number of shares, we never have more than 100 common shares out. One worker could have five percent of the value of the business which could be $500,000, which means that as soon as she leaves we are bust.

CM: You better not tell them.

SH: That is part of what we are not telling them. What we wanted to do initially was have non-voting common shares in a trust, so that there were more common shares and the value of each one was less. Then there would be some financial benefit to the worker when she leaves for having contributed to the business success, but not as high as $10,000, for instance. These women are still making $4 an hour; if they're going to make $10,000 by quitting, most of them would do it. I would do it. So one plan was to have this trust fund.

But you can't have a non-voting common share. Somebody has to vote the common shares. Actually, it was LEAP that said this wasn't really legal. I personally think that they were wrong; we could just say that the trust share votes with the majority. Then the workers would still be in control, but there wouldn't be such strong temptation to dissolve the business.

At one point we had another LEAP officer come in and say we really should be non-profit. Now I have incorporated a lot of non-profit corporations and I really don't see how a restaurant that is trying to make money could ever be a god damned non-profit corporation, and incorporating under that act would really be foolish. To buy and sell and grow and expand — I just couldn't see it. And it would mean always having a community board of directors, but what would be the incentive for the waitresses to be on the board? Basically LEAP was saying that they were going to close us down if we didn't hurry up and get this agreement together, but they never liked the agreement that we came up with. And so finally they said you have to do it this way, so we did. As far as I'm concerned, the day we are finished with LEAP we re-do the agreement.

CM: Is there any way you could have made it go without LEAP?
SH: I doubt it. It would have meant taking personal loans. The 10 of us who gathered together didn't have any money, and personally I have no interest in having any money that I might have tied up in a restaurant. I was interested in having a natural food restaurant, I had done a lot of work on getting government grants, I know all that kind of stuff — and I was interested in having a worker co-op. But I had no idea it was going to be as much of my life as it has been.

CM: Could you have got good legal advice? Is there a lawyer around here that knows anything about co-ops?
SH: I tried to talk to Brian Iler when I was in Toronto, but I never succeeded.

The present board is about half workers and half community members, three of us being originals from day one. We are not very sure what we do. Our main role has been to deal with LEAP; now that will be eliminated. Vaguely, the board makes policies and the staff carry them out. Staff has meetings too, and makes decisions. They decide what they want brought to us. It is still confused; we have not defined what constitutes policy and what doesn't. So suddenly they want to know how often they should wash the walls or something which is not policy. We spent 45 minutes yesterday discussing how we are going to move the door and then there wasn't time to look at the financial statement.

As more and more workers come on the board, it seems there is less need for meetings and more need to carry on the restaurant. The waitresses take every opportunity they can to express their opinions. Last night, the board was meeting here and the waitress who brought us some coffee lit in about what we should be doing.

It's running better than before. We ask the staff "How do you do it?" and they say, "We don't know — we just do it."

In some ways I think those of us who come at it with a theory about what being cooperative really means are mostly here because we think we will have a lot of say, and we want a say in everything, which means that decisions take forever, and people get very frustrated. It's the same with a lot of middle class liberals who think it would be fun to work in a co-op, and have all this individualism which does not really suit. Whereas the women here, they don't have all that. They say, "We want to work in a place that's nice to work in; we want to have a comfortable environment; we don't want anyone breathing down our throats. But we also want to get on with it, so things get done." Nobody says, "Who gave you the authority to make that decision?" Whatever theoretical base we were trying to operate from was never very clear.

I think that although we were taking the money from LEAP, and although LEAP was laying out the criteria for who we would hire, people never understood that. They had this notion that there was this sort of hippy group of people in town who would love to work for $4 an hour doing restaurant work because it would be a co-op and because it was natural food. Well, as near as I can make out, that group was never there. And the two women who began it were very quickly saying, "We want to be equal, but if equal means low wages then we do not want to be equal."

"We began talking about $7 an hour, but when it came down to how many people we would need and how much money we were eligible for — there were a lot of things that were unsolved — for instance, the manager would only work for a certain amount of money. And I feel that not very many people were committed to the worker-owner concept from the start. They seemed to be backing the idea, but when it came right down to really turning this restaurant over to the women who are what you call our target group, they didn't help it happen. It wasn't really a worker co-op. In fact we had managers with fairly traditional management ideas or poor personnel skills. There was very little encouragement for people to get more involved, to express more opinions, to give more thought to the whole operation.

CM: Where did those managers come from?

SH: The two women who began the idea didn't have management experience; they couldn't manage. Then we advertised and hired a fairly traditional manager out of a management school, who was expressly *not* committed to worker ownership. As soon as we gave out the first shares, she left. And there were members of the board who mistrusted the worker co-op idea too. Some weren't willing to have one-person/one-vote. They felt that the waitresses would ruin it, that they would make all the wrong decisions.

One of the first things was that the workers voted not to share tips. Frankly, I think what you do is education. You don't just throw up your arms and say, "These women are horrible, they never will get anywhere, never make the right decisions, we'll have to protect ourselves against them!" But that was the feeling of many on the board.

For a while the board would offer training, but the waitresses wouldn't come, and the management was always dumping on the workers. A lot of anger got generated in the board about that. Finally the workers said, "We would like this information and we would like it in this form," which I think is wonderful.

There were really two of us on the board who supported the move to have the workers do the managing, and try to give them the kind of information they wanted. It's turning around now so that the waitresses are doing it. We've made one of them, Della, the coordinator. Della is doing it, God knows how, but I think she is getting very tired, and one of the main support people for her is moving and that leaves a big gap. I think she is fabulous, but Della is 19 years old! I wonder if she can hold it together on her own. But mostly I just want to leave them alone because things are better than they have ever been and the board is very tired and very fragmented and very put down. The workers are going to do it or they are not.

I will try to answer whatever calls they make to me for advice, but I don't have the time or the energy anymore to try and push them in one direction or another. They call fairly often. Often I've spent 40 hours a week on this place, and this is over two and a half years, and it's just too much. It is some fun now and the thing that I like is that Della phones and asks a question, and then gets on with it, and gets it done. At least there is a sense that you are appreciated and that things are under control. I still look after the art shows and I still look after all the shares and so those things have to be turned over, probably to Della. Those are probably the major things that we have been doing.

CM: What is your own regular work?

SH: I'm completing an M.A. and I'm a sessional lecturer at the university in sociology. People kept asking me why I wasn't writing my thesis on this place and I said, "Because it is the bane of my existence and I only go to the university to get away.'"

CM: What has made you hang in?

SH: I'm stubborn. I felt like I was the only one that was pushing worker ownership and I wasn't going to walk away and let them turn it into a non-profit corporation or one where the workers had no say. In February, we first said, "OK workers, do you want to try it? Then let's go for it!" Then it was all worth it; everything had come together. It was very exciting. I think it is vaguely possible that they can make a go of it. We have got maybe eight months to do it.

CHAPTER FIVE
Wheat Song Bakery
Winnipeg, Manitoba

"We learned how to start a business from nothing . . . ."

It's easy to be wise after the fact and easier still to analyse someone else's errors. All the easier when you have an informant as open as Bruce Inglis, one of three partner-owners at the Wheat Song Bakery when I visited in a late fall afternoon. The Broadway Street shop and bakery is a block away from the Parliament Buildings in Winnipeg, Manitoba. A couple of customers and a service man with a bill to collect interrupted us, but mostly Bruce continued his clean-up as we talked. I helped him cover the trays of goodies and move them into the back just before he locked the door for the day.

Given the factors against the enterprise, it's a wonder it's operating today — and even more a wonder that the three partners are all members of the original collective. That collective was idealism personified. Among its many goals were to:

— produce a good, morally correct product
— maintain good jobs
— maintain good working conditions
— learn how to bake, to do business, and to get along
— teach other people how to bake
— control the job environment.

Whew! And this was to be done by a large, amorphous group of people, who had no knowledge of how to bake bread (a perishable product taxing to turn out right), no business management skills, and very little discipline. (The collective was conceived and born in the 70s by people who had entered adulthood mostly in the permissive 60s.)

Moreover, they had no place to turn — no legal advice, no appropriate business advice, no consultation about personnel management. If those resources were available in Winnipeg in 1978, which they probably were not, the group didn't know how to find them.

Their structure was shaky. They had literally scores of people on different levels: volunteers, part time workers, full time paid, unpaid — all wanting a piece not only of the action, but of the decision-making.

Wheat Song is no longer a cooperative, but the bakery is still there. The product is better, more varied, and reliable. Four people make a living from it. Three of them control the job environment within the demands of the product and the store. They call it a partnership.

Bruce Inglis left Wheat Song less than a year after our interview, in 1985. His partners continued the business with two employees, Eve who bakes the goodies and keeps the store, and Keith, who had been in the original collective and came back to be the overnight baker.

Business continues to stabilize and grow at about 10 percent a year. There is a new cheery orange canopy out front, and some new products on the racks. Eve, who suffers allergic reactions herself, has developed and bakes her own recipes for gluten- and yeast-free breads and cookies for the growing market of people with allergies and diabetes. They are delicious.

Does the fact that Wheat Song began as a collective make any difference today? It does, says Eve. The old members are a loyal core group of customers. Some still drop in to lend a hand. And one of their best sellers, a multi-grain bread loaf, was developed and tested in the shop ovens last year by Carolyn Ackerman, the instigator of the whole idea.

Bruce Inglis: It started in 1978 as a collective. The original idea was a restaurant, but I think because of the licensing it was too difficult, so we decided to start a bakery. I heard about it through some friends. There was one woman, Carolyn Ackerman, it was originally her idea, and we used to go to her house and discuss how we were going to arrange it. We started baking bread in her kitchen and selling it to a grocery collective. There was a core of maybe 10 people who were actually active in baking, and then there were a lot of supporting people, sort of like associates who had all donated some money to get things rolling. For a long time we baked out of this kitchen. None of us were bakers — only Carolyn Ackerman knew how — she was a trained nutritionist. The rest of us learned on the job.

I had been involved with an amusement company — operated machines — owned part of that, and I had had other jobs. A lot of the first members were out of work or they were doing jobs like bartending, and they wanted work where they would have a direct say in what was going on. That was a major factor for a lot of people. Working for large companies, they had no say in what was going on. So some people quit their jobs and came to work here. There were both men and women. Ages from late teens to sixties.

Then we decided we should try and get a little bigger, so I phoned around to all the bakeries in the city and asked them if we could rent their premises one day a week. One said sure, he would rent it to us for $50 on Wednesday afternoons. So several people went out there once a week and baked 800 loaves of bread in one afternoon, within eight hours. It is a huge oven so you could do a lot of bread.

By that time we had customers all around the city so we had a delivery route; once a week we'd deliver the bread. It worked pretty good; it looked like there was a reasonably good business there because nobody else was specializing in whole grain breads. From there we started looking for a location and we found this place. It was a fish restaurant called The Pirates' Wharf. The place was in an absolute mess and we fixed it up. Got a bunch of people together and came in and tore out walls and rebuilt it and brought this oven in.

There was still the basic 10 people. Things were rolling then and we wanted to keep it together.

We started with whole wheat bread; it was the main line, 100 percent stone ground, and then we started to branch into other types like rye, raisin, apricot and some specialty breads like gluten-free, health diet breads, and then the goodies.

The original idea was to have a place for people to learn how to bake. It was not only a business, but to bring in people from the community who wanted to learn. So we got a lot of people in here who just wanted to learn how to bake and then they took off.

Baking is taxing because you start at midnight and work all night. It's hot and fairly heavy, so you have to be in pretty good shape to stick at it; that is a factor in this business. I know from other collectives that they have a very high burnout rate, not from the physical work but from the tensions of running the collective. But here it's a combination of the physical and the interpersonal, and that has always been a problem. That's one reason why so many people left the collective. They couldn't handle it. The women would find it much too heavy and so they would leave.

It still is a challenge to get this bread to turn out properly because it's a very delicate operation; it's not like an ordinary bakery where they use chemicals to make the dough rise. If the temperature is a little bit off then the stuff isn't going to turn out, so this is a continuous challenge.

You can't make whole wheat bread commercially; it's too hard to make, that's why nobody is doing it. Regular bakers go to bakery school and they learn how to put chemicals in it. But eventually we developed a loaf that looks like a regular loaf of bread. So we are proud of that; we did this when everybody said we couldn't do it.

Constance Mungall: How did you get your initial working capital? Did members invest?

BI: Some members made a very small donation — $5 or something — a few hundred in total. But we started so small — all the overhead we had was $50 to rent the bakery once a week.

Nobody was getting any pay; we did it all voluntarily. To buy the equipment here — everything we got was second-hand. We got this counter from an old school that was being torn down; the sink was minimal; the oven cost $1,000; the mixer is rented. So the only start-up cost was the rent on this building which was $250, plus a license and some ingredients.

CM: And at that point you began to pay yourselves salaries?

BI: We did get some money and some of it was held back. We would be paid $4 an hour, but $2 would be held back. And to start with there were only two people full time. I was doing something else as well as working here, and there were other people who were volunteering. There was a lot of free labour still going into it.

The big thing with almost everybody was the fact that this was a unique business because nobody else was producing whole wheat bread without additives, and the people who were buying it seemed very happy with it. Here we were creating something that didn't exist in this city and people seemed to really want it. The bread being sold in the grocery stores was not a good product, not even healthy, and we wanted to do something about that. So that made everybody happy.

But business wasn't very steady. Every once in a while a reporter would come along and do an article, and business would just skyrocket. But that wouldn't last because you got a lot of curious people, but they wouldn't bother coming back.

CM: Did you choose this area because it is within close walking distance of the Parliament Buildings and a lot of people who would buy your products?

BI: This spot was available, it was central, and it was cheap. Cheapness was the major factor; I recall I wanted a more expensive building down the street that was bigger and in better shape, but we decided on this one because it was more affordable. It looked like a pretty good location at the time because there were a lot of university students in the area, but the residents have changed; the neighbourhood is deteriorating so we don't get the clientele that we thought we were going to get from the immediate area. We get people from all over the city.

We actually had a map posted for a long time, and we would ask customers when they came in to put a sticker on where they lived. That's how we found out where they came from. More live in areas like Fort Rouge, but they come from all over.

CM: What was your legal structure?

BI: We incorporated as a collective, which is something looser than a co-op. One of our problems was that we never had any policies or by-laws. We set out to do that, but we could never decide on what to write in. Also, we never had a lawyer. One fellow considered himself to be knowledgeable in legal matters, and we assumed that he was, but he wasn't. We made a lot of mistakes hiring people who were not qualified because we couldn't afford to pay proper lawyers. A lawyer came to a meeting once and gave suggestions, but it was such an unusual situation that he didn't know what to do.

Collectives are not really covered by legislation, but a co-op is. Everything is laid out; you can just plug into it, I guess.

CM: But anybody who was working here had one vote.

BI: In theory, yes. I guess legally they would have one vote. Everybody who worked here was on an equal basis. We all had equal say. But that brought some problems. Everyone wanted their own way. For a time a lot of people enjoyed it. There were a lot of good things about it, but conflicts began to build up. The pressure became too much somewhere along the line. People got upset and left.

CM: Why did people want to work here if it was so . . . ?

BI: They were sort of fascinated by the idea of a collective, and a lot of them were interested in baking; I think most people enjoyed the actual work, but the hours were a problem, too, because you have to work all night baking bread. Some people were unemployed and would come here until they got a job somewhere else with more money and better hours.

CM: And when people left they would draw out their unpaid wages?

BI: In some cases they demanded it immediately and in others they took it over a period of time. We went through a number of bookkeepers. Most of the workers had no direct contact with the books because they had no interest in them. We would give the job to a worker to look after, and three months later they would throw their hands up and say they couldn't do it. Some did have training, but it's incredible the number of bills that come into a tiny place like this. And then people spend money out of their own pocket and come along to collect — "Where is the bill? I haven't got it." And there were so many people on the payroll that it was very difficult. They'd come and they'd get paid for awhile and they'd quit and you'd have to do all this income tax; it just got out of hand. In six months about 40 people had come and gone, which gives you an idea of the turnover of people and the record-keeping involved there.

There was nobody with a really sound business knowledge, although the last bookkeeper was experienced, but he didn't have any knowledge of business management. In that case, he thought that because he was the bookkeeper he should run the whole show, so that was another problem. People should not be involved in business without the basic skills of business management.

CM: How about some training in the basic skills of conflict resolution?

BI: I was thinking about that today, that there doesn't seem to be anywhere to learn. We get involved in a collective and have to resolve these problems and nobody knows how to go about it. Once you are actually involved in a conflict your emotions take over and you can't be rational; you try to be, but it's difficult.

Where do we learn these things? Maybe it's something that has to be learned early in life, and we're not being taught that. Something is missing because the people that I have been involved with are reasonably intelligent, and yet in most of the cases where people left, they left angry; their emotions sort of carried them away. They didn't seem to be able to handle a certain stress, and it seems to me we are not learning that. So maybe it has nothing to do with collectives, but is general in society. When the collective was running into trouble, those who were left would say all we needed was the right people, but we went through a lot of people here and it seemed that the right people never did get together.

CM: Did you ever identify the kind of people that would be right?

BI: Different people identify different qualities. Generally I think everybody would agree on certain things; they should be hard-working, cooperative workers. But hard-working cooperative people seem to be stubborn as well.

CM: Did you ever set up regulations, by-laws? "This is the way we are going to work together, this is how we are going to make decisions, these decisions are made by this group."

BI: We tried to set out by-laws, but it got bogged down. We couldn't agree on what should go into them.

We did try organizing with a coordinator, but then people would become upset with the way things were going, or they would feel that they had too much work and other people weren't pulling their weight — this was a common problem. Some of the full time workers got very ugly with the part time workers, who would come in and do things their way and wouldn't consult because they thought they had the run of the place. This was the major problem: people not cooperating. Or they thought they were cooperating, but they weren't really; they kept doing things independently, making decisions independently, working, baking. Another problem was that with so many people making the product, it was not consistent. One night the bread was really good, and the next night it would be flat as a pancake. Customers didn't like this and they complained.

A coordinator was to take over for a year, to commit himself to running the business for one year. He was fairly successful — the business built up, we went on TV and pleaded to the public that here was a community business that was going broke and got in the newspapers on the same basis — so people were curious and came down here and the business made a fortune. We built up a huge bank account. But at the same time, there was such a state of confusion, the way it was organized — people were literally hating each other, they were angry with each other, they were in little groups lobbying to get things done. In one case one of the bakers left so upset that she took some of the recipes with her. She claimed that she had developed them — they were hers, they didn't belong to the collective. That was the sort of thing that was happening and kept on happening. On one occasion there was a physical fight and just incredible anger so they couldn't even be in the same room, and some of them quit after that.

After six months the coordinator had had enough with all the personal conflicts. It didn't matter about the commitment, he had just had enough. And when he quit the money went just like that. After all the publicity died down there was nothing to maintain the business, and no more advertising. The people who were left used up all the money in wages and there was no business coming in. So they were going bankrupt. The coordinator who had quit approached me and said I should buy it. I thought it would be a good business, so I went to a woman who had been a member, a baker, and she was interested, and another woman who was a baker plus her boy-friend who had also been a member and bookkeeper, and the four of us decided to take it over.

Buying it was very tricky because in Manitoba you cannot sell a non-profit organization, but we consulted a lawyer. It had never come up before so nobody knew what to do.

There was no money left in the accounts of the collective. They owed money. The three women who were left paid themselves off. The bakery owed $3,000 to a group called Harmony Foods, set up to fund community projects. So we assumed the loan and there were still some outstanding bills from the collective which we assumed. The total value of the equipment we took over was under $3,000. We didn't lay out money to purchase the equipment because there was nobody to give the money to; we just assumed the debts. Each of the four partners put in $500 to get things rolling again.

We did check to see if we were eligible for government loans, and we did check with banks to see how much we could borrow if necessary. We don't foresee getting a loan or a grant right away.

I don't think we want to deal with the Federal Business Development Bank. We could; we have checked into that; if we wanted the bank would give us a loan on the strength of our business.

As far as grants go, like Department of Regional Industrial Expansion grants, they would like us to hire more people — that is one of their stipulations — and I don't think we are prepared to go along with that. We have shied away from that for the time being.

CM: What percentage profit do you make now?

BI: Around 20 percent. Our own store is the major outlet. We sell to one restaurant, Good Old Days, and we supply Vita-Health. They have six stores and they take quite a bit of our bread, about 10 percent of bread sales. We also sell to a collective grocery store, Harvest Collective. We do some advertising in small newspapers, local magazines, no radio or TV.

CM: Do you have a tie-in with other community groups, other collectives that give you support?

BI: There aren't many left as collectives — the only one that I am aware of is the Harvest Collective which we get along with very well. That is about our only connection, plus Harmony Foods, that loaned the bakery collective money. It's a very loose organization. We're still paying off their loan.

Our customers give us support because they obviously like our product, and some have been coming since the bakery opened. They don't care whether it's a collective, a co-op, a private business or what; all they are coming for is the bread.

CM: But other groups, I'm thinking of big groups like Co-operators insurance or Cooperative Wheat Pool?

BI: No. We have no connection with them at all, never did.

CM: Have you ever thought of talking to people there and seeing if there could be advice or if they have in-house courses?

BI: No, it never occurred . . . you mean as far as operating as a co-op? It is something we may look into.

CM: Are you able to make a living out of the business now?

BI: Yes, we all make a living. I make $900 a month. I work about 55 hours a week, sometimes less; it depends on how busy we are. If I work overtime, that extra pay goes into an account as back wages so that if I leave or quit I take it out, but for the time being I leave it in so the company can use it.

The guy that is doing the bookkeeping bakes as well. He has so many hours a week to do the bookkeeping but he doesn't get any more for doing it than I would for talking to a newspaper for advertising for example. He's never asked for more money. We get along fairly well, that's why we are still together; it's almost three years, which is pretty good. So generally we can get along.

The present system of the partnership is not much different from the collective except that there are fewer people; there were four partners but one left. There are three partners and one employee, and I think it's very confusing for her. We have a partnership which is basically a collective or a cooperative. We run into the same problems that the collective had, because you have three people who are three bosses. You have fewer people to conflict with, but it is still there, mainly management decisions like, what are we going to do with this business, are we going to stay here or move? We should move; this is a key issue right now, but we can't find a place. One says we are doing all right here, why should we move? And the other two say they want to move, so you've got conflict there. The two accuse the third of not being ambitious or progressive.

This is one example, but it's the kind of conflict that runs through the whole thing, right down to cleaning up the place. Someone has not cleaned off the counter — and these things build up. When that happens repeatedly with a lot of people you have trouble. That's probably why people leave a collective; they can't put up with the aggravation. When you're working for somebody and the boss makes a decision, you quite often might say, "He's the boss. I don't like it, but I got to do it, otherwise I'll get fired." In a collective it's different; you feel that you have enough power to say, "I want this done," but if you're out-voted then you don't get what you want. We actually get along fairly well now. But when you get more than one person in a business, the potential for conflict is there. I've never been married, but I don't think after being in a collective that I would be if it's anything like this.

CM: It doesn't sound like much fun.

BI: The stress factor is very high, or it was, but even now I would rather be in this situation than working for somebody where I had no control, where if I did certain things I would be fired. I enjoy the work. I'm making this fine product, so that sort of keeps me going. But the work is becoming more and more tedious because it is repetitive. It's not challenging intellectually at all.

CM: Could you get challenge in some other way, by diversifying your product or by expanding the business?

BI: That is what we talk about, but at this point I think we're all a little reluctant to expand the business because we don't know if we want to stay with it and to go personally into debt. As far as a challenge, yes in a way it is. It's still going. For the people who want this product it's still here. It's still providing jobs for four people and it has provided jobs for a lot of people along the way. It is actually pretty amazing to consider that nobody with any particular baking skills or business skills started this and we are still carrying on. Maybe the odd thing is that the original members of the collective are now the owners.

This bakery could keep going indefinitely. I think it will. If we eventually leave someone will come along and take over. The collective didn't work out, but there were some good things — plus a lot of people met other people and continued to be friends. I've met people through this that I'm still friends with. A lot of people learned how to bake and maybe they picked up some other skills too — management skills; by observing all the things that didn't work out, they learned how to do them. And those of us who started it learned how to start a business from nothing, with no money or business skill.

CHAPTER SIX
Wild West Organic Harvest Co-operative
Richmond, British Columbia

"We're going to see it through."

Darcy Hamilton met me in an East Vancouver co-op house — there was a bus strike on and I couldn't get out to the warehouse on the outskirts of the city. Darcy is small and slight — doesn't look big enough to drive the truck and unload crates of fruit and vegetables. But that's her role in operating the wholesale organic produce distributor — as well as functioning as a director of the co-op.

Wild West is now a women's collective, although it didn't start as one. And it has established and operates the only certification program for organic produce in Canada, with its own farm inspections, reports, and educational program.

Wild West had been operating seven years when I visited, had weathered two financial crises, and was about to face another. The first crisis was when a founder, burnt out, withdrew and took an important chunk of the market with him. The second was when the warehouse opened a retail outlet on Granville Island, the trendy housing and market area near downtown Vancouver. Overstaffed and badly managed, the store put the co-op in the red, and CCEC, the Vancouver credit union that is a major funder for all the worker co-ops in the area, withdrew its loan.

When I visited, a number of short-term loans that had been negotiated privately to tide the co-op over the second crisis were coming due. Darcy felt they could be paid off, but the co-op wanted a further loan to finance a cooler for apples, which would put the whole business on a firmer footing. Both their former lenders, CCEC and the Federal Business Development Bank, took a dim view of their chances, and refused.

Darcy made no attempt to whitewash all the trials the co-op has faced. She's proud of its survival and its experimental approach. I got the impression the whole enterprise runs on guts, commitment, ingenuity, idealism and optimism — as well as a lot of hard work. Whatever the combination, it seems to be working. After my visit, Wild West succeeded in finding the money to increase their storage capacity, building a 1,200-square-foot walk-in cooler, mainly for apples. Its staff has doubled, to eight, five full members and three awaiting membership. Co-op sales for 1985 were around one million.

Darcy Hamilton: I got involved about a year after it started; it didn't start as a worker co-op, it started as wholesale distribution for organic produce. In 1977, they decided to incorporate as a co-op; I think they decided that partly because they had experience in food co-ops and liked that form of ownership.

Our main focus is still the distribution of organic produce. In Canada we are the only people who have a certification program. We developed our own standards and we have an affidavit and a farm report. We buy as much as we can around B.C., in the Gulf Islands, Vancouver Island, the Fraser Valley and the Okanagan. When we import or buy from other people we try and buy from people who are part of organizations like California Certified Organic Farmers or distributors who have checked out growers. We've had our certification program about four years. We're going to make some changes this year to change the emphasis from "no chemicals" to soil building, because that is where the difference really is.

Constance Mungall: You must have to provide educational material to your suppliers?

DH: We do, and we learn a lot from growers. We can help them switch to organic, and get supplies. We have a very limited budget, but we try to do some consumer education.

Most of our market is small health food stores and co-ops and concerned individuals — people who have to eat food that has not been sprayed. We try to encourage individual buyers because they are very loyal. The retail outlets have been really fickle. Even the health food stores. We are competing with the standard-grown product, which is cheaper to produce, so we have to charge more. A big part is that food is priced below the producer's cost in a lot of cases, so people think they are getting cheap food, but they are just not paying the real cost. So when you have a whole different network with organically grown, and you pay the producer more of his costs, you have a higher priced product.

CM: But you nevertheless have been able to survive for six or seven years.

DH: We had a really rough year two years ago and it has taken us that time to come back. In the beginning there were about 10 or 12 of us. When it was incorporated in May 1977 we just had the wholesale outlet. That fall some of the originals went. The people left were newer in the business, learning the ropes. The business had not been run really tight; the book-keeping had not been kept properly and so we did not know where we were at. So we had to learn how to run a business and work at the same time. After two years the business had lost a lot of money, people were feeling very discouraged, and decided to quit. Then one of the men who was a key figure left and took with him a chunk of the distribution area and called it his own. He had just put in too much energy and was burnt out. We had to build it up again in different areas and we made some big changes in our market structure and management, and turned it around. Within a five-month period, we had come from a $30,000 loss to a $5,000 profit.

Then we had another opportunity. Granville Island was just being built as a farmers' market, and they wanted us to have a place there. So we said sure, and started a store. We started it at first as a separate worker co-op because we did not know how it would go, and we did not want it tied into the wholesale. That went on for a couple of years, steadily losing a little bit of money and changing personnel a lot. The store people thought the wholesale was evading responsibility, and if it was all one big business we'd do more about it. So we changed the incorporation so that it all became one big business. That was really a mistake; we should have left it as it was. The store was badly managed and overstaffed and not getting enough sales and kept losing money.

After it had been running for four years and had lost nearly $40,000 in the last two, we decided to contract out management of the store to two of the women who had been working there and who had a commitment to it as their own business. It has worked out better for us because they take care of all the expenses. They manage it a lot tighter.

We tried to get advice from the government, but we had a hard time getting help. We had a couple of CASE workers from the Federal Business Development Bank. They didn't tell us anything we didn't already know, but they helped focus things a bit. We found when we went to outside people that the produce business is really different from regular wholesale. We can't go by the statistics and we have higher labour costs and because we are working with perishable foods our focus is different. As far as business help is concerned, we relied mostly on our own ideas. We made the best changes when we could try out an idea and evaluate it to see if it would work. The advisors did not know what a worker co-op was or how it ran.

But I think in the beginning the main problem was that we did not have any basic business skills, like good bookkeeping. After we had hired our third or fourth bookkeeper we began to look for someone with specific skills who could do a trial balance and statements. We knew better what we were looking for because we knew what information we needed to decide what the business was doing.

Wild West has for a long time had specialized jobs. We hire bookkeepers and warehouse workers, and that is the person's function, at least until they have been here for awhile and can take on other responsibilities. I started as a truck driver and a warehouse worker. Now I am the buyer and I still drive the truck and do the deliveries. We have changed from just hiring anybody to being more specific about what we need and also asking for much more commitment. We ask for a financial commitment and also a two-year commitment to work with Wild West.

We have been a woman-run business for the past five years. Now we are four women. It's a requirement now that you be a woman, but it wasn't in the beginning.

We work together really differently than a mixed group. Women bring more of their hearts into their decisions. We make decisions with more factors thrown in and we understand each other better, communicate better in general. In my experience women put more energy into communicating and so in a collective where communication is important, it makes a big difference. It's run more smoothly since it's been only women. A man would have to have a pretty strong feminist outlook to be accepted by us at present.

I really enjoy the work a lot — working with women, I find them really concerned about their work environment and the health of the people that work here. We've had a good time. We don't meet outside work a lot although one of the women has a farm and we go there and visit.

We range in age from 26 to late 30s. I've been in food co-ops for 12 years. I came from working with a food and distribution co-op as part of the paid coordinating staff. Jane came from a health food store, concerned about health and food. The other two women have worked with women in social services.

Most people have two main jobs right now — I'm a buyer just sitting at the desk and making phone calls and thinking about what we're going to sell. But I also drive the truck and move boxes into the stores. Jane is a buyer, but she works in the warehouse and her main focus is the certification program. Sue does mostly office work, bookkeeping and telephone sales. And Alf does mostly warehouse work. That's the way we're working right now. It's really a good experience, a really strengthening experience for the group.

Our hiring process has been the same for a long time now. We put out that we need workers through handbills and notices in places like co-ops, alternate bakeries, health food stores and in our catalogue. We need people who know what organically grown food is and have that kind of interest. We interview the applicants and they have a three-month trial period with two evaluations before it's decided whether they become a member. If they do, they have a $400 share to put into the business. That can come off their pay.

Right now the pay is very low, because we are recovering from this low period. It's $5 an hour, and we average 40 to 50 hours a week. When things were better we paid about $5.75 an hour, and when we made small profits, we paid bonuses. We pay sick leave and we have a dental plan, and the workers can buy food wholesale. But our pay is really low compared to wages in this area. In B.C., a lot of the wholesalers are unionized and a lot more mechanized, so they are more highly paid. We are capital-poor and use a lot of hand labour. It's hard to get applicants, because we pay so low. Also, it is more difficult to hire in the summer because people just want to have fun then. When it gets cold and raining they start thinking about getting a job for the winter.

We need somebody now right away because the woman who does part time bookkeeping for us went back to school. We are covering our extra warehouse work with casual labour, friends and people who have worked here before for a day or two at a time. We'll do that until we find someone who will fill the slot.

For a while we were really going through staff: hiring, quitting, hiring and quitting all the time. We had a hard time keeping people for a year even. I personally had been with the business for four or five years at that point, and I felt ripped off that I was getting the same amount of money as this person who had been here two weeks and had so little commitment to the business.

That's the hardest part with getting the same money. The people that I work with now are putting in so much energy and so much personal commitment that I don't feel that at all. But when we were going through that period with a lot of new and inexperienced people it was really hard to take home the same pay. I didn't feel good about that.

CM: Even now, you've made a larger investment to the company than the new person that is coming in for instance. Have you talked about how to look after that?

DH: No, not really. Because our business has been in really hard times, we consciously made that commitment, "Okay we're going to do this; we're going to see it through." When you've put that much in and you've seen it work out, that itself is a reward. I think if the business gets comfortable again pay differences might become an issue. We've discussed it in the past. There are a couple of people in the group right now, and it's really important to them that people get the same amount of money. It would be a really big decision if we changed that.

It's not an issue with me right now. I just want everyone to get more money because I think we pay low wages, to survive in these times.

We've always paid a bit more to people with children, but the business is so weak it's hard to do that, now. You have to look at, can you afford to hire someone with kids, and pay the extra 50 cents or dollar an hour? None of the people who work here now have dependents, but that could be a factor if someone applies. There was a women's group in Seattle and it got to be really bad; a woman with three or four children would take home a lot more than someone who had been in the business for 10 years, with no dependents. That got to be a big issue there.

Wild West started initially just on its working capital and got a short-term $5,000 loan for a year to do the initial purchase for importing. When that was paid back, we got a small loan to buy a little truck and got a line of credit for $10,000 from a local credit union. The dollar volume of wholesale sales stayed about the same over a two- or three-year period, but the actual number of cases dropped considerably. Even last year we weren't increasing. So the wholesale wasn't making a lot of money, and the store was losing money, and we weren't able to put any aside. The loan was called when we lost all the money on the store, and it almost did us in. We had to get more funding, but the banks wouldn't come anywhere near us, so we got more private money. We got one private loan for $10,000, and we still owe that money. Then we put out a community letter and got $100 loans for a long period. We got a reasonable response. We got one really big loan and quite a number of small ones totalling about $17,000. That helped us to pay off debts to suppliers and give us operating capital. The interest we paid varied according to what people wanted, from 5 percent to 13 percent. Those loans to individuals are due next spring. We have been running the business very carefully, and we will be able to pay the money back then, but we went back to the banks this summer for money to build a cooler to store apples, but they still wouldn't give us any. The credit union won't, and the Federal Business Development Bank won't either. It's really amazing. They say that we won't be able to pay it back, that we don't have enough spare money to make the payments. It's a Catch-22 situation, because if we have the cooler we will make enough money and if we don't we won't. We need to borrow $15,000. We have projections that show that from apple sales alone from the cooler we could show a profit of $25,000. Isn't that amazing? Plus our regular sales are doing real good. They have been at least five to six percent over projections for the whole of this year.

So what we are going to do again is to appeal to private funding to get this cooler. It is a bit time constraining because it needs to be done by the end of September. We'll go the bank when we are making millions, and see if they will lend us any then! It's such a hard situation.

CM: What kind of assets do you have?

DH: Hardly any. We lease our warehouse — 6,500 square feet — in Richmond.

Basically, the truck company still owns the truck. We bought a new big truck two years ago which cost us $42,000. We scraped together the down payment mostly from our personal investment in the business. That's when our shares went up. When everybody put in their money plus a couple of small loans from individuals we had enough for the down payment, and the truck company lent us the rest of the money. It was a really tight time; they needed to sell trucks very badly or they wouldn't have come near us, and we're still paying 21 percent interest on the loan because we can't find anyone to re-finance it for us. The credit unions are just like the banks sometimes.

Lack of capital has been our hardest problem — to buy even basic delivery equipment, and hand trucks and electric trucks for the warehouse, and coolers to keep our product in — really basic stuff. The business can make money to pay people, but to make a lot of extra money to buy those big purchases . . . you can't do it in the food business.

CM: How do you make decisions?

DH: We have business meetings every Wednesday afternoon. When you are so small — four people — and when you have worked together so long, decision-making is much more simplified. One person has worked here a year, myself and another seven or eight years, and the other for three. We make a lot of day-to-day decisions really; we don't have to wait for the meeting. Over the years it has evolved that a person can make a lot of decisions without having to take them to the group. We trust each other.

Our business meetings usually last three or four hours — paid time. Wednesday is usually a slow day so we just close down for the meeting. It has worked out really well. We all share management responsibilities. We pretty much make decisions by consensus. At one point we had more people who were concerned about the political aspects of worker co-ops. It was really difficult to make decisions then because they wanted decisions that were socially important, and the business decisions suffered. For example, should we sell to Safeway stores? It's a big corporation that sort of represents a lot of what's wrong in the food business. We discussed it for a long time. We changed our decision-making process so that we had to have a 75 percent majority because we were having such a hard time reaching consensus on issues like that. We had eight or ten people at the time and it was really hard. The people whose focus was on the social or political implications and the others who wanted to make a profit and survive, those two groups just really bashed heads.

CM: So the ideologues quit?

DH: Yes, withdrew. They were almost forced to because the business kept getting in financial trouble. The group that's here right now hasn't really strong ideology about the world and how agriculture and business should be run. We have to prove our ideals by surviving as a business. Now 99 percent of our decisions are by consensus. We work out a decision that will work for all of us, but we can go to a majority if necessary. The truck was our first major purchase and for some people it was a big struggle to think about owing that much money. What to do with our product line was another: should we expand into other things like dry goods, nonperishable food? At one point we even considered handling produce that wasn't organically grown, in the winter, for example, tomatoes; in the produce business you are expected to have tomatoes 52 weeks of the year. So we decided to do that. We never actually did, partly because we just couldn't compete with the commercial food handlers. It wasn't an ideological decision, but economic. I think we actually made a consensus decision on that.

I think the breaking point in trying for consensus is when we can't make a decision for a long time. Then we say, "We have to decide something. Why don't we just put it to majority vote?" In seven years it has happened on maybe five decisions, and the bigger the group the more you have to use it.

It's very amicable right now, but when we hire the new person she may have a hard time working into the group, we have to be really conscious of that. Also, you tend to let things slide more than you would in a big group, where you can use constructive criticism more conscientiously. In a small group you are closer together and you don't want to hurt feelings; you even get to a point that you accept the person, and you give up trying to change them. But it's not good to let that kind of thing go on. It always gets strange in the end.

Even with constructive criticism and meetings every week it is really hard not to just force out people who aren't working well. Instead of firing them you make it so hard for them that they just quit. Firing is hard for collectives to do. We've fired a couple of people and it was hard, even though they couldn't do their work.

It would have to be a whole group thing to fire someone — we have never been a big enough group to delegate the job. Of course they would know it was coming because they would have had an evaluation, been told where they had to improve . . . evaluations should happen regularly. It's one of the things we've let slide but it is something that we should still do, even with a stable group and four people. We used to evaluate everybody once a year.

CM: When somebody goes do they take their share with them?
DH: Yes. We make an agreement with them on how much notice they get. How soon we can pay them back depends on our financial situation; we try to do it as soon as we can. Some people have been real easy when they quit, they just got their shares back in food over a period of time. Others needed the cash right away. It hasn't been a problem, but if a person had thousands invested it would be.

CM: You are incorporated as a co-op, so that means that you have a constitution. How did you write that?
DH: The constitution is the one the original group wrote at the very beginning, so it has a really big focus on agriculture and communities and buying land. The possibility was there of buying land and operating a

farm as a group and doing more distribution. So that is still the main thrust of the constitution. There is not much on how we operate, which has just evolved over the years.

CM: Have there been any disadvantages to being incorporated as a co-op?

DH: No. I think we are discriminated against as women in getting funds, not because we are a co-op, although it's hard to tell. There's an alternative credit union here called CCEC and we've dealt with them pretty much ever since we've been in business. They're the people that called the credit line in on us and nearly closed us down. When we went to them for capital for the cooler they still said they didn't think we could do it. I think being a group of women has been a factor in our dealing with financial institutions. When I first came across that idea it really amused me. All they look at is your financial statements, and it should be apparent what's there, but they deal mostly with men, and there are very few banks or credit unions that have women managers. A woman has to really act like a man and use their operating modes to get into those positions. It's interesting.

Being a worker co-op might have been a bit of an advantage in getting customers because we've been able to work pretty closely with other co-op wholesalers. That's provided us with buying clubs and co-ops and contacts. But most of the people we deal with, it doesn't really make a big difference to them. I don't know if it has helped or hindered in getting capital.

The only people who care how you manage are the FBDB people; one of the factors in considering their loans is how the company is managed and how much equity the people who own it put in. We usually approach them every time we need money. When we started the Granville Island retail store they put up an equal amount of money, a $4,000 loan at current interest rates. We had to pay that back.

CM: What are your plans for the future?

DH: We've been working so hard at making the business survive that we haven't gone into any kind of expansion plan. I guess the plans for the future are basically to build a strong connection with local growers, it works sort of haphazardly right now. We need more markets and we need to build up a grower base here, a base of supply. We worked this year on our certification program and getting that stronger and expanding that so that we can certify in the States. We want to improve our distribution system too; we added a new delivery route this summer. We're trying to give better service so that people will buy more from us. We're not trying to create a market, we're just trying to serve better what we have, and to educate consumers.

In the last two or three years we've tried to put out as much information on organically grown produce as we could. We've put out brochures about our activity as a co-op and our focus on organically grown, and little things that stores can hang in their produce department — take-home things, bag stuffers with information on organically grown. Those have been three main successes.

There's more of an awareness now because there have been so many pesticide scandals over the last few years. We buy from suppliers whose focus is organic growing, and we sell to people who know about it, care about it and so we get really isolated. That's an interesting part of the education thing, having some kind of grasp on what people don't know. Having successes is really important. Turning around a bad financial situation when everybody thinks it's really gloomy, it's really interesting. Even the experts say that's the biggest factor. You can look absolutely the worst possible and everybody will say there is no hope. But if the people who are in the business are committed to it and want to make it work, then it will work, nine times out of ten. It's that kind of energy that makes all the difference.

That's what happened again in our second financial crisis, around the store issue. We knew it was losing money and we kept thinking that it was going to change around. I'm an optimist and a hopeful person personally, so even though the whole group was saying, "Look, this is the point where we have to stop," I really felt strongly that it could make it. When these two women took the store over and ran it properly, it made it. They don't make a lot of money, but it makes wages for them and it's not losing money any more.

With the people who worked at the warehouse the personal commitment has always been there. You take it really personally when the business is not making money. It's mine and I'm going to take responsibility for the fact that's it's losing money and do something about it.

CHAPTER SEVEN
Northern Breweries Ltd.
Sault Ste. Marie, Thunder Bay, Timmins, Sudbury, Ontario

"We had to get off our butt and make a proposal."

My sojourn across Canada took me to Thunder Bay, where I interviewed one of the branch managers of Northern Breweries Ltd., Eric Holm. Later, I talked with Ross Eaket, the president of the company at headquarters in Sault Ste. Marie. Northern Breweries has seven plants, four breweries and three soft drink bottling plants, in four northern Ontario cities. When I talked with Ross Eaket in 1986, the company had annual sales of $27 million, up from $12 million when the employees took it over from Canadian Breweries Ltd. in September 1978. Both Eaket and Holm had been with the company before the change-over. They kept their jobs, but also became shareholders then. Eric Holm has since retired.

It was the then president Mac Coulter in Sault Ste. Marie who, within 10 days, obtained the necessary financing to make a successful bid. He had tried once before, in 1971, to buy the hundred-year-old family-owned business from Dorans, the founders, but Canadian Breweries had outbid him. In 1978, Coulter went to a Friday afternoon employees' meeting asking for pledges. He was hoping for $800,000 to $900,000. Before the deadline, he had $1.2 million, and cooperation from the banks.

When the majority — 85 percent — of Northern Breweries' employees put their money where their jobs were, the label was losing its identity, becoming just another Carling O'Keefe brand, and markets were slumping. Now, with employee pride and identity re-established, the company is holding its own, and more.

Eaket doesn't fault the former owners for the slump, but he does point out that a small unit of a large company can get lost, have trouble conforming to national policy.

Northern Breweries is not a worker co-op — voting is according to number of shares held, not one-man/one-vote, and the membership on the board of directors is not a reflection of the number of management, office and plant employees, but rather of the number of shares each category holds. Nevertheless, it is truly employee-owned: 85 percent of the workers are shareholders. They do have input, and the company does benefit from their participation.

Employee take-overs were discussed at length at a national workers' co-op conference in Saskatoon in 1985. Richard Long, head of the Department of Organizational Behaviour and Industrial Relations at the University of Saskatchewan, reported on several studies he and others have done in the field.

As at Northern Breweries, it is often the manager who initiates the takeover. "In some cases, management benefits more than anybody else," he said. But in firms where employee participation is in truth enhanced, "they are generally financially viable and their success rate is very good." One study showed that majority employee-owned companies are 50 percent more profitable than conventional corporations in the same industry. Some of these companies, like Northern Breweries, were already unionized when they were taken over by the employees, and again like N.B., they almost all retained the union.

"The only reason we have a union is we're in the beer business."
— Eric Holm, Branch Manager, July 1984

Eric Holm: Our president, Mac Coulter, he arranged it. He negotiated the purchase and then got in touch with the employees and said how would you like to go along with it? You got to give him credit. He's the one that put it together.

What he did was to go around in all the plants and explain the whole situation. There were big meetings in the plants in each city — Sudbury, Sault Ste. Marie, Timmins and here in Thunder Bay. We didn't have too long to make the purchase because there were others who wanted to buy it too. We had less than a couple of months' notice, because all of a sudden Carlings said they wanted to sell, and we had to get off our butt and make our proposal.

It was a big undertaking on the part of the employees and I think we did one heck of a job. I know I was a little skeptical because we didn't have that much money. We all had to borrow it. The managers and probably the brewmasters put in more money than the ordinary employee, although it was surprising how much money some of the employees invested. Some of them put in $50,000.

The annual Shareholders' meeting has always been held at the head office in Sault Ste. Marie up until now. A lot of the shareholders go; all the employees can take that day off with pay to go to the meeting, but not everybody can go because we can't close down the whole plant for two days. Anyway, they have input because they have directors on the board, who come back and report to the union. The union — the hourly people

— they get a statement the same as I do. Then directors meet during the year. We haven't had a directors' meeting here yet, but maybe we will have one here next year.

The executive staff — the president, the vice-president and the secretary — they are the ones who make the decisions. They are in contact with the office all the time anyway, so if anything comes up you just phone the president. He pretty well looks after the day-to-day operations, except for major spending; then they have their meeting.

The rank-and-file would give their two representatives their ideas, and they would go down to the directors' meeting and say, "We should do this." Some of the ideas are pretty far-fetched. But it's pretty well run by the board and the executive staff. We are a close knit company; we haven't got that many people, about 155 altogether.

CM: What are relations like with the union?

EH: Good. People feel this is their place. They are now a part of the company, and if they don't make it then we are all in trouble, so I think we have better relations. We still have the union, but the only reason we have it is because we are in the beer business. We could have an association or something like that. It doesn't make any difference. I think the workers are more happy now. Their shares are going up; the company is well run. I don't see any problem.

CM: Have you had any people who try to swing their weight because they are owners of the company?

EH: No. I don't think so. We have monthly meetings with the management staff, and if anything comes up that is reasonable we hope to have it fixed by the next meeting. Also, employees can give their ideas to their foreman. They have their shop stewards and meetings with two from management and two from the hourly.

CM: Those meetings would be focussed on working conditions and possible grievances, not on production or management decisions?

EH: True, but the input is there. They can make whatever input they like because they are also on the board.

CM: And you have a pretty stable product. Even in bad times people buy beer and soft drinks.

EH: In soft drinks we have the four major franchises, outside of Coke, of course: Pepsicola, Seven-up, Orange Crush and Canada Dry. We have a good share of the market in this area.

In the brewery, we supply northern Ontario and part of eastern Ontario, but our share is probably about one percent of the market. We run things on a small scale, and as long as we get our fair share we're happy. We'd like to get more sales, but we are in tough competition. Our slogan is BE PROUD THAT YOU'RE A NORTHERNER. We have all the draft in northern Ontario. Nobody sells draft but us.

We are very stable. We hire extra from May to September, a number of students, because that's our busy season, and at Christmas-time, too. But the crew is pretty well the same. We haven't had lay-offs. Nobody leaves, either. We have a few old-time employees and father-and-son combinations, too.

"Like living in a fish-bowl . . . all your shareholders are watching."
— Ross Eaket, President, July 1986

Ross Eaket: I guess the unique part of the company is that it's not just an executive group of employees that bought out, it's all the employees, union employees, plus the salaried office staff, plus the management group. Everyone can buy shares, whatever they can financially handle.
CM: You mean it's up to the employees how many shares they buy?
RE: At the start, we went to all the employees and everybody put their money together, whatever we could borrow from banks, from credit unions, whatever. At that time there was basically no limit. Since then we have decided for new employees with two years' service, we have a standard amount of shares that they can buy. Right now it's 100 shares.
CM: And what would 100 shares be worth at present?
RE: Now about $4,000. After two years we can sell new stock to new employees, and we do it by payroll deduction to make it easy. Everybody's circumstances are not the same, some are raising young families and they don't have a great amount, but we're trying to have everybody be employee-shareholders.
All employees that retire or quit have a time limit of two years in which they must sell their shares. This applies to everybody, whether it's myself or any other employee. Actually we've extended that time limit a little bit because of possible changes in the income tax act, the capital gains legislation, so we don't penalize the employees who are retiring. We can sell back to the company, or to other employees, so that it will be a perpetually employee-owned company. Once the employee's a shareholder, he can purchase shares from other employees that are retiring. Mind you any stock purchase must be approved by the board of directors, I guess to stop maybe one person from trying to take over the company, but it's more a formality, to try and keep it to a number of employee-shareholders.
CM: In effect, does management have more shares than a labourer, for instance, or a sweeper?
RE: Actually the management group has about half of the shares . . . about 20 employees. There are three-sixths of the shares for the manage-

ment, two-sixths are held by the hourly employees, and one-sixth by the office group. That just happens to be basically what they bought in at. However, it made sense then that the board of directors be elected separately. The management group can vote only for three management directors. The union group can vote only for two directors from their group, and the office group then elects one. We then have six directors. It's basically one vote per share, and the numbers happened to work out fairly evenly in the groupings.

CM: So one individual who holds more stock would have more votes?
RE: Oh yes, definitely, it's one vote for each share held, and each employee holds a different number of shares.

We also have two public directors, who are appointed to the board by the six elected directors. That works two ways. It gives us outside help: we have a lawyer from Sudbury right now as a member of our board. It gives us a bit of balance there. A long-time businessman from Thunder Bay also acts as a public director. These men do not have any shares in the company, but they act as a sounding board. It also keeps it so that management does not control the board of directors.

CM: But management has half the directors, and then they have half the vote to appoint the outside directors, so the dice is really loaded?
RE: The public directors must act on behalf of the shareholders, not on behalf of any particular group. The two public directors basically *could* control if you had a power struggle. Not that we're expecting any, but I think it makes it a lot easier to live with.

Everyone gets financial statements, every employee-shareholder — right now we have 140. Shareholders are about 83 percent right now of the total working force. The numbers change, and recently we have had quite a number of retired employees. Now with the replacement employees coming in, they have that two-year waiting period. They're starting to fill up the ranks, and it's encouraging to have the young ones come in . . . they don't have a large amount of money, but in time . . . . It's working very well.

CM: What about the increase in the value of shares? They've gone up quite a bit since you first started.
RE: Yes, the share values have increased rapidly, from one dollar in 1978 to $40 each today. They will level off a bit, but we expect them to continue increasing. I guess the main reason is that we're not paying dividends. Everything the company makes is being plowed back in to pay off the debt and for capital expenditures, buildings, land, that are required for proper operation.

We have a mortgage with the Bank of Montreal as a big part of our debt. And employee-shareholder "notes" were part of their original investment, at the time of the take-over. At that time, in 1978, each employee's investment was five percent in shares and 95 percent in promissory notes. This was to make it easier for everybody to buy in. For example for a $1,000 unit you would have $50 in common shares and $950 in a shareholder promissory note. The note could then be taken to a financial institution by the employee to borrow against; the company paid interest on the note monthly, at two percent above prime. So the employee then could pay the bank interest monthly on his note, and his basic cost was really a $50 investment. And yet the borrowing power was $1,000.

CM: Very clever financing! No wonder the Bank of Montreal has you on their advisory board for your region! So those promissory notes are now being paid back?

RE: They will be. First is the outside debt to pay off, then we'll start gradually paying the notes back. They are financed over long term, through till September of '89. Some of that will likely be refinanced. Because it's at an excellent rate, some employees like them as an investment. But for new employees, as of this year we've eliminated the note part, because the share values are getting high; it's costing too much. So we've wiped the note part out. You don't have to invest in the note, just buy 100 shares.

CM: The cost was eliminating some people who would have liked to join?

RE: Yes, it got just a little too pricey. Also we've lowered the numbers of shares that had to be bought by an established employee. Now if you want to make additional purchases, you can buy 25 shares. We'll likely split the share values to make it easier for new employees and also to trade in on retirement. As time goes on the system has to change, but the principle is still basically there.

CM: As far as financing goes, do you have any trouble getting the bank loans you need?

RE: Not really, no. The company was established when we took over and some of our capital was borrowed through the employees. In that time period, from '77 through to now, we've spent over $5 million in fixing up our plants, which is a lot of money. The equipment has got a fairly long lifespan, but it just needed to be upgraded.

CM: The fact that the shares have increased in value so much indicates that business has been really good. What would your gross annual take be?

RE: Right now about $27 million a year. It was about $12 million when we started. I would guess in the next five years we should be able to get another half of what we have in total sales, to $40 million. The company relied in the past on draft sales in northern Ontario, but times have changed, draft sales have decreased rapidly in all of Ontario, and very rapidly in the north. Now bottled beer sales outstrip the draft.

CM: Was that a crisis, when you realized that the market for draft was not there?

RE: It was part of a heavy decline even up to Carlings days, and then when we bought it we thought we could get sufficient bottled beer sales, and perhaps get some of the draft sales back . . . the heavy drop in draft sales hurt badly. So we went into bottled beer . . . .

CM: Did you do that right after taking over?

RE: Yes, immediately. Actually, we hired sales staff and then started into additional market areas piece by piece.

CM: When you decided to engineer the take-over, did you make business plans, and analyse the ins and outs of it all beforehand?

RE: Very definitely. A lot of it was done beforehand, back when Carlings bought the company from Dorans. I was an employee then and we considered a possible take-over at that time, but nothing happened . . . . It was just a bit of a seed at that time. Then things moved very quickly once it became known that Carlings were selling out. The business plans were made up very quickly, but they were based on the day-to-day operations, which we were all involved with. So it became a matter of putting it down on paper, getting our firm of chartered accountants, getting the appraisals in, and really, "Let's get this thing mobile." Nothing was that flowery, no grand expectations; I think we made very conservative forecasts. If it was better than that, great, everybody'd be happier . . . . And it *has* been much better.

CM: So when you organized the take-over you had changes in mind?

RE: Oh definitely.

CM: It must have been fun.

RE: Very much so. And again with some of the new products. For example we're producing non-alcoholic beer, and we went into a new package, a draft beer ball for home consumers, again to try and spur the market.

CM: So you were able to put into effect all the ideas that you'd been bubbling away, but as part of a big company didn't have a chance to try out.

RE: That's right. Smaller companies can do these things. They can even start, and if doesn't look right, OK, back up and get out of it. You can experiment more, and try new products and so on.

The first two years of operation, we were into fairly heavy losses, but those were expected. It takes time to get operating; the sales volumes were not good, we had to train a sales force — a number of problems of getting going. All of the beer brands had slid in actual sales amount, but I don't really blame Carling O'Keefe for letting it go. You have to remember that large companies generally operate with Ontario-wide or Canada-wide policies. Small companies like we were didn't really fit. It wasn't an intentional thing that they were trying to close it down. They had an investment there; they wanted to make money, but it's just their marketing practices didn't fit a small or medium-sized business.

And we're again looking at plans of expansion. We've gradually expanded our beer market into southern Ontario, into Toronto first, and the Hamilton area, the golden horseshoe area, then into Ottawa. Just this spring we moved into the London area, and Guelph. We'll gradually cover the rest of the province.

CM: Are you plugging it as a northern beer?

RE: Yes. We have the Northern Ale, and Superior Lager, and Northern Extra Light. We plug the northern image, the good water, the clean water, which we do have . . . . We have a director of marketing for beer, who handles most of the promotion and sales representations, and also a director of marketing in soft drinks, because they are basically different fields. Then the management group of myself and the vice-president as operating managers, and the plant managers, keep it going. We have one plant manager in each area, and some of them wear two hats. In Thunder Bay the soft drinks plant manager is also the director of marketing. Our director of production for all the plants is also plant manager in Sudbury. We're trying to keep our manpower down . . . .

CM: You imply that employee-owned operations, which are likely to be smaller, can actually be more efficient.

RE: I think they can be efficient. From a marketing point of view, if you have 250 employees, you have 250 salesmen out there! The same in your plant operations . . . the little things, the extra half-hour of work that they're not charging for overtime. It's just, "Well, it needs to be done, let's go and do it!" And the employees will work on all these weekends where our products are being handled at city or club functions, maybe dispensing soft drinks, selling, handling beer kegs, that sort of thing. That's strictly volunteer time.

CM: Have you any figures for the increase in productivity?

RE: Not really, I guess it's more of a feeling . . . talking to the employees. One thing about a company of that nature — if there's any complaints or whatever, I hear about them, because the employees are part of it. They walk into my office and tell me . . . or if I'm in the plants. It hasn't been easy on all the employees either; it's been some tough times, hard work . . . the extra hours put in . . . it doesn't come easy. But I think everybody's happy, they're really proud of what they've accomplished; it doesn't matter what department you're in, whether it's production or selling, or . . .

CM: How much extra time would they put in?

RE: A lot of weekends; a few hours extra at night, but summertime is when the business is heavy . . . . This is volunteer time, not part of the normal working job.

CM: And they don't get overtime? What does the union think about that?

RE: Most of it is not in-plant type of thing, it's as I say, working various functions.

CM: And is there any objection if someone refuses the extra work?

RE: Well, they'll bug each other about it rather than complain to me. And I think it has to be remembered that you're not *forced* to be a shareholder. Employees that don't want to buy shares, or possibly don't have the money, they're not forced to. And they're not treated any differently, they're not outsiders.

CM: But they would presumably have a bit less of a sense of commitment?

RE: Yes, usually they do. I think most of them are at one or the other end of the spectrum. They're either just reaching retirement and don't really see any great short-time gain, or very young trying to get along, buy a house, raise a family, and they don't have the money. Of course, the part-timers are not eligible.

CM: What is your proportion of part time workers?

RE: Actually it runs very low in the wintertime, end of September through to about the first part of April, we probably have 25, 30 part time employees. During the summer, this would jump to 75, at times 100, employees. We usually try to hire students, university students. But both beer and soft drinks are seasonal, and if you get a good hot summer, it adds a lot of jobs. We're running just over 200 workers in the four cities I guess about now. That includes management and office staff.

CM: What was your role when the switch-over to employee-owned was made?

RE: I was secretary-treasurer of the company then. I'd worked here about 25 years, first for Dorans before it was bought by Carlings. The continuity was I guess one of the strongest points of it. Mac Coulter had been president; Dick Waas was vice-president of production, then myself as secretary-treasurer, we all had been there for quite a while. It's not as if we were starting new — we knew the business. Mr. Coulter guaranteed he would stay for a time before he retired; and he stayed two years. It kept us with a bit of experience there rather than a bunch of rookies coming in. It meant a lot in stability. Now Mr. Coulter's retired; Dick Wass, our director of production, has retired and been replaced; Eric Holm who was our manager in Thunder Bay, he's retired . . . we've had a number of employees retire because of age . . . we're at that stage. But we have an excellent group of young employees coming up. We've been bringing them up through the ranks, and hope we can continue that. You never know; it depends on the position open and who's trained and who's available, but we're trying to train them. We offer to pay for university courses and whatever. The company will pay if you want to take night courses as long as it's somewhat job-related; it could be almost anything as long as it's helping the employee.

CM: Did you have to learn a new management style when you took over?

RE: Very much so. It's no longer ordering people to do things, although at times you still basically have to. I like it. It's a lot more cooperative effort. It's almost like living in a fish-bowl because all your shareholders are right there, watching.

CM: Was the adjustment hard?

RE: Not to me it wasn't, no.

CM: And the people who have come up to replace the old-timers who are retiring, are they able to take on that cooperative style too, without any trouble?

RE: Yes, they will. I think with some difficulty, but nothing really serious. And I think the younger ones, it'll become really habit — this is the way to operate.

CM: You mentioned taking courses; can you find that kind of style modelled in management courses that you might take today?

RE: Not that I'm aware of. I guess most of it comes by the seat of the pants . . . experience. It's hard really to try and guess beforehand how you'd do it. I don't know as you can take everything by teamwork committee approach; nothing would get done! It's almost like writing . . . whether it's a brief or whatever, if you've got 15 people trying to dot the i's and cross the t's you'll never get anything done. Yet you do have input. And then you have to say, "OK, here's the input. Now this is what we're going to do." Then somebody has to direct, "Let's go do it!"

CM: How often do you have director's meetings?

RE: We try to have them quarterly. And we have an annual shareholders' meeting. We try to have our board of directors' meetings in a different place each time. We'll go to one of the plant areas.

CM: And do the other shareholders have the right to attend those?

RE: Not the actual director's meeting itself, but we normally have a meeting afterwards with all the employees, and then you have the whole board of directors on the firing line, just to ask questions, bring them up to date as to what's going on, really off-the-cuff type of thing.

CM: Is that on company time or is that after hours?

RE: Usually company time or a combination of both, depending on how it will fit with most of the employees, when it's best for them.

One of the problems . . . it can be difficult to get sufficient information across to employees. You find yourself caught up in the day-to-day routine, and especially with a lot of travelling . . . you know darn well you should be getting them more information, and that becomes a steady, ongoing problem.

CM: Are these meetings your main mode of communication?

RE: A lot of it is meetings, a lot of it is just standing around with a group of employees . . . the meetings don't have to be formally structured, in fact it's better if they're not. They're more open.

We are also setting up a newsletter now and it should be going in October. This came out of our last directors' meeting and shareholders' meeting. It had been tried awhile ago but without too much enthusiasm. Now we've got volunteers. In fact two of the members of the board of directors, one of the hourly and one of the salary group, have volunteered to make sure it's going. You have to have someone from each plant enthused about it, they have to gather the information.

CM: Do you have committees in addition to your board of directors' meetings as a decision-making body?

RE: No. We have an audit committee which is made up of an hourly employees' director and the salary director and one of the public directors. No management can be on it. They go over everything with the accounting firm and meet separately, without the influence of management, to check the total audit and any problems that might come up, anything that management is maybe not doing right. That's really the only other committee that's formal.

CM: How does the union fit in there?

RE: We meet and negotiate union contracts, the same as any other company. We have a local of United Brewery Workers of Canada, a separate local which will vote separately in our plants only, and negotiate for rates and so on separately. The union representatives are also shareholders, so they also have members on the board of directors.

CM: Does that make for any awkwardness?

RE: No, actually perhaps it makes it easier.

They have the financial statements; they know the shape the company's in. I think the demands become a little more reasonable; you don't get the outrageous ones. We find both ends of the spectrum and eventually we'll meet in the middle. I think you get a little more common sense, a little more give and take, perhaps more thought to what different groups of their membership need — pensions or wage increases — which are their priorities? I think they get a little more thinking among themselves there than before . . . . But we never really had any major problems, I think, when I look back on the company's history with unions. We had disagreements and so on naturally, at times in the past almost to the point of strikes. But you knew it wasn't going to reach that stage. I think they've been fairly treated. Wage rates are high, they're well-covered in employee benefits, from dental to glasses to guaranteed wage plans . . . just about everything you can think of is covered under benefits negotiated by the union before the take-over. Since the take-over, we've had additions and upgrading of the contract.

CM: How do the wages compare with wages in the cities where you have plants?
RE: Quite favourably. I guess we probably pay about the highest wages in each of the cities, compared to other industries. We're slightly under the wages that the major breweries are paying in say Toronto or Hamilton, but it isn't that much difference. I think our base rate of pay is around $14 an hour, for what we call unskilled or regular daily worker, and then there's categories up from there. We figure benefits are around 40 percent of our wage costs, in addition to the $14 . . . that's costly. Those are all negotiated with the union. The rest of your salaried employees' increases — I would determine those.

CM: What about grievances that come up in the plant?
RE: They're handled the normal way. You try to have them settled by the foreman in that area. Then you have the regular union steps that you go through, to arbitration if you have to. We did have one case, on interpretation of the contract, and we had to go through to arbitration to get it settled.

You have to remember that the union covers all employees whether they're shareholders or not. Also if an employee comes up with a grievance, the union is really obligated, whether they fully agree with it or not, to carry it through, so you can still have a problem with one disgruntled employee. It doesn't mean that the entire work force is upset. You have to live with it. We don't have a separate personnel manager who deals with these things. Being a small company we all wear a lot of hats, have different titles and different jobs.

CM: Are you automating?
RE: In some areas but not that much, no.
CM: Not enough to cut back staff?
RE: No, we intend to be adding staff. We'll be going into additional markets, I would hope we'll go into the U.S. in another month, so we're looking for gradually increasing staff, not decreasing.
CM: Is this what you see mainly in the future?
RE: I think it is. Nothing that major or large, it's not that you're going to take the market by storm. But if you get a small percentage of a large market, then you're fine. I would guess the next couple of years we would be probably adding workers at the rate of between five and ten percent. We've reached the level where with just a little additional production and expansion, we have to hire more employees, a very thin line. We've got just enough workers, but boy not too many! It's very labour-related, so that as you add additional production, you do start adding manpower in a hurry. And being very lean, we're in that position.
CM: The Ontario government is just instituting an Employee Share Ownership Plan, to encourage employees of small and medium-sized

businesses to buy in. It was announced in the 1986 Ontario budget and I'm sure you know something about it. Can you see that as relevant to your company?

RE: Yes I can. The only thing wrong with the plan, I think, is the small amount of investment allowed . . . $2,000 a year. But even that's encouraging, at least it's a step in the right direction. The limitation of course is that you can't be a major shareholder. You have to hold under five percent of the shares to get a tax concession. Well, there's nothing wrong with that limitation. The whole idea is to get a number of people that are employees to be shareholders. Maybe the limitation's a little small, but . . .

CM: Would that affect any one of your shareholders? You do have some shareholders that have more than five percent?

RE: Yes, but I think the dollar amount is low. It has to be new shares issued. I think it will be a boost, really, to a number of employees, ours included.

CM: So your new employees becoming shareholders could get this tax benefit on half of their shares, if they're buying the minimum $4,000 worth?

RE: Actually we are changing the amount so that they can buy maybe $2,000 a year. Whatever . . . we're very flexible, we'll make it fit, whatever the government wants to change in the rules.

CM: Do you foresee your kind of solution of an employee-owned company becoming more popular?

RE: Definitely I think it will be more popular. And I think with the scheme the government's coming in with now, in spite of its limitations, will encourage it. Some medium-sized companies — not necessarily just very small — this is their way of operating already. Employee ownership — the U.S has a number of schemes that are different — or I believe our government is contemplating changes to pension plans, where you can invest some back into your own company. Pension plans do not have to be such a scary thing. Why can't you use a portion of an employee's Registered Retirement Savings Plan, to invest back into a company, if that is what the employees want to do?

CM: I guess some groups are afraid that if a company went under, the employees would lose their jobs and they'd lose their pensions, too.

RE: Correct. And I don't see our regular pension plan being part of it. However, using tax incentives to encourage investing an additional Registered Retirement Savings Plan back into the company . . .

CM: Have you any links with the cooperative movement, with say the big Co-operators insurance company or with Federated Co-operatives?

RE: No, we don't have.

CM: **You don't think of yourself as a cooperative, really, do you?**

RE: Not really I guess, I don't know what we are . . . we're a hybrid. Some of the union members were stating that we're making capitalists out of their union members. And yet to me it's the reverse of that . . . we're making socialists out of a bunch of capitalists!

CM: **Do your business colleagues in Toronto know your set-up, that you are an employee-owned company?**

RE: Oh yes. We've had a number of people really interested, and it's surprising how much detail they get into. I think there are a fair number maybe going to get into this type of thing if the opportunity arises; the circumstances have to be right. There are probably three or four that I know have gone for it and actually made it, they're operating . . . .

CM: **You mean they've come to you for advice and gone ahead?**

RE: Yes. Awhile ago I spoke to the profit-sharing council, which is setting up employee profit-sharing plans, and they've published an article I wrote. It's an open field . . . I guess the biggest thing is that employee. ownership will not work if you're buying a company that's not going to make it anyway. There's no point in kidding anybody. It's not a magic that's going to revive anything that's not profitable. There has to be the possibility there. It may not be profitable at the moment, but it has to have the makings of being profitable, and in a common business sense, not as a dream.

CM: **Do you see yourself as staying with the company? Or would you be tempted away?**

RE: I don't know what would tempt me away, I like the challenge.

CM: **But with your experience, you would be a valuable acquisition for other companies.**

RE: Well I think I can do a lot, really, with the company from here-on in. I think we've got a lot of future. It's a bit grinding at times, but it's there, even in the next few weeks or so, a lot of work to be done that could make it very successful.

CM: **And is it worth your while financially, too?**

RE: Oh yes, I'm a shareholder too.

CM: **You said the employees' wages were high for the area, but not as high as they'd make in Toronto. How about your pay as an executive?**

RE: I don't want to get into pay discussions, really. My pay is controlled by the public directors, and the audit committee, so I don't set it. And it's not anywhere near what the market would be.

CM: **So you could do better?**

RE: Oh yeah. But money isn't everything. As my daughters say — and I've taught them, I keep telling them — "Remember, money's only a commodity." It's not the end-all. It's worth it, yes definitely.

PART III
Publishing is Mightier Than the Sword

CHAPTER EIGHT
Dreadnaught Publishing Company
Toronto, Ontario

"There is nothing more important than Dreadnaught in our lives."

I met Elizabeth Abraham, the business manager of Dreadnaught Publishing Company, at their shop in an old house on Harbord Avenue near the University of Toronto campus. The location is important, because the group, working long and erratic hours, needs to live and work in the same area. Six years in their present premises, close to clients, research facilities, art supply stores, and home, they are looking for another, larger, site in the same area, big enough to shelter both home and workplace.

Elizabeth Abraham is a strong, purposeful, contained woman, clear about what she wants and how to get it. Her office is in the front of the house, behind her the business office with constant telephone and typewriter noises, behind that the works, with sounds of typesetting and presses. I never got to see the shop, because Elizabeth dismissed me firmly, and correctly, after an hour of discussion, with, "I must get back to work." Her dedication to the purpose and the quality of the work is never forgotten.

Established in 1970, Dreadnaught now combines the functions of publisher and creative studio. Three friends started it with no money, and no business organization or savvy, with the name Dreadnaught, from James Joyce (and the name of an underground newspaper once published by one of the founders). Their home was their part time workplace. Their salaries from their daily jobs paid the expenses.

The business has been through many phases since then, from publisher of limited edition books, set and printed by hand, to graphic design services and book packaging for other publishers. But always in the past 15 years the format has been the same: a cooperative of workers, focussed on quality production, on excellence. They achieve it by dedication, to quality and to the group, an almost religious fervour. And high energy. As a result, they have an enviable and established reputation, prestige clients, and high job satisfaction. They have an emphasis that puts interpersonal problems into perspective and disposes of them simply and rationally. But they don't have much material reward. Elizabeth herself says it's hard to make money when you're working to that kind of quality. "You want to do everything twice," to perfection.

She is optimistic about future gains. After 15 years, she knows how to plan, to analyse, to restructure, and she thinks they're on the track. She's a little bitter about the time it's taken, and the lack of support, from government, from financial institutions, and especially from the established cooperative movement. One contract from a big institution like Co-operators insurance, or United Co-operatives' of Ontario, and Dreadnaught would have it made financially. But as Elizabeth sees it, those established cooperatives have forgotten their roots, have become big business, "are not in practice interested whatsoever."

When I contacted Dreadnaught for an update in September 1986, I had to call back twice, because I'd hit them first just as they were taking delivery of their new computer. It's for office use initially, but they look forward to using it for manuscript preparation in the future. The group had decided to go for the computer rather than for a new building.

There have been other changes. Elizabeth now has an assistant to do most of the office management, freeing her to concentrate on sales and marketing. The staff has increased to five and a half — one worker had a baby and is still on part time. They have extended their activities to include consulting to publishers. Robert MacDonald, one of the founders, runs the publishing workshop at the Banff School of Fine Arts, and the consulting contract came to the co-op as a result. Annual turnover is about $350,000, and the outstanding loans are being paid off at a higher rate than projected.

Dreadnaught still lacks the support of the established cooperative movement, but they have done a couple of very small jobs, a book for Credit Union Central, the cover for *Starting a Worker Co-operative*, a manual of Toronto's Worker Ownership Development Foundation. "We're moving ahead," Elizabeth Abraham said.

Elizabeth Abraham: We started out in 1972 doing limited edition books and doing all the work by hand. We cast our own type and printed by hand on a letterpress. All our early publications were letterpress limited editions. A lot of people were changing over to cold type from hot metal then and every week places were going out of business; we would hear about them and go and buy the type.

We all had other jobs. Two of us were in graphic design. I used to do all the hand typesetting, learning as I was working. We worked full time during the day, and then we worked all evening and every weekend. When we could afford to, about three years after we began, we quit our jobs, but for a long time we were just able to pay the rent and food. We didn't get salaries for many, many years. And then eventually we started paying salaries and hiring people.

We never had a boss — we always worked as a co-op. Everybody had different functions, but we worked together and made decisions together. When the three of us started we had to register as a business. We knew even less then, so in order to set up a business account, we just registered it in the name of one of the people, as a sole proprietorship.

In 1980 we felt that we wanted to incorporate. I forget where the impetus came from; there were a number of new people there at the time and I think that we just wanted to solidify this cooperative. Working for other non-profit organizations, we were committed philosophically to helping them, and we thought if we incorporated as a cooperative ourselves that would help us. So we looked at different ways — there are lots of ways to be a co-op; you don't have to do it the way we did. We incorporated as a non-share capital, non-profit cooperative. We didn't want shares that could then be sold off to other people who were not really interested, and we didn't want to have anybody take anything away from the cooperative.

In our present structure, you come in as a member and you work as long as you want to work, and when you go away you just go away, and everything you have put in is left in the co-op. Now we have grown so much that we want outside investment, but in the structure we have it's just not feasible to do that. As a cooperative the investment rates we're allowed to pay are limited. So far a bank loan is all we've got.

We never had any capital; we just started working.

Constance Mungall: It sounds as if your personal lives were very much intertwined in the beginning. Is that still the way? Your own savings are not separate from the business?

EA: We are the business. There is no separation.

The three original members are all still here, and one other has been here for about seven years. Everybody else comes and goes. One person has always been responsible for the business end of it. Now I am that person. The business that we are doing changes all the time, so there are needs for personnel changes. Two years ago we were doing a lot of publishing and we needed a large editorial staff, so we had eleven full time people. Now we've got five because we're not putting together as many editorial projects.

That was a conscious choice. We all decided together on the direction that the company should take. The people whose jobs were not really going to be necessary any more decided to do freelance editorial work.

We do some publishing now, but mostly we are doing graphic design services, and book packaging. We come up with a concept, do all the design work, because that is where we are really strong, put together a proposal, and then take that to a major publisher. Sometimes we do the printing and provide the publisher with finished copies, or sometimes we just provide them with artwork, and they print. They do all the sales, distribution, promotion, publicity.

We use freelancers to put together a concept — freelancers rather than people on staff. Some of those same people who used to be on staff are used on a freelance basis.

Doing a financial analysis we realized that what consistently made money was the graphic design — the services aspect. Book packaging and publishing is viable, but it's a longer term kind of thing.

The salaries are pretty low. We're not making money — we are a non-profit organization and we do a lot of work for other non-profit organizations, and so we don't bring in really big money.

Salaries are steadily going up. We are becoming much more profitable. We started out with absolutely no business sense whatsoever, just a creative sense. We were doing what we wanted to do, and producing works of art, typographic works of art. Learning the business aspect of it has been the most difficult, time consuming part. We've taught ourselves, by reading and trying to talk to the kinds of people that know what we need to learn.

It's taken a number of years, but we finally know what we want to do, and we're going for it. I estimate we'll be making a profit in two years.

CM: Do you all pay each other the same amount, or does that vary?

EA: When we first started, we were all paid the same amount, but that didn't seem to be fair because the four of us who are the original people are all signed up for loans; we have all worked for a number of years without any salary and we all worked much longer hours. New people tend to come in at nine and leave at five, because that's what they're used to, so it didn't really seem very fair. Now we have got a system based on length of service. The base salary when you start is $10,000, and then every year you increase by $1,000.

CM: So the people that have been here seven years would make $17,000?

EA: If we had made that decision seven years ago — but we didn't. We just decided that a couple of years ago.

CM: Was that a difficult decision to make? Was it something that took a long time?

EA: Yes, but only because we had 11 people then, and the majority of them were new. Now we don't have any trouble at all making decisions because we have all lived and worked together for many years. We know each other perfectly and there is no problem; everything is done by consensus. Everybody has the best interests of Dreadnaught at heart; there is nothing more important than Dreadnaught in our lives, so all decisions are extremely easy to make. When you get new people they all have different ideas and it was at that time that the question of salary came up. It wouldn't even have come up with the original group. We don't have any entertainment costs or anything like that because we are just here and we work. We don't live in this house now, but at that time we were living and working out of a house on Sussex Avenue.

I think that's why we're not typical. It's so much easier to start a business with a group of people who are friends already and have worked for a number of years together in various ways. A number of us make up a core group, and it's so obvious that we have the expertise that people respect that.

CM: Your core group is distinguished by the fact that you get an extra $1,000 a year for each year you work.

EA: And we work longer hours . . . .

CM: I'm trying to look for ways that you get more in return for your investment, and you tell me that you are allowed to work longer hours!

EA: I think that for everybody here, the work itself is more important than any financial reward.

Our first objective is quality work. At a time when more and more people are working to industry standards, we won't accept that. We are interested in really high quality work in our concepts, in our design work, in our typesetting, in our printing. We push everybody that works with us to work harder, to do better quality work than they think they can.

But at the same time, very often it is really hard to make money when you are working to that kind of quality because you want to do everything twice, to spend more hours on it than you should. Then the challenge comes to make the business economically feasible without compromising quality.

We have to find clients that are interested in quality; to quote realistically so that we can make money; to know exactly what the bottom line is, what our profit margin will be — and all of that means controls.

Right now we are happy if we are just making 10 percent. It depends. On some jobs for a really large corporation, we hope to make more, so that we can afford to work for non-profit organizations on a cost-plus basis,

just to cover our overhead. But what our overall profit margin should be
I'm trying to work out now, in terms of long-term goals.

A raise in salary would come from the profit margin. So we are trying to
cut costs and increase sales and not sacrifice quality. I think of business as
being just as creative as the art side of it.

CM: How do you recruit new members?

EA: They come clamouring to us. It's a very creative environment in
which to work. You don't do just assembly, or typing, or printing. You
get to take a project and see its development all the way through, and in
this society, that doesn't happen very often; people are so compartmen-
talized. There are a lot of people who really want to work at Dreadnaught
badly.

The people in the particular department that need help are the ones who
first interview the job applicants. Very often we know them personally;
we cast around amongst the people we know who have the skills and who
want to work. Sometimes we advertise. We are looking for a new assembly person now and we are getting somebody from the Ontario Art
Council's summer program. They'll come for the summer, and that will
give us a chance to check them out. If it works out there will be a perma-
nent job.

No one is actually hired until it's OK'd with everybody. They come and
work with us for six months. There's no way that you can tell until you
start working with them whether they're cooperatively minded or not. A
lot of people will say they've always been interested in co-ops, but they
just don't have any idea of what it means. So it's much better to hire them
for their professional abilities and then tell them what it's all about theoretically. They don't have to join as members; they can just be employees
if they want. We just had one that did that.

Some just come for the training and go. They'd rather just work nine to
five.

You can't push a deep commitment on anybody. Some others have come
as regular employees, and then made it their life work.

You have to be very open personally; you can't have secrets from each
other and you can't pretend to be something that you are not. And you
have to be prepared to work extremely hard, as hard as it takes. If you
have to work all night and all the next day and all the next night, then you
just have to work that time, to find the energy somehow. The people who
have done that, who have been able to tap their internal energies, are the
people who have stayed. If you burn out, it's because you haven't learned
how to use your energy with other people.

There are no prima donnas here — some people are respected more than
others and get more concessions than others because of the level of their
work, but that is just understood. Some people can get away with more

because they give more and everybody knows it. They're at a higher level of development, or they have more experience, or more energy and they work differently. Some people will give energy like crazy and then cut it off for a long time. They deserve to revamp themselves. Everybody works with different energy.

That's why I say we're not typical; we've lived together and worked all those things out. Nothing needs to be talked about anymore.

CM: Did you have a lot of meetings, do a lot of talking in your process of setting up?

EA: Oh yes. Interminable meetings. Now it comes and goes. We don't have really regular co-op meetings, but we meet informally about specific things. If I want to discuss something I'll call a meeting, or if the production or the art department wants to discuss something about their work, they call a meeting. But it's all the same people anyway. We meet here usually in the evenings.

CM: Is that a drain on your energy?

EA: Meetings? Well not now because we know each other so well. It was awful when there were so many new people. I hated it because it was so hard to communicate and it's so important. You can decide a specific item of business fairly simply, but when you start talking about philosophy and salary structure and all that kind of stuff, everybody brings so much from previous jobs, so many fears and expectations, that it just goes on and on. It takes hours. That's extremely draining.

CM: Learning how to work together with 11 new people — was that the major challenge in the 12 years you have been together? And you continued to operate by consensus at that time too. Did you have problems with that?

EA: No. It always worked out in the end, but it was just that it took so many hours. Everybody was coming from a different place, so you had to explain over again, and then each time you bring in a new person you have to start from the beginning again.

CM: The five that you have now are a doughty group that have made a closer commitment. Do they have to put money in too?

EA: They don't have to invest; it is just the original ones who have the investment. And we have two people as well who signed to guarantee loans. They don't work here any more, but they still are committed. The loans will be repaid in five years, but if anything happened to Dreadnaught before then, they'd still have to pay even though they're not working here any more.

CM: What about other benefits?

EA: Well, it depends what you're working on. Helen there, we need her from 8:45 until 5:00 every day, otherwise we'd die. She does the telephone and the bookkeeping and the typing and all that kind of thing, so it's really important that she be there between those hours. But people working on artwork often work all night. They work by the job and mostly they're here early in the morning because there are phone calls and typesetters, and printers wanting to ask questions. So if they're a little bit slack at any time they can take time off.

We all work for ourselves, in a way. That's what's so nice about working for a co-op; we are our own boss and we have the sense of being self-employed. Even though we're getting a regular salary, we're working for ourselves.

Buying a house is the next step. We're trying to figure out now where and how long before we're going to be able to buy. We'd like to get back to living and working in the same house again, so we want a huge great house. When we were on Sussex, we could have clients come to read galleys at seven a.m. because we just lived upstairs. Some of us have young children and it's ideal; when the kids come back from school you can continue work, put them to bed in the evening, keep working without having to go out and find a baby sitter. And also it's extremely important for the children to see their parents working. At the same time, we work under high pressure so we can't have them running the office. That's impossible.

CM: How do you deal with interpersonal problems?

EA: We just talk. It's not really been any problem. Dreadnaught is all that matters, getting the work done is all that matters. If one person is interfering with another getting their work done, then you have to talk about it. Maybe one person can't work without the radio, and the other person can't work with it. Then you give them separate offices, or one will decide not to play the radio between such and such hours. As long as you have a larger view in mind, there's no problem that can't be solved.

CM: Did you get help from outside agencies, educational or provincial advisors?

EA: Most people working with co-ops only know about them theoretically; they don't know anything about what it really means. And most of the people who know about business don't know anything about co-ops. So I have really had a lot of trouble finding the kind of help that I need. Even accountants — it's extremely difficult to find an accountant who knows what a co-op is, or understands, or could care less. As soon as they find out that you are non-profit they don't even want to bother with you. They just can't understand that a group of people would want to work for a motivation other than making profits. It is extremely difficult because you don't know until you have been working with an accountant for a year or so that he doesn't really understand what's going on.

CM: Do you feel that you have had any back-up or nurturing support from the co-op movement itself?

EA: No. Definitely not. It is really a problem. We should be getting all the design work from cooperatives. Co-operators insurance should use us, but they don't. They know about us, and they don't use us. They make it as difficult as any private organization does to get contracts. It's shameful. We should be supporting each other, and any co-op around should be committed to using other co-ops to do their work, but they are not.

CM: Why do you think that is?

EA: They think co-ops do not give high class work. And they are lazy. They've used the same people for a number of years; changing to a new design company when you are as large as Co-operators is a big deal. You have to learn how to work with the other group and you have to be really committed to do it. In their annual reports they say how interested they are in working with other co-ops and supporting the co-op sector, but it's just theory; they are not in practice interested whatsoever.

CM: So you feel really alienated from the co-op movement?

EA: Yes. I'm just going to this co-op resource group this evening. I know a lot of people in it, but I haven't been involved because it just seems to be so much theory, but I wanted to go tonight to see if they're doing anything on a more practical level.

CM: Have any government agencies been able to give you more help — the provincial co-op department, Federal Business Development Bank, etc.?

EA: The FBDB is useless. We have got loans from them, but they don't care. I don't think the people that are working there have ever been in business; they are just bureaucrats. No I have not had any help at all from government agencies. Every once in a while I make a foray into that area and try to get some help, but it just takes so long to talk to them. To explain who you are takes half a day, and then they fiddle around and are no use in the end. I'm too busy. It's better to find out myself.

The bank manager has been good, but that's just because he sees me every day going in and out, chats with me about my business. The bank is interested in supporting the small businesses in its neighbourhood and helping as much as possible. They are obviously serious, dedicated, hard-working people, but they're not interested in our structure at all.

CM: Have you been open with the bank that you are a non-profit organization — that you are a cooperative?

EA: Yes. We've dealt with the same bank since we started; they've been pretty good to us. Longevity means something with those guys. We pay 1½ over prime for a line of credit; we don't have a long-term loan. And we have a loan with Bread and Roses. We just negotiated a new loan — it went up to 14 percent — that's their standard rate.

It would certainly have sped the whole process along enormously if there had been a resource group that could really give practical help. The type of people who are interested in co-ops are not, a lot of them, terribly practical. They're coming to it from a theoretical, idealistic point of view. Their idealism is wonderful, but they're not going to get anywhere if they don't have that practical experience, and the more co-ops that start up and fail, the less likely the co-op movement is to be successful. It's better not to start at all than to start and fail, from that point of view.

CM: Have you any advice for a group starting out?

EA: You have to have a larger purpose. If you're just working for your salary or just working for the store or the small immediate goals, you'll never make it. There always has to be something else. For us it's the quality of our work. A real dedication to the co-op movement as the way to save the world is another larger purpose. As far as being successful in a business sense, I would give the same advice to any small business: make sure you know what your market is, what your goals are and that you have a proper business plan. And do not just start out doing it, like we did!

CHAPTER NINE
Dumont Press
Kitchener, Ontario

"A social experiment in the workplace."

I visited Dumont Press at a significant time for this worker co-op — both immediately before and after their annual weekend retreat to discuss working relationships and the future of the shop. As a result, these matters, and an awareness of their basic goals, their philosophy, were in the thoughts of the people I interviewed. Once again, as at other, although not all, the worker co-ops I visited, I found people who were very conscious of the social changes they were part of and helping to bring about.

Their method of incorporation was a good expression of both their ideals and their business savvy — and the good legal advice they had at the beginning. Dumont is a business corporation with all its common shares held by a separately incorporated non-profit employees' association which guarantees one-person/one-vote. This arrangement gives them the advantages of business incorporation, including the right to pay interest rates on loans from the members at the going market rate rather than at the restricted rate for cooperatives in Ontario. And it makes control by one individual legally impossible.

Nevertheless, Dumont has been strongly influenced by one remarkable person, Steve Isma, part of the group for 17 years. Now 37, he is well read as a philosopher and historian, able in electronics as well as in the publications trade. He is strong, clear and committed, with a quick and deep intelligence.

"Could the co-op survive without him?" I wondered. The three workers I talked to initially referred me to Steve Isma several times in their conversation, but they themselves obviously had their own strengths. Bruce voiced their awareness that Steve could become dominant because of his strength and the multiplicity of his skills. But my question was answered when I got in touch with Dumont a year later. A new worker-member informed me that Steve had left to work for a computer consulting company — and Dumont was flourishing, thank you very much.

I met Mo, Mary and Bruce first, in the corner of the shop furnished with beat-up sofas and easy chairs as a lounge. A few days later, after their retreat, I met Steve there too. The initial conversation was less structured, and Steve had some information about the original founding and incorporation that gives it form, so I've presented it here first.

"A way to change the system that creates *the problems."*
— Steve Isma

Steve Isma: We started out being involved in a fairly radical student newspaper around 1968. Then in 1970 we decided to produce a community newspaper, and for seven or eight months we put out *On The Line,* doing all the writing here, but having to go pretty far afield for the typesetting and printing. When we ran out of energy one of the ideas left over was the notion of a typesetting co-op or publishing of some sort. So one or two people, not including myself, did a lot of the groundwork over that winter, 1970-71, to look at equipment, decide what was necessary, find the money for it and find work in order to set up a shop. Everything came together in April or May 1971, along with a major contract to do the student newspaper at the University of Waterloo.

There was very little discussion at first about how the place was going to be set up, except that everybody assumed that it was going to be a worker co-op without any bosses — no division of labour or hierarchical structure. And we had a great deal of confidence as to how quickly we could learn the techniques. Only one person had any kind of experience in a typesetting shop. A few others knew the basic principles, but had no real hands on experience, but we had a pretty good grip on how to do things. There was a fair mix of students. The main thing that we had in common was an interest in social change. We were involved in activities at the university, and in the community. Some were engineers, some dropped out of school, there was an interesting mix of experience in terms of journalism and electronics, and since typesetting equipment at the time was getting more and more computerized, we needed people who had a leaning towards electronics to help get the thing going.

Constance Mungall: The co-op legal structure was assumed from the beginning, then?

SI: Yes and no. We figured there must be a way of assuring that no one would get a disproportionate amount of control, but we were not exactly sure how. Fortunately, we had a good friend who was a lawyer, and who over a couple of years worked out a corporate structure for us.

We weren't in a big hurry because we had established a cooperative way of operating to begin with. What we wanted to ultimately assure was that no small group of people could gain control of the assets. So Dumont was set up as a corporation — a regular Ontario corporation — and still is not a co-op.

Within a couple of years a second corporation was set up — a non-profit corporation called the Employees' Association of Dumont Press Graphics. It took control of all the common shares of the corporation, so that all legal control rests in it. It is non-profit: no individual can buy or sell parts or gain control of it. It exists only as an Association of employees of Dumont. There are particular by-laws that define membership. Everyone who works here full time is a member. Basically, once you have worked here for a few months you become a member of the Association. All the decisions that affect Dumont are made by that group in a democratic way — one person, one vote.

In fact, the way things have always worked has been more or less by consensus. As soon as someone starts to work here, he participates in all the meetings and in the administrative decision-making through the general meetings — about once every two weeks. So the Employees' Association is kind of like a formal definition of what in fact happens. It is the everyday practice that really reinforces the way things work.

CM: How do you decide when you want someone to come in — when it is time to hire someone?

SI: When we have the work to do and the resources to hire someone. We generally advertise among groups that we know — development education groups, public interest research groups, certain more cooperatively inclined areas of the university. Word spreads, and we rarely have a problem attracting applicants.

There is a fair turnover. Since presently the collective is about 7 people, and it has stayed between 5 and 12 for the past five or six years, I'd say that of that number two a year will leave. Sometimes we will hire four people at a time.

CM: What is your salary policy?

SI: In practice, we pay ourselves what is available, every two weeks. There has only been one exception during the last year and a half. Over the last four years, the payroll has been somewhat difficult, but over the last 13 years there have not been a lot of problems, and frequently we end up paying bonuses at the end of the year.

CM: Is your pay comparable to pay in other enterprises of this sort?

SI: It's $5 an hour, much lower than a professional typesetting shop, but probably the same or higher than other co-ops. Plus another couple of dollars for fringe benefits of all sorts. We take a month of paid summer vacation a year and a week off at Christmas, sometimes two weeks, and at least one statutory holiday a month besides that. We have a full medical plan, including dentist, naturopaths, sick leave, including time off for over-stress.

When you take the amount of time we actually work over the year, I think we do pretty good.

CM: Meetings are considered a part of your work input. Do they ever get interminable and a pain in the ass?

SI: Yes. People will frequently think, "Let's get this meeting over with," so we wind it up quickly, but the general meeting every two weeks can be difficult. It's usually about three hours.

CM: How do you solve interpersonal difficulties?

SI: We are getting better and better. Either two people talk to each other directly or we have various mechanisms to encourage people to say how they feel at the beginning of meetings, and at various other times. The retreat is a mechanism for that. When new people come into the collective, they often bring in new ideas around that. I think most of the new ideas come from the people we hire, not from outside counsellors.

CM: How about other kinds of advice, business advice and government agencies?

SI: We've had little. Generally they say our books are in pretty good shape, that we could use a little more capital; they really can't tell us a whole lot. We've had accountants who've given us some ideas, and our friend who did our legal work 13 years ago still does it. But that's pretty rare. We don't have legal difficulties but we know we have him to fall back on, and that's reassuring.

CM: Do you have any trouble meeting government requirements like income tax, Unemployment Insurance returns, etc.?

SI: Well, we have learned. We didn't used to take it as seriously as we should have. We would treat it as just another bill. But the government is much more strict, so it's generally the first to get paid. Almost all our relations with the government are as a small business, and there is a lot of flexibility. Whether the government has interfered with our cooperative process is hard to say. It would be better if we had more flexibility over payroll. The regulations assume that employees are always different from management and that there is always an antagonism. The government has been brought kicking and screaming to that legislation by labour, so what they have established is a compromise between the needs of workers and needs of industry. Where workers control, those dynamics are not necessarily appropriate.

Our situation is not so much between employees and management, but employees and the market, employees and the economic system. That is really more fundamental. The government does not really deal with that except through make-work programs and certain business incentives, which are hard to get at. There are supposedly government programs for investing in microelectronics, say, or in computers, which could apply to us. I tried to find out where they are. It's really obscure. I phoned the office in Toronto dealing with the graphic arts trade. They had just transferred the person dealing with that to Ottawa, and weren't going to fill that office.

CM: How did you get your original financing?

SI: We got a loan from the Federal Business Development Bank. It's now called the Industrial Development Bank. The regular chartered banks weren't interested in us without a government guarantee. They required us to raise as much money on our own as we required from them — an equal amount. So we went to friends. Our budget must have been $20,000 to $24,000 when we started up because we got about $10,000 to $12,000 from FBDB. That was not a lot of money, and we were able to pay off our friends within three years. Since then, we take out loans from regular banks under a special government guarantee for equipment purchases, usually $10,000 to $12,000 every few years. We take the loan, buy the equipment, pay it off, and then acquire a new loan. It's the easiest way of being capitalized, it seems. We are paying off a loan of $50,000 at 11 percent now.

CM: Is this a provision for all small businesses, or just for co-ops?

SI: All small business. In fact when they learned that we were a co-op, they had some difficulty with it. But once they looked at our record for paying off previous loans, they shrugged off their doubts. The bank inevitably finds out our structure. In fact, we are not a co-op on paper, legally. What they want to know is who owns it, and when we point out that no individual owns it, then usually the next step is to see what they can collect if there is a default, in terms of assets. So any time we have a loan outstanding, the equipment is held in mortgage by the bank. But even if we lost all that equipment, it wouldn't make too much difference to the survival of the company.

CM: Do certain people take responsibility in specific areas?

SI: Yes. Administrative functions are generally longer term responsibilities. In production, everyone tries to learn how to do everything. Some people end up better at certain areas, but rotation isn't usually a big problem, even within a day, from morning to afternoon. Since each one takes on all the responsibilities for a small job, one worker will do everything it requires.

Administrative functions have also been rotated frequently over the years, but usually someone will take on an administrative task for a year. It's decided from time to time who will do what, at general meetings. We realize that it has to be done. It's no big deal.

The administrative tasks around here are accounts receivable and payable, deposits, ordering supplies. The actual management decisions like dealing with the bank will be made by the meeting. I do the year end statement every year, largely because I'm familiar with the books, but I don't do any of the daily and monthly work on the books, so I'm just checking what somebody else has done. I learned everything I know about accounting from other people who used to work here.

CM: And because you make management decisions together, is there any need for a mechanism to modify them?

SI: You mean do we ever have to suddenly negate some decision? That rarely happens. If something goes wrong, it usually is pointed out by the person who made the decision, who realizes they did something wrong. So we have to have an emergency meeting and sort it out. There's rarely a serious error in judgement. Everything gets decided at a general meeting, and if we decide something with utmost confidence one week, and two weeks later we decide that was a bad move, we will change it, and that flexibility is not chaotic. It's the best way of trying something out and assuring a more reasonable decision. It's a matter of careful experimenting. We aren't afraid to try something out, and we aren't afraid to recognize that we are going off in the wrong direction and have to modify it.

CM: You do seem to be good at hanging in there, going with the flow. Is everybody able to do it that well?

SI: No. I think that's why there is turnover. The procedure has bothered some people, but I think they have different goals in mind. Then there have been people who have worked here for years and they just want to do something else. People leave for all sorts of reasons, but there have definitely been occasions where people have been frustrated by the decision-making process, because they need to have hard-and-fast decisions and hard-and-fast directions.

Consensus has not been a problem because we never get into fights. I know of situations where splits occur and things break down because people refuse to come to some sort of an agreement. That hasn't happened here in ages, and it's never happened problematically enough to close the place down.

I think it has a lot to do with the kind of people who work here, and that's a function of how we do our hiring. We just do not hire people who are bureaucratic.

CM: And how do you evaluate that?

SI: Seat of the pants, I guess; I don't know. Some sort of sensitivity. Having known enough people in circumstances like this over the years, we just collectively know how easy people are going to be in a consensus decision. Half the time, we know the people personally before they come in. We've often debated whether that's an advantage or a disadvantage. When you know someone, you know their problems. But when you don't know someone, you tend to look at what's most interesting or exciting about them, and that can throw you out of whack if you aren't careful. I'm not sure how that works. The other thing that makes the whole process work well is the way in which we want to live our lives. We don't make a whole lot of money, but nobody *wants* to make a whole lot of money.

CM: You don't have to buy in when you come to work at Dumont? And when you leave, do you take anything with you?

SI: No equity at all. The debts are really the corporation's debts, of Dumont Press Graphics. If that were to go under, the Employees' Association would not be liable for the debts of Dumont. The Association only owns shares, and its shares are really worthless, worth less than a hundred dollars total. All the debts, the cash assets and so on, rest with the corporation. The assets are ultimately owned by the Association, but no one owns the Association, so what we have created, in effect, is a situation where there is no property that can be owned by an individual, and that was intended. The idea was not to see this place as property, but rather as resource, and I think that's a big difference. Resources are something that people can use, that have value only in use, not really in terms of buying and selling.

CM: In fact, you yourself have put a tremendous investment in time and thought in this place, plus your electronics skills. I saw the new machine waiting to be put into use and heard that you were rebuilding part of it yourself.

SI: OK, but another way of looking at it is that I have learned all these skills here, and I certainly don't know everything. We depend on other people's skills a lot, outside the collective. I can't do everything myself, although I can do a fair bit. The other question, of what have I invested in here, that is a concept of private property, and I do not see it that way — I do not want to see it that way. Part of being here is an exercise in challenging the values of corporations in general, the economy in general.

To me, a co-op is not just a little entity that makes things convenient, comfortable and interesting for the people who work there, but is somehow integrated into a larger sense of community. It is best if it is ongoing; seen as something that passes on to other people's use, other people's benefit. For me to think in terms of property or energy that I have invested here and that I can withdraw as from a bank is very contradictory to that notion. I am satisfied with the skills that I have learned and my access to resources here for doing things that I find interesting and satisfying and exciting.

The community this cooperative is a part of is not easy to define and is pretty scattered. There is most definitely a community that we fit into, in this geographical area as well as in the more nebulous community outside the area. Around here, friends are involved in workplaces that have some similarity to co-ops, often research or academic groups, or the community radio station . . . .

Most of them differ from us in that they are not really producers; they are in service or research. But the relationships within each group are similar, and our social values are very similar. So that we will often find ourselves involved in common activities around, say, peace groups, anti-nuclear stuff and alternatives of various sorts — food co-ops, etc. In a sense, that constitutes our community of like people.

CM: Do any of these people have any input into your decision-making?

SI: At Dumont? No. Actually, that brings up an interesting point. I suddenly flashed on how consensus works here. To a great extent when we make decisions we tend to think of other situations and other people. I wonder how in fact that works? For example, to reach consensus, we sit around and talk over a particular problem. We may talk about it for quite awhile, and realize that we do not have a ready solution. If we need to come to a decision, we generally agree to choose the best available, but people are not necessarily going to feel in their hearts that is the best possible solution, it's just the best available at the time. Everyone realizes that we will try it out; if it doesn't work, we'll try something else. If we still, after discussion, can't reach a decision, it probably means that the problem is not so urgent and that we can put it off to some other time. That has worked for a long time. It does have an effect on how efficiently things get done, but what we are doing is making a choice — that this decision-making process is more important than efficiency or than the perfect solution. We generally agree it is a very important part of our cohesion, the thing that keeps us here.

In a similar way, we see that the things we do, the way in which we make Dumont's resources available, has an effect on our larger community. It does not necessarily get together to decide how Dumont is going to work, but there is an interchange of ideas.

CM: How do you communicate with this larger community? Meetings, chatting with people who come in with jobs, participating in some of the groups yourselves?

SI: Yes. I am fairly active in the food co-op; not everyone there even knows about Dumont, but the ones I know best do because I tell them. We all interact with other people.

CM: The resources you have offered have changed a bit from the beginning?

SI: Not much, except in the equipment that is available. Right from the beginning, if the collective at Dumont agreed, people could come in and use our equipment for their own purposes, under certain conditions. For example, if what you are doing is interesting to us, socially relevant, and you do not have money to pay for it commercially, you can learn to use our camera set-up and our typesetting equipment yourself. That covers a lot of people. Sometimes a group has lots of money, so we do the work commercially.

CM: You let people use your typesetting, your design and camera facilities, but you also do commercial work on contract. You began with contracts with two university papers, but you don't have them now. What is the bulk of your business now?

SI: A lot of our work is books for publishers and some journals. I generally estimate that the commercial work is about 20 to 25 percent.

CM: Are they always within your political philosophy?

SI: No. The commercial work is straight. I would say more often than not we may be somewhat antagonistic to it, not in tune with it. I don't like advertising, I think it tries to con, but unless it's outrageous, like sexist or racist, we accept it. Sometimes there's something offensive that the customer didn't notice and doesn't mind changing. Other times they are insulted at being confronted.

CM: Is your market local, in Kitchener?

SI: Not really. The trade work is local, but most of the publishing work is from outside of town. Given the number of people we know in publishing, and the alternate press across the country, it's pretty easy to hear about a new publication. We get in touch with them about it. Often people will come to us directly because we have been around so long they know us as typesetters. That can be on a national basis. We get phonecalls from out west. One of our regular jobs is based in Newfoundland.

CM: And these would all be in the alternate community?

SI: Usually, yes. The main reason that something good happens is relationships among people. In a sense it's customer relations, the quality of our interactions. We give them feedback on things they do. Often it involves content; frequently it involves style: this won't work; this doesn't look very good, you should try this. We usually spend a lot of time with customers, helping them design things or choose elements of typesetting that give them choices.

CM: Do you give more service than your competitors do?

SI: I would say so. Often we suspect that we are spending too much time. There has been some overlap with other cooperatives. It does seem that a lot of people who want to set up a co-op think of some aspect of publishing. But we don't want to see ourselves as competing, at least not in an aggressive way.

There is some relationship between the profit we make and our working conditions, our day-to-day practice. These are primary. If we decided, for example, to schedule work to be done much faster, and go out and look for more work, we could probably make more money. But we are not so interested in money that we want to change patterns. I am quite sure that a typesetting business involving people who are as skilled as ours could make a lot of money, but it means pretty constant gruelling work.

I was just at a conference of worker co-ops in Edmonton. There was a strong tendency to think of a worker co-op as a business, as something that a group of people construct for themselves as a way of making a living. They might as well set up a small business, a small corporation, a partnership or something, if that's what they want. I really think that people should see cooperatives as part of a larger community — something that relies on, in various ways, economically as well as socially, other cooperative activities. Not see it as something that props up a way of life that we have become used to, but as a way to change the system that *creates* the problems and the way of life. It is a very old form of relating, and it was part of communities that used to exist with much more integrity as communities.

In the Middle Ages, people held property in common and shared the resources of their area without anyone accumulating a disproportionate amount of wealth or power. There are an incredible number of examples in history.

I have done a lot of reading about that. I'm very interested as to why non-hierarchical structures broke down, because I think at one point they were the norm, before times of war-lords and city states. The cooperative form is really a residue from something very old. It can be used to patch things that exist right now, disparities in wealth, in industrial development. But unless a cooperative venture is tied into a larger sense of cooperativeness, a larger sense of community, the patching-up job is not going to hold. I am interested in profound social change, not just a temporary patching job.

CM: It seems to me that this is part of our culture, too, that we do have, as part of our beliefs and part of our ways of acting, the cooperative mode. In the west, co-ops have been important for generations, but it seems to me that the big and successful co-ops have lost a sense of that themselves, that they have become businesses, like The Co-operators insurance company, the co-op grain companies. But we can reach back and remind people that this is part of our history, too, that we are not just successful as individual enterprises, but together. Maybe we can build on that more. It is old; we have been doing it; we just did not always identify it that way.

SI: Well, there is a lot of work to be done in history. Too often we only think back to Robert Owen. That is really false, because the history really goes back to the travel societies. The Mennonites and the Moravians predate Robert Owen by about 500 years. They lasted far longer than civilization as we know it. They were communities that had some strength, some kind of integral strength that allowed them to maintain themselves over generations and generations with dynamics that militated against the accumulation of wealth. They did not want someone to become more powerful in the tribe, which did not mean that everyone was the same because there were elders — people who retained the tradition or people who knew medicine and understood the ecology of their particular areas. But the knowledge was available to all within the community.

The history of the state is, I think, the history of attempts to break down that kind of community, but despite that, aspects of it have persisted. To cooperate is a human need. I think it is related to the love and enjoyment that individuals have of other people, sharing and stuff like that. But at the same time, some of the older communities in Europe, who were resisting the attempts of the new nation states to suppress their values, left, emigrated, and were able to establish in different parts of Canada and to retain some of those values.

What unfortunately has happened in the last one or two hundred years is that in a climate of liberalism, the values have been more easily eroded than they would have been under repression. Which is not to say that repression would be preferable. I think that is what happened to the co-op movement. It learned techniques — financial techniques — to deal with its enterprises. It was not critical enough of those dimensions, and felt that these tools were merely ways of evaluating their wealth, their assets, ways of establishing efficient work relations within their enterprises. They learned these techniques from capitalists, not from ancient communities. Mondragon is a good example. They assume that a production line under worker control does not erode ancient cooperative principles, but it does. The nature of a production line is such that it gives certain people more authority than others.

"People's temperaments often dictate what they do that day."
— Mo, Mary and Bruce

Mo: We are a typesetting shop. We take rough material, like typed copy, and we turn it into full type, and then we take that and assemble it into a book, a magazine, poster or whatever. Sometimes we do design work and sometimes we don't. We rarely print. We do the production from rough copy to the negative stage and the negatives are then sent to a printer for printing and distribution.

We have two presses, but we use them for current political work; we rarely use them for commercial work. People who have an interest in turning stuff out use the shop on a non-commercial basis. That is, they pay for use of materials and a minimal shop charge for overhead, and they do their own work here. Generally, what we do is set them up with a Dumont volunteer who works with them until they are able to do their own work on their own, and then they proceed to do it.

The commercial work keeps the shops going; it pays the overhead.

Constance Mungall: How did the funding group come together?

Mo: A lot of the people who were involved originally, in the late 1960s, lived in a house on King Street. They called themselves the Dumont Brigade, after Gabe Dumont, Louis Riel's guerilla leader. It was seen as a romantic Canadian connection. They got a Department of Regional Economic Expansion grant, and in order to get the funding they had to raise the same amount of money. A number of people who had family money were politically involved at that stage; basically, they bought shares in Dumont. They were preferred shares with no vote. If the company folded, their money would be given back to them, but there is no power. There is a certain amount of guilt in having inherited money, and it was alleviated by a little revolutionary enterprise. They also got a guarantee from the *Chevron* and from the *Court,* which are the University of Waterloo and Wilfred Laurier University newspapers, that Dumont would do their production. That guarantee was considered as money that Dumont had raised to match the DREE funding.

Initially they got a typesetting machine that was just terrible, really slow and couldn't do the work; they never did pay for it. Then they switched to the typesetting system which we have now. At that point, it was very advanced; there were a number of places that could produce paper tapes on perforators, but they had no way of running them out. So at that time the shop made a lot of money running tapes through the machine.

Mary: What we have efficiently done over the years is operate with second-hand equipment, so that we're really one stage behind the state of the art. We've never been abreast of technology. But now we are evolving our own systems, our own computer systems, to do typesetting which should be able to interface with other computer systems. The only reason we can afford to develop that technology is that Steve Isma, one member of the collective, along with others not in the collective, have the knowledge and are willing to work with us to develop the systems.

Two of us are now working half time. Steve and I both go to school part time and work here part time. It's a relatively new situation — we have yet to figure out how it can work both to the benefit of the collective and the part time people.

CM: And do you have as much say in the operation of the business?

Mary: As collective members I think essentially we do. Yeah, we attend the meeting; we have long afternoon meetings where we make major decisions every two weeks. Being collective members, we fully participate in the decision-making. Once a year, we go on a retreat for the weekend where we talk more intensely about major stuff.

CM: What's the background of people now?

Mary: It's pretty varied. Joe is the only person now who has had any kind of formal schooling in this area, otherwise we've all learned by doing it.

Mo: Training on the job is a significant part of what we want to do here, both in terms of people who come to work here as a job and others who come to work on various projects — skill sharing, making it possible for people to print materials to promote their particular cause or interests. It used to be sufficient that a person had an interest in working collectively, but over the years that's altered somewhat, for one thing because of the pressure of production.

Bruce: I've been here a year and a half. I was in integrated studies at the University of Waterloo, which is a sort of lefty independent study program and that's where I met Steve. I was studying mainly psychology in education. I never finished; I had some disagreements with getting a degree. When the job came up I sort of jumped at it.

I like design work; I have an artistic sense; I'm not a good artist but in design work I can be very artistic without needing technical drawing skills. I seem to have a natural predilection for it. I used to type resumés and proposals for others at university; people came to me because I had a sense of how to set it up, and that sort of expanded here, and that's what I enjoy doing the most. I didn't like working for a boss — I used to work for General Motors, at three times the money I'm getting here, and it gave me nightmares. My father and both my grandfathers spent their lives in GM. It was home, and that was scary. I'd give up that extra money for the working conditions here any day.

Mo: We have one basic requirement now, which is that a person should be able to type. We didn't mind teaching people to typeset and do design, but learning how to type before you even got started was too much for the shop to absorb. Also we found that some people had an attachment to the idea of working collectively but didn't like the work. Since we are production-oriented, we have to produce the product in order to continue to survive, so you have an interest in the task as well as in the process. There has to be a balance.

Once we put an ad in the paper, but it didn't work because the people who had been involved with the trade thought we were completely out to lunch working cooperatively. They couldn't figure out what we were talking about. So we decided not to bother with that any more, particularly since there is a considerable pool of articulate people who can type and are interested in alternative ways of working, a large enough pool to draw from.

We set up a hiring committee; the whole collective doesn't interview all of the applicants.

CM: Can you describe the procedure for managing the shop?

Bruce: We all make collective decisions on the major issues. We do split up some of the administrative functions. One person does the bookkeeping; I do payroll, but I don't sign cheques. These are the administrative functions. Twice a month, every other Monday afternoon, we have a meeting where we deal with major issues.

The decisions that have to be made day-to-day are usually around production. A job comes in — who's going to do it? We have a system of docketing so that anybody can see what stage a job is at. A larger job — a book, a magazine — has a coordinator, usually picked at the bi-weekly meeting. They make sure that it gets done, schedule it always in consultation. Then we have a lot of small jobs — fliers, etc. — we have to make sure that work gets done, because we don't have a boss that keeps it all going.

When we get near a deadline, we might pull people off another job. Day to day we have at least two production meetings. We work very flexible hours, so around 11:00 or 11:30 in the morning, when most people are in, we have a production meeting about what is in the shop, who wants to do what, who wants to make lunch — even when we aren't being paid, making lunch is a way of taking care of ourselves. This meeting usually lasts five or ten minutes every day. Production meetings don't need everyone there. We just need to be able to cover all the jobs. We try not to give something to somebody who's not there, or if we do to check it out when she comes in.

It's good that way — peoples' temperaments often dictate what they want to do on a given day. Some days you come in and sit at a keyboard and type all day. Other days, you want to paste up or do camera work. You can always be doing something new, within limits — when you have a job at deadline you know it has to be followed through. Very seldom something falls through a crack — a little job may get overlooked at some stage; it's a minor irritation and you may get teed off at somebody. Very occasionally we get into trouble on a big job.

Mo: We once hired a CASE counsellor. They came and looked at the books and said that they couldn't give us any advice, that we were doing pretty well for what we were doing, and went away.

CM: Have you had any help from provincial government?

Mary: No. We wouldn't want it.

Bruce: There used to be a man who kept the machines going and he seemed to feel that gave him a special authority. Sometimes new employees bring patterns from the straight workplace and try to apply them here — look for a boss, look for a power figure, look for authority, look for something to strike back against. Steve Isma for instance has an awful lot of skills, so there is the fear that could turn to power. Often it's a long process for people to finally realize that those figures just aren't here. We are a social experiment in the workplace. This is what we are.

Mary: People hardly ever override each other or talk over top of each other. Partly that's because there are always new people and it's important they feel that they can speak. Somebody who hasn't talked for awhile and suddenly starts to say something, people shut up because it's time for that person to speak.

CM: Have you consciously learned techniques for dealing with them? Have you had training in conflict resolution?

Bruce: Some of us have.

CM: Are the goals being maintained as in the beginning?

Mo: I think that is virtually impossible to answer. There were 24 people involved when it started, at least 12 different opinions about what could ultimately happen. The shop evolved, but to me it feels much the same. When someone who used to work here 10 years ago came in the other day, I said, "Does it look different to you?" He said, "It looks different, and it looks exactly the same!" It's not the same political climate as it was. There's not the student activist base; there's not the same kind of connection to the student population, partly because we're older. I'm 37, Bruce is 21, Steve is 35, Bill is 33 . . . .

We used to worry about gender; now we worry about sexual orientation as well and try to keep a balance. The question of sexual politics is more important. It has become much more of a gay and lesbian shop because it's a safer place for us to be.

CM: And is that a factor when you recruit new members? Do they have to be gay or lesbian?

Mary: No. The point is that we don't want to be exclusive, but we want to be able to work with people who will feel comfortable with us.

Mo: These are the questions you have to address if you're working in a collective. Mary was talking about hanging around for a year and paying attention to what's going on. That's because learning to work collectively is a process; half of what you're learning here is how to work collectively and half of what you learn is how to do the production work — however long it takes a person to figure out how it works is their particular learning process. The community changes all the time, and we're always having to change our ways of thinking about how we work individually and together. It's never-ending.

Doing an interview at this particular juncture, today, you're going to have people feeling a lot more and thinking a lot more about interpersonal stuff because we're leaving tonight for a retreat weekend to explore these very questions.

CHAPTER TEN
Baseline Type and Graphics Cooperative
Vancouver, British Columbia

"We are all really isolated."

Baseline Graphics occupies a big bright open floor space in a renovated warehouse in downtown Vancouver. I met David Lach, the leader in founding the co-op two and a half years before, in the corner room which forms the workers' lounge, with couches, a coffee-maker, plants and sunlight, a good place to relax and chat. In the shop, several women were busy on computerized typography machines. One man was pasting up a layout. Since our interview, membership has increased from six to seven. The business is stable, and is making it on its own — no government grants or even useful advice. As with many worker co-ops, Baseline's attempts to get relevant advice from the Federal Business Development Bank were fruitless.

The only problem Baseline seemed to face, like many small businesses and most worker co-ops, was undercapitalization. "We need $15,000 more long-term money," says Lach. Their $20,000 line of credit is from the CCEC, Vancouver's forward-looking credit union which funds many worker-owned enterprises. A five-year loan for typesetting equipment is at 20 percent interest, and to get that, the six original founders signed personal guarantees, sometimes committing joint assets held with a spouse.

David Lach has some creative ideas about how to overcome this kind of requirement, while encouraging worker co-op formation: a coalition of co-ops that would provide stability, define a general statement of the principles under which worker co-ops operate, and give help in financing. This coalition would establish a business development fund, so a co-op could start itself off with a reasonable amount of financing from its own members. The fund would underwrite commercial loans with regular banking institutions, and the risk would be covered by an insurance premium of 5 to 10 percent. Credit unions could then make relatively long-term loans to help create new worker-owned businesses.

In return for the benefits in the initial stages of financing, successful worker co-ops would agree to put part of their surplus into common funds for development. Through the coalition, they could also have access to central research organizations and relevant business advice.

As he talked with me, David Lach struck me as cheerful, optimistic, energetic, with a handle not only on his own worker co-op, but on the movement as a whole.

David Lach: We started in May of '82. At the beginning there were seven of us, and we have reduced to six. We were the workers in an existing business that did design and typesetting and layout. We wanted to run the place in a democratic fashion, but in fact it was controlled by two people who had the major investment. There was some dissatisfaction that we were controlling the business in name, but not in practice, and when we heard that it had financial problems and was going to close and we were going to be laid off, we decided to carry it on.

We came to an agreement with the owners to assume the lease and the payments on the equipment and various accounts outstanding, and pay some good will. Basically we carried on in the same premises with mostly the same people, but as a new business, with some of the existing clientele.

I had some background in housing and food co-ops and some contacts with other worker co-ops, so I was the one who was instrumental in setting up as a co-op. I knew the ropes in terms of incorporation so we did that fairly fast; everyone really agreed that was how they wanted to work. That was one of the many reasons why people wanted to work here anyway; there was a freer atmosphere than in a conventional business. But we didn't necessarily all come in with very strong ideas about what it really meant.

We all did make a commitment that we were going to work here for a year when we started up. Two people in fact left after the first year . . . it wasn't what they wanted to do. One in particular found our meetings very difficult, very difficult to sit through other people's points of view, so she left.

I guess over the year we learned that if we had things to say we had to say them. We had to do a fair amount of writing up policies in order to get a loan from credit unions, so that forced us to lay down in detail how we were going to operate, how we were going to hire new people, what probation periods, what membership investments, on what terms members get their investments repaid and those kind of things. That was a very useful discipline, although at the time it was quite hard.

Constance Mungall: How did you fund the business when you took over? Two owners had had the money in it and they withdrew that, did they?

DL: Basically they used existing accounts receivable to pay off their bank loans. At the same time, we assumed the existing loans for the equipment, and paid rent for the premises and the equipment, so we didn't actually have to come up with a cash lump sum, with operating money on a monthly basis. About a year later we actually purchased the typesetting equipment and the camera from the company. We did that by assuming the balance of the mortgage loan and paying some cash.

We didn't get a bank loan. We all dug as deep as we could in our own relatives' pockets to come up with some start-up capital, close to $10,000 altogether. For some people it was $500 and for others it was $4,000. We couldn't require an equal amount from everyone, because some had no way of getting it. We have a policy that you have to invest a minimum of $500 by the time you have been here one year, and with maximum long-term investment of $1,250. Any more is in short-term loans to Baseline, not locked in the way the long term loan is. We pay 10 percent interest. Our total assets would be about $65,000 for typesetting equipment and the camera, and about $7,000 for leasehold improvements. So our total long-term investment is in the range of $72,000 to $75,000. That is supported by a line of credit loan of $20,000 from CCEC which is being converted into a five-year term loan, and member investment of about $10,000. Individual loans from friends are around $8,000.

Our biggest piece of typesetting equipment was purchased on a five-year term at 20 percent interest. The only reason we got that loan was because the typesetting company wanted to sell equipment and guaranteed the loan to the bank. If we had had more capital we would have been able to get started far cheaper and we would be in a better cash situation now. We are totally undercapitalized. We need $15,000 more long-term money. Because money is tight we have to juggle it in order to pay on time. There has been an awful lot of overhead. We have bought equipment; we have moved; we have renovated; a lot of things that you don't do very often we compressed into our first year and a half. At the end of our first year we got a month's notice to move from the premises we were in because the transit company was building a station there. That was a major disruption because we had to find premises in a very short time. We moved here and we had about five months of construction to actually create the space. From now on it should go easier because we can now concentrate on the business instead of the physical space.

CM: But you are fairly stable?

DL: Reasonably stable. We could do with about 20 percent more business. The printing business in general is not in good shape in B.C. There hasn't been any growth for three years.

We do typesetting, camera work and graphics. We don't do any printing, so that limits us. We do a lot of publication work, magazines, books, newspapers and a relatively small amount of trade work. Both the universities in Vancouver, Simon Fraser and U.B.C., have purchased typesetting equipment so the work on academic publications essentially dried up.

On the other hand, I have a good computing background, and we have a computer that can hook up with outside computers. So we are beginning to get seriously into receiving books that people have keyboarded on their own computers and have transmitted by modem to our computer and run through our typesetting system. We become a manufacturer of type rather than doing so much labour-intensive keyboarding, and that is the way the business is going to go. If you get the bulk of the books and magazines by modem, then you can charge a good rate for the more complicated specialized typesetting, and produce good quality detailed work.

CM: And you can keep up with that kind of technical change?

DL: On our level. Obviously we can't deal with a major newspaper publisher or the yellow pages! Our equipment is not fast enough, not large enough, but for small publishers and small magazines we can provide technological support that they can't get from most places. We can provide them with a good service cheaper than by any other means. I think we have a niche there.

CM: How did you learn to do what you do?

DL: I started a magazine in 1974 that I published myself until I ran out of money. So I started to typeset and lay out other peoples' magazines and gradually converted that into a business. On staff, we have myself with experience in publishing magazines and computer systems, an experienced layout person, Dennis in production from camera work and printing, a bookkeeper who trained with one of the main accounting firms, two experienced typesetters and one other person for camera and layout. It's necessary to be versatile because if someone is sick or away, you have to be able to fill that spot. We will hire people to fill in, but we prefer to create a job rather than hire part time.

The production manager coordinates all the work that involves more than one department and does all the outside buying. We distinguish between small jobs that go out in about a day where there is not much coordination and large jobs like books and magazines which require much more coordination of typesetting, layout, camera work, outside buying.

All six of us meet at lunch-time on Tuesdays for about an hour in weekly production meetings and go over all the major jobs in the shop. After we have reviewed the status of all the jobs we do the scheduling: how are we going to avoid overloading, who is going to do what? Sometimes we have to move people's hours so that we can get two shifts on a machine instead of one. Then the small jobs come in across the front desk and they go straight into production. Feedback is only needed if typesetting or paste-up or camera is overloaded and you have to alert customers so they know they have to wait another day or so.

Those are weekly production meetings. Any major discussions take place in directors' meetings every three weeks to a month; the schedule always gets interrupted — someone is sick or on vacation or taking courses. We are all directors, and meetings happen after the work day; we tried to reduce our daily work hours to compensate. At one point we each got a day off every five or six weeks on a rotating basis to compensate for the meetings, but we have suspended that temporarily. It's too small an organization; if everyone's not here, other people's time gets really disrupted.

We all get the same rate of pay, currently $1,050 a month. And we have a dependency allowance of 7½ percent for a shared dependent and 15 percent for a totally dependent child. We pay the B.C. medical plan and a medical-dental plan as well, so we've got good medical benefits but the pay is too low. Some people have a quite tight situation with that kind of money, particularly people with families.

At this point we are just about on the verge of where we could take on another person, but we should resist that for a while. We work 9:00 till 4:30, theoretically a six-hour day, but in fact we work closer to seven hours and a five-day week — about 35 hours a week, not counting meeting times.

CM: Do you foresee being able to pay yourselves more?

DL: We haven't budgeted for an increase this year, but we would dearly like to do that when our budget shows we are able to. A 30 percent increase would be reasonable. We have difficulty hiring qualified people at the rates we pay, even in the depression that we are in.

Three people have left since we started, and we have hired three. We have two men and four women, from 28 to 43. We would like to maintain a mix, and obviously that is harder to do with a small group. We advertise for replacements and we had 150 applicants for our last job.

CM: Do you look for people who know what a worker co-op is or do you look for expertise?

DL: Very few people know what a worker co-op is, so if we only looked for those we would rule out a lot. You have to look for experience primarily, because everyone has to produce, and training is really lengthy, particularly in typesetting.

So now we look for experience in a person with compatible personality; that would be our main goal.

For hiring, we set up a committee of three which does preliminary interviews, and then we all interview the two or three leading contenders. We have always been more or less unanimous in our final decision. At the end of the three-month probation period we have an evaluation and we have to have 75 percent in favour, which is essentially everyone except one. We could decide to get rid of somebody, but we never have. Each of the people we've hired has gone on through the probation period and stayed. As soon as they are admitted as co-op members they have to buy a share. That is only $10, but they have to come up with the $500 within the first year, so some people pay in installments by taking $50 off each cheque.

CM: Do you have any problems making decisions with a group of six?

DL: We defer things too much. We fail to make decisions in our own areas and instead give them to the whole group. All that does is make six people sit around talking about something they shouldn't really need to talk about. The group decision is usually better, but it depends on the area. In the wording of some form, for instance, it's better just to do it than to wait two months until everyone has had a look at it and agreed. It's only experience that tells how much of that participation is needed and how much is redundant, so it is a kind of learning process that a new person has to go through. We talk about this process, but usually relatively informally, at a directors' meeting or sitting around having lunch. We have tried to say, "so-and-so is responsible for that," and go do it.

CM: Have you had any guidance or counselling about the decision-making process?

DL: Not external, no. One person took the community business training course at CCEC, a group decision-making workshop. A lot of the ideas she got from that were related to working out things together and having formal procedures so you don't re-invent each time.

We almost never take a vote. It's very rare to decide something with opposition, because the opposition usually has some valid reason and it ceases as soon as whatever it is is adjusted. I don't think we have any causes of violent disagreement. If we don't agree we say so; most of the time the questions do get raised and dealt with. I think we are a reasonably good group at this point in terms of working together.

CM: If you decided to close up shop, there would be some assets to divide. How would you look after that?

DL: All the assets belong to various banking institutions! We don't have very much in the way of accumulated assets, and we have obligations outstanding. To close up shop and pay off everyone would be difficult, but then any business is in that shape. The initial investment is pretty much taken up by getting the business going and you don't really see the results until after the business has paid off its major first indebtedness. Members' share of the business consists of their $10 share and any loans they have made. According to our rules, long-term loans have to be repaid within three months of the person leaving, although several have left them longer. Also under the credit union lending policy, we are not allowed to refund without their permission; in a way they are part of the security for the credit union loan. No individual owns a portion of the collective assets; these belong to the present members of the co-op.

CM: After you get over this hump, you will have put in a lot of sweat equity. You will have invested a lot in getting it going. New people coming in will benefit from your input. Will that be a problem?
DL: That raised itself at one point. I guess the answer is that it can't be because of the way we incorporated; the only people who can be members are the workers, and all workers should be members. If you cease to work for the co-op then you cease to be a member and you are no longer realizing benefits, so those people who did put in some work during the first years when it was hard going will not be there to reap the benefits in three years. One person raised it as a problem, one of the beginning founders who was leaving, but it wasn't solved. It was left, and that is the way it is.
CM: Have you found it an advantage or a disadvantage to be a worker co-op?
DL: It is difficult to say in terms of getting business. I think we are getting an increasing proportion of the business from co-ops and community groups. There was a woman's collective running a magazine and also typesetting and camera work that closed down about a year ago, so we took over some work from them. I guess we are now the only typesetting and layout co-op in the city.
I think the word co-op has not very good connotations. In the business community it means relatively disorganized. To some degree we have tried to defuse that by putting on our flyer, "owned and operated by the people who do your work," which makes it an advantage rather than a disadvantage, particularly for small business people who own their business. I think we are reasonably business-like and highly skilled and we provide better than average service, so the connotations don't apply.
If you use the word "cooperative" you have to be incorporated under B.C. law as a co-op, which is a limited liability company. The alternative was to incorporate as a company, with votes in accordance with the number of shares. We wanted the people who work here to control the company with one-vote/one-person, which is exactly the way a co-op is set up.
We haven't seen any disadvantages to being incorporated under the Act. The recording requirements are probably less than for a private company. You have less options in terms of financing, I think. You can't issue preferred shares, so you probably have less options in the capital market than you do as a company. Other than that . . . we have never tried to deal with banks; I don't know how they would react to an application for a loan. We have dealt with CCEC as the bank and lender all along.
CM: Are there any big cooperators here like the Wheat Pools or Co-operators insurance or credit unions that could be markets for you?
DL: The central credit union did have its own print shop which closed recently and they have signed an agreement with the union local to go through a union shop. It doesn't seem reasonable, yet we are excluded. We are not unionized, although we have discussed the question; it's not

necessarily incompatible. I don't think that unions really know what worker co-ops are, or treat them as other than competitors, so I'm not sure what the results will be. There are problems in terms of hiring policies; I think that under union agreements you have to hire from a union pool, and I'm not sure how seniority affects your choice of staff. Things of that sort would be problematic.

The highest priority on our list is to reduce the amount of overhead of administration and accounting. We are in the process of computerizing our accounting system. And we have to find some new customers. It is a problem because we don't have a person full time on sales, and it's very difficult to see how we could, with a group this small. It has got to be a part time occupation and it is one we tend to let slide. We tend to be either too busy or not busy enough.

CM: What are your plans now?

DL: To make more money and expand up to about eight people. We are too small now to be efficient. We run into problems with too much paste-up work, and too much camera work, and we can't deal with that as well as if there were more people. We've got the space, all we need is business. The very successful typesetting companies operate on shifts, using their equipment 16 or 24 hours a day.

We have to keep up with technological advances by being smarter. We can do things with our computer equipment that most people have to spend a lot of money to do, because we have computer background. We are in the top third of the quality market in terms of the type we produce. We have two people taking apprenticeship courses and others are taking design and camera work courses. The apprenticeship courses are B.C. government funded, so there is actually no cost other than the time of the person involved. I'm supervising the person who is doing the typesetting apprenticeship. It involves a series of courses over three to five years, so they are bringing in new ideas and meeting people from other companies.

CM: With your background you could probably get a job with higher pay somewhere else?

DL: Probably, but it's worth it to stay here. I enjoy the environment and creating and developing something new. It's true there won't be any equity because the money investment that you put in is what you get back, plus interest. The business belongs to the workers so if we make a lot of money in the future then the company could increase our pay or we could pay bonuses.

CM: Have you had any support at all from government agencies?

DL: We called in a CASE consultant from the Federal Business Development Bank with specific questions about sales and internal operations. He came in and read us his prepared speech; there was no consultation at all; it was a lecture, essentially, so we didn't really get what we wanted. He told us that co-ops were inefficient and that what we really wanted was a manager who ran everything. We got the pitch, but it wasn't related to the business — I mean we are not selling to individuals, we are selling to businesses who don't know that they need us and it's difficult to identify where that market is. It is out there, but to zero in on the best strategy is difficult. He did not really help us in that area. That is the only government consultation we have had.

It would be nice to find someone who had some experience of identifying type, and knew where to go and sell it. When we made the original loan CCEC had a credit committee that went through our procedures and policies and that was very useful. We put together a 20-page document that we always refer back to, laying down in writing a lot of these things. We are all really isolated. Vancouver is relatively well endowed compared with some other cities, but the group interested in co-ops is relatively tiny, and the amount of exchange is relatively tiny, and we are all so busy with our own businesses that we don't have time to do more. But we do need reinforcement of worker co-op structures and some clarification of what a reasonable level of investment is.

There are problems with obtaining loans from organizations, particularly in the amount of personal guarantees that are required. Not only are you working for the business, investing money in it, but you are also signing a personal guarantee that if the company goes out of business all of your assets are at stake too. That is what the lending institutions want. And that is very difficult, particularly for married people with joint assets. When they sign the personal guarantee the wife's or husband's house is at stake. You even get to the point where people threaten to leave if they have to sign a personal guarantee.

Two people haven't signed because of jointly owned property. In the early days, six of us signed personal guarantees on the equipment loan, which is $53,000, but at that time we were all unemployed so we had more incentive.

CHAPTER ELEVEN
Accu-Graphics Co-op Ltd.
Winnipeg, Manitoba

"We were already unionized . . . we believe in the common good."

The three men who formed the Winnipeg co-op Accu-Graphics had worked together for between 20 and 30 years. When their employer threatened to close up, they had two choices: find new jobs, or take responsibility for the ones they had. They chose the latter, and went worker co-op rather than partnership in order to qualify for guaranteed loans and for advice and support from the Manitoba Department of Co-operative Development.

Accu-Graphics became a worker co-op November 4, 1985. It had been the graphics art department of a large printing company, responsible for all the preparatory work involved in printing, up to the press run. Then as now, the group did typography, artwork, paste-up, positioning of pages into a book, photographing the artwork, placing the negatives into a proper format, making the plates.

The parent company, Wallingford Press, had overreached itself in an amalgamation, and was being pushed by the bank to reduce staff and operating costs. The owner was happy to unload a part of the operations, and gave his old employees a good deal on the equipment.

Becoming a co-op wasn't a difficult adjustment. As Jim Livingstone, one of the founders, said when I visited in July 1986, "I liked the idea . . . we were already unionized . . . we believe in the common good."

Nevertheless, their grasp of cooperative philosophy and practice does seem a little more tenuous than in the older "established" co-ops which were formed not only because of need for a job, but because of belief in the cooperative way. When considering the procedure for buy-in for a new member, for instance, Jim Livingstone admits, "We start to think like private businessmen" — not about to give away to the new guy the profits made by work and worry (as well as the immeasurable value of Manitoba government support in guaranteeing loans, gaining a reduced interest rate, training and business advice). Compare this with Steve Isma's attitude to the personal knowledge and growth he himself had gained by similar risks and hard work at Dumont Press, another graphics operation. But then, compare also the time — early1970s vs. mid-1980s — and the age of the participants — early 20s vs. 50s.

The Accu-Graphics workers were and still are unionized — and proud of it. They pay themselves less than the union contract stipulates, but they've had no hassle from their local. They expect negotiations for their new contract to be tricky — "We'll jump from one side of the table to the other" — but not impossible.

They look for continuing support not to the union, but to the Manitoba department which guided them through the seven months of negotiation with the original owner and potential financiers.

"Writing their business plan was an excellent learning process for them," says Ken Bourquin, the government development officer who worked with them from the start. "They did it. They came up with the figures." Bourquin is still standing by, but he hopes the group will be independent once their first year is out. He was on hand during the interview, and cleared up a misunderstanding in Jim's mind about share value. I got the impression it wouldn't be the last time Ken would take that role.

Jim Livingstone: Originally Wallingford Press was the company that we worked for, and they appeared to be in a great deal of trouble, both in loss of accounts and a shrinking complement of people, and we were concerned for our well-being and our jobs. At one time in this department alone we had eleven people, and there were only four remaining and one fellow was just more or less filling in; his forte wasn't in this area.

In effect Wallingford Press laid all four of us off, and three of us assumed the role of starting up Accu-Graphics. I contacted my MLA, Eugene Kostyra who was Minister of Cultural Affairs, but in close contact with Jay Collin who is the Minister of Co-operative Development, and I made contacts to see what the program was all about. That was when I met Ken first; he was the first contact we had with Co-operative Development. When we first talked to Co-op Development they told us what they could do for us. There were no grants available, but they would in fact guarantee a bank loan if we couldn't get one on our own. We visited four or five financial institutions, none of which were prepared to forward the money to us unless we put up personal guarantees for 100 percent of the money. We didn't really want to do that; having worked for Wallingford and seen the shrinking process we didn't feel that we wanted to take the risk of signing our houses away. I think finally we probably put up 30 percent of the cash. And even at that the banks and the credit unions were not interested in loaning us the other 70 percent. I think the financial institutions aren't interested in owning printing equipment. It's not the kind of tangible that you can unload easily and they felt the best they could do if something happened to Accu-Graphics would be 25 cents on the dollar.

And we went back to Co-op Development and explained the situation and they decided they could guarantee the difference.

Constance Mungall: So you couldn't have done it without that guarantee?

JL: Definitely not. And thanks to Co-op Development, we received our money from the credit union at 1/4 percent over prime, which is optimum.

I guess initially there was probably — I'm guessing now because I can't even remember — but it would be under $60,000 that we needed to have guaranteed. That included money for cash flow which wasn't really part of the purchase price of the equipment . . . we did need money to operate on for a three-month period, and I believe $22,000 was allocated for cash flow. It wasn't enough. It was probably one area where Co-op Development was short-sighted and I think that it was a learning experience for them as well as for us. We were one of the first groups that went through this process. We did quite well in the first three months and by the time we realized the cash flow problem, we were overdrawn at the bank. We did have enough receivables that they loaned us additional money on them, which saw us over the hump. Actually it toughens you up a bit . . . to have to do these things on your own.

CM: How long did it take you to get all of this together, from the first discussions?

JL: I think we probably started discussing it first in about May, early May. I remember my holidays were to be the first three weeks in July, and I was wondering if in fact I was going to take holidays because we may be doing this, and we had already had meetings with Co-op Development through May and June and we made Wallingford's an offer. It took a desperately long time for them to come back with a counter-offer, and when they did they wanted an answer tomorrow so we did our little bit and gave them an answer and then it took another month and a half for them to get back to us again. We were surprised frankly that he accepted our offer. He just wanted to get rid of the whole thing, that was fairly obvious. So it did take a period from May through November to achieve this. We incorporated probably in October and we started on November 4th, our first day. There was no slow-down of work; it was a very smooth transition. We had been bargaining back and forth with Wallingford with the help of Co-op Development. By the time that was all done it was just — one day we were Wallingford Press and the next day we were Accu-Graphics and we just carried right on doing the work.

There's always rumours about Wallingford Press being up for sale, and just how that would affect us we're not entirely sure. We have an agreement right now for a three-year period to do all of their work. From day one our contract with Wallingford covered 100 percent of our work.

CM: Do you have any other contracts now?

JL: We have been building on our other clientele. Between five and ten percent would be other accounts now. We assumed even at the beginning that at least a two-year period would be necessary to build enough of a clientele to survive if something happened to Wallingford, and we went into it knowing that if Wallingford was to close their doors, we would probably close ours one day after that, because they were our only customer. Only time will tell, if they stay in it long enough, whether we will in fact be able to survive without them. I think we probably will. When Wallingford was shrinking, they cut staff because the bank was after them, and they cut past the point they should have so that they were farming a lot of their work out to other companies. We assumed all that work back, but without increasing staff. Consequently we've been working 50 hours a week.

CM: Have you become more productive as well as working longer hours?

JL: I would say yes, to a degree. You do seem to have a little different point of view when you're doing it for yourself, and we do a lot now that we wouldn't have done then. In the old days, if you came two minutes late you'd be docked for ten minutes, and so you wouldn't be too prepared to stay longer at the end of the day and not get paid for it. Now we'll stay for an extra couple of hours to finish a job.

In the early going we became less productive because we assumed a larger work-load in an area that we weren't too familiar with: the invoicing, the bookkeeping aspect of running a company. Co-op Development showed me how to set up books and how to keep them, and the invoicing we picked up on our own, but in the early going it just about floored us because we just short-sightedly assumed that we would carry on doing what we always did best and produce at 100 percent. We found the first week that we produced at less than 50 percent because we had all this paperwork and we didn't know how to do it. So after the first week we really wondered if we had made the right decision and whether we could in fact do the job. That became quite a lot easier as the weeks progressed. Now I take the invoicing home and my wife types them and I just add them up and enter them and do the month-end statements . . . .

CM: So that's extra, unpaid time, is it?

JL: Well, we don't *not* pay ourselves for it, but we are paying ourselves less than we would have been making at Wallingford Press. I think they've had two increases since we left and we haven't given ourselves an increase. It's not that we couldn't, but we're just kind of laying low . . . . I think we're all surviving quite nicely without the money and we'd like to see the company grow so a large portion of that money would be put back into the business.

CM: You were unionized when all this happened?

JL: Yes we were and we still are; we're a union shop . . . Graphic Communications International Union. We're a member and we have a union.

CM: Was the union involved at all in your take-over?

JL: No, they were informed after the fact. We were good union members then and we still are, so I don't think they were opposed to . . .

CM: How about the fact that you are getting less money than other union members?

JL: Well you see we're living actually by Wallingford's contract as far as the union is concerned. Until that contract is expired, we would operate under it, and then we would have to negotiate a new contract with the graphic arts union ourselves. As I say we're paying ourselves actually less than the contract spells out but there's nobody to complain because the three of us are the entire company and we're not complaining! We agreed from the outset that we would do that.

CM: How are you going to conduct negotiations with the graphic arts union when you're the union and you're also the bosses?

JL: We expect to drive the union president nuts! We're going to jump from side to side of the table and discuss both sides at once . . . no, I don't think there will be a problem. There is no other staff to consider at this time and so I've gone through the contract. We'd like to retain everything that's in it, but as a new company that doesn't have the financial capabilities of the one we left behind, we may leave some stuff out just because we can't afford . . . it's too rich for our blood.

CM: What are you thinking of?

JL: The company was paying three percent into an early-retirement pension on our behalf, and I've never been a fan of union pensions. One of them that I belonged to and paid several thousand dollars into went bankrupt. It's a compulsory thing, when you join the union you join the pension. We had a chance when we made this transition to opt out of the plan and just leave the money there, whatever it may be, till we retire and we decided to do that, because we as owners of the company can take a portion of the profits and buy RRSPs on our own behalf instead of letting somebody else manage our financial future.

CM: Are you doing that?

JL: We haven't had a year end yet but we would expect to. I think we're all buying RRSPs on a personal basis but possibly we'll do something through the company profits as well.

CM: You can't get access to that pension money to use in your operations now?

JL: No. I'd just as soon not do that. Any money that I have set aside might as well remain set aside. It wouldn't amount to very much anyhow.

CM: There has neither been help nor hindrance from the union, really?

JL: No, they've really adopted a "laissez-faire" attitude; they haven't bothered us. Any questions that we've had, we've discussed with them, and they've obliged us by answering them and . . .

CM: So they know what's going on?

JL: Oh, yes, very definitely. They're not opposed to it. I couldn't really see a union being opposed to people that wanted to stay in the union and start a new company and be a union-contract shop — I can't see them being opposed.

CM: In what ways are you different from just a partnership of three people?

JL: Well just the fact that we're a worker co-op. It's not a partnership that has a legal agreement that partners may want to get out of in future years. We're bound by different rules and regulations. A worker co-op would have to have 50 percent of its workers as owners — a minimum of 50 percent — right now we have 100 percent.

We may hire two people in the next year and not really want to take them in as partners until we see whether they fit in. We do have some money behind us now, so we're looking at hiring a typesetter. We can in fact save money, because we're having our type farmed out right now and we're paying probably double what we would pay in wages — but we also have an agreement not to pay the typesetting company for 60 to 90 days. If we hired somebody for $2,500 a month, we would still have to pay $3,500 a month to the other company for the next two to three months, so again it's money. But I'd say in the next month to six weeks we'll be looking for a typesetter full time. I would expect if they were to be offered a chance at becoming an equal shareholder in the co-op that it would be probably at our year end, which would be in another four months.

CM: It sounds as if you're thinking of hiring somebody and then seeing if they fit in rather than hiring somebody with a contract for probation.

JL: There will be no contract but they will be told of our operation and what could happen if they fit into our scheme of things.

CM: And will they be part of the team in terms of decision-making from the beginning?

JL: No, the directors set the policies, and the voting members of the cooperative would be the three of us. Until such time as the new man was accepted as a shareholder in the company he wouldn't have a vote. Except we'd probably ask him for his opinions, but he wouldn't really have a vote.

CM: Would you have to hire through the union?

JL: I wouldn't have to hire through the union, but anybody that I hired would have to join the union. The union does say that you should come to them first, and if they have any people out of work that you should hire them before you go to outside sources, but they've never been a stickler for that. And really I would rather pick and choose who I hired and then have them join the union.

CM: Would you pick somebody who had co-op experience?

JL: Probably not. I don't imagine there are too many printers in Winnipeg that have co-op experience; we're probably the only shop right now that is a cooperative. I would probably draw from people that I knew were excellent tradespeople and not opposed to joining a union.

CM: What do you estimate will be your intake for the year?

JL: Our financial statement for the first six months projects that through to the end of the year we should do roughly a quarter of a million dollars in gross sales.

CM: Do you see that increasing in the future?

JL: Yes. Providing nothing happens to Wallingford Press, I would see that increasing. Not so much from Wallingford but from outside sources.

CM: Do you each have a share worth so much?

JL: Yes, we've basically valued the shares at one dollar and we all have an equal number of shares. There's no difference between any one of us. We have $3,500 each.

CM: And you each have one vote.

JL: That's right.

CM: If you take in new members will they each be required to put in $3,500?

JL: We haven't really thought that out entirely. We have discussed it, and in all likelihood it wouldn't be enough in the future. I guess in that respect we start to think like private businessmen. We took a risk and we have worked without increases and we've taken less holidays than we're entitled to, to get this off the ground. And we've also put in many hours of our own time. I wouldn't think that we'd take somebody in a year down the road and let him have an equal share in the company for the same value. What we will have done by that time will be worth something in dollars and cents, so we would have to look at what we would value as an equal share in the company at that time.

CM: So he or she might have to put in another few thousand dollars?

JL: Quite possibly. We haven't decided because we haven't had to cross that bridge yet.

CM: Is there any limit on how far the shares can increase?

JL: Well, I suppose the sky's the limit. We did projections that the company was supposed to do, let me take a guess, $160,000 worth of gross sales a year. And in the first year we do a quarter of a million dollars in gross sales, and maybe 10 years down the way we might do $6,000,000 — then why in fact should a share be worth $3,500, in a company that's survived and grown to that extent? So yes, we'd definitely be looking at shares that were worth more. Just what that figure might be would depend on the size of the company at the time.

CM: Have you thought of the effect on new members coming in?

JL: Well, I suppose that if you made the value of your shares too high you may have trouble getting somebody with that kind of money. It's a grey area, we don't know how high the share might be. It's difficult to say. If I was out looking for work or looking for a change in my life and I was offered a chance to purchase an equal share in a company that was doing really well and worth several million dollars we'll say — delusions of grandeur! — then I might not balk at spending $65,000 or whatever. It might be attractive; I'm really guessing because I don't know what size we would grow to or what the shares . . .

Ken Bourquin: I think you're talking about two different things. One thing to be remembered in a co-op, in Manitoba anyway, is the hard value of the share doesn't change, so when Jim is talking about a person buying a share into the company he's not saying the value of the shares have increased, but the person would have to purchase more shares to become an equal member.

JL: See, our shares are valued at one dollar apiece, that won't change, but we purchased 3,500 shares each . . . we would in fact have to re-assess, we'd have to concede that we had more than 3,500 shares. I don't know the logistics of it but possibly Ken you could help us out on that.

KB: Yes . . . in time they may feel that for the contribution they put in, both in money and in time and sweat, it may be $6,000 for a new member to come in. Well that new member is buying 6,000 one-dollar shares.

JL: What happens though then on paper? He owns 6,000 shares and we own 3,500 shares?

KB: Well you're going to be having your allocation out of the profits to build that up, allocating the profits in the form of more shares.

CM: How do you share the work? Do you have different responsibilities or do you all do the same thing?

JL: We're all versatile in all respects — we can fill in for each other and perform any operation in the department. Carl does most of the estimating although he's on holidays and now I'm doing some of it, and I do most of the invoicing and books. When I go on holidays I just get it all done in advance.

CM: Will you switch the administrative responsibilities — next year, for instance, will Carl take over the invoicing and you do the estimating?

JL: Probably not, no. But as officers in the company we may switch. I'm the vice-president and treasurer now. Carl is the president.

CM: Do you meet all the time to make decisions?

JL: It really isn't necessary. We're too close. Most of our problems can be ironed out in a minute or two. We just kind of get together and discuss things for five minutes and that's usually all it takes. We get along really well and there's never been a difference of opinion as to where we're going or what we want to do. So we want to maintain that if we take in more people. We're obliged to have an annual meeting to vote on certain things and we'll do that to meet the commitments of the cooperative.

CM: How did you go about incorporation?

JL: Probably the cost of incorporating for a company that wanted to start up in the private sector would be in the neighbourhood of $800 to $1,000. Because Co-op Development has people trained in that field, legal and financial, they were able to do most of the work for us and we incorporated for a sum of $65 . . . . We had meetings to go over the rules and regulations of becoming a cooperative and what their requirements were, and the philosophies behind being a cooperative. After that there were papers to fill out and election of officers and stuff that was necessary to be an incorporated company and we did all that — the paperwork was done by the cooperative, actually — and we just paid them the $65.

CM: Would you have gone the co-op route without Co-op Development pointing you in that direction? Because you could have just been a partnership.

JL: We couldn't have been a partnership, for the simple reason that we couldn't have received the financing to start the company. We would have investigated the possibilities of becoming a private company, found that we couldn't receive the financing, and probably wouldn't have gone any further. So I would say that probably if Co-operative Development didn't have a program in place at that time that we wouldn't be in business today.

CM: It sounds as if you made concessions to Co-op Development in order to get their guarantee.

JL: No, we made no concessions. We weren't opposed to being a worker co-op, I liked the idea. All of us being union workers and having the common good in our own best interest — the cooperative philosophy doesn't stray too far from that — you work together towards a common goal and we didn't make any concessions to become a cooperative, no.

CM: If any of you want to get out of the business how will you handle that?

JL: We probably couldn't get out of the business and remain a worker co-op. The minimum complement is three people, and that's all there are, so if one of us wanted to leave we'd have to find a replacement who wanted to purchase that share and be part of the cooperative. I don't think that's likely to happen; right now nobody's thinking of leaving. But I believe it's covered in the bylaws . . . the share would revert back to the cooperative; it's not handed down to people that aren't working at the trade. In other words my wife wouldn't assume my share, the cooperative would buy it from her, at whatever the going rate was at the time.

CM: You've got a lot of electronic equipment around here.

JL: This is only one room, we have a lot in two other rooms that is an impressive amount of equipment for the purchase price. It does become obsolete over a period of time. Perhaps the equipment that we have is bordering on being obsolete now. Our typesetting equipment is very close to ten years old; for computerized typesetting probably it would become obsolete in six years. What you see here filling half of the room could probably take up one small corner in the equipment that they have today in digital typesetting. It's fairly expensive, and although we could receive a fair trade-in for this equipment, we would still have to put in a considerable amount to update and we're not prepared to do that at this time. Probably one of the first things that we would replace would be the typesetting equipment. We'd certainly avail ourselves of any incentives or grants made available by the different governments. If there was no such grant available, if we felt that we had grown and we had enough money in the bank, we would probably still purchase the equipment.

CM: You lease the building, do you?

JL: We lease our portion of the building on a three-year agreement. That's from Wallingford Press as well. So the two three-year leases, for space and for business, go hand in hand.

CM: Have you approached the federal government for any help?

JL: I did at the beginning. I was contacting several people to see what . . . not necessarily grants or financial help, but even advice or expertise in starting a small business. To tell the truth I didn't really feel that any-body else was very much help to us. What's the name of that bank? The Federal Business Development Bank — I approached them, only by phone, and the Chamber of Commerce, and there was another group that was assisting small businesses get started at the time. There was probably a total of six people that I did contact and I really didn't think that they had anything to offer except they sent me a few pamphlets . . . . FBDB weren't any more help than any private financial institution. They wanted us to put up 100 percent personal security, same as every other bank.

CM: How about your hopes for the future, aside from buying new typesetting equipment . . .?

JL: Our hopes are to grow and survive and be happy and expand . . . .

CM: Do you have a real push on sales, getting other contracts?

JL: No, that's another area where we're short of money. It would be awfully nice to be able to hire one more person to just go and push and sell and do some of the paperwork instead of doing it at home, but the three of us are kept busy 120 percent of the time, we can't do it all in regular hours and if we had more money behind us we probably would have hired somebody a long time ago, to help out. I guess we were stuck in a Catch-22 situation where we didn't have the money to hire somebody so we did the work ourselves, so we didn't have any spare time to go and solicit new customers.

CM: Can you keep that up, working 120 percent of the time?

JL: Well, we don't feel any older or worse for wear but we probably would like to take it a little easier, not pick up the pace; we're not 18 or 20 years old anymore!

CM: Do you have any support or business from the co-op movement itself?

JL: Not really, Co-op Development approached the Queen's Printer on our behalf to make sure that we would get a chance to tender on their publications. And I approached the central credit union; they have a printing operating in the basement of their building, but they seem to be self-sufficient, they have their own artists. I haven't really approached any other cooperatives. Probably we could realize more work more quickly by approaching other printers. That would be a direct source for an increase in work, but we haven't really had the man-hours to do that. The odd customer from Wallingford finds out that we're on our own and comes to us direct and they'll get the word out and because of things like that we have been getting a little bit more work each month, actually. As a matter of fact I'd probably rather go and solicit the work myself, and hire somebody qualified at the trade, but I don't know how it's going to evolve. Anyway it's going to be a while before we can just hire somebody. We'll probably prepare a printed promotional piece and get the word out that way. We've already formulated our price lists and it's just a matter of making people aware of our services.

There's actually several areas . . . to end the year with a profit is probably a blessed situation and it looks like we will do that. But there's probably a few areas and we're not really 100 percent sure what we're going to do. We would again rely on Co-operative Development to help us as far as allocating profits, whether we wanted to turn it back into more shares . . . certainly we have to put money aside for the eventual replacement of equipment. Or whether we might want to actually purchase equipment at that time, or to purchase RRSPs for the shareholders . . .

CM: Or pay yourself a bonus.

JL: . . . or a bonus or all of those things. Probably the bonus wouldn't be a factor . . . . I think we're content with just trying to get by on whatever it takes to get by, we'd rather leave the money in the company.

CM: Do you enjoy working here more than you did before?

JL: I do, it's something different, it's a little more exciting and we are working for ourselves. I always thought life should get easier as you get a little older but I'm working more and more (laughs) and I do question my sanity at times but I think we've done the right thing. But my golf life is cut in half. I don't golf half as much as I used to — my score reflects that.

PART IV
And So is Service . . .

CHAPTER TWELVE
Atlantic Employees' Co-op
St. John's, Newfoundland

"The most satisfying . . . I'm doing it from scratch to finish."

In Newfoundland, a marginal economic area where the unemployment rate was 26 percent and rising last year, a cooperative that creates jobs by selling the services of its members looks good. The Atlantic Employees' Co-op is one of two worker cooperatives in the St. John's area of Newfoundland, although there are more fishermen's producer co-ops and community development cooperatives throughout the province.

Started in 1983, AEC operated in the black in its second year, paying wages averaging $10 an hour for about 20 weeks of the year — good on both counts in the construction business in St. John's. Moreover, this work is not "under the table," as offered by so many labourers in home restoration and maintenance. Because the workers are employed by the co-op, they have Unemployment Insurance, Workers' Compensation, liability insurance, Canada Pension Plan, holiday pay, income tax deductions, and a clear conscience.

Paul Martin, a founder and president of AEC when I visited their offices in the attic of his house in downtown St. John's, overflows with good will and energy. Like some other co-op members, his practice is to bid on contracts, and if he gets the job, to share the work with other members, at the same rate of pay. His home is central and handy as a meeting place — a crew gathered in his living room downstairs as we talked upstairs. As president, it was his year to accommodate the business, rent-free.

Along with other founders, Paul sometimes turned his pay cheque right back to the co-op during the first year, to pay expenses. As a result, he now owns $700 worth of shares in the association, more than the $5 deduction from every pay cheque required from new members. Despite this imbalance, his voice doesn't seem to be louder than the others'; the co-op sticks to one-person/one-vote.

The co-op finished its first year with a debt of about $3,000. Paul Martin says he would be happy to give up at least half of the equity he accumulated in the business to help pay off that debt, a solution common in older co-ops like Mondragon. This seems fair, he says, since the expenses came about partly because of the founders' lack of experience and judgement. But the Newfoundland/Labrador Federation of Cooperatives and the Registrar of Co-ops, used to dealing with producer co-ops in the fishing industry, were puzzled by this solution, and advised against it. Ironically, this has meant that banks, seeing the $3,000 debt to the co-op's own members, have refused credit. Suppliers give credit on materials, but without a line of credit at the bank, the co-op has not been able to go after bigger jobs, that would pay off only after months of work. The credit union has been as conservative as the traditional banks.

AEC has a fairly complicated structure, with members, associate members and volunteers. Its work is mostly in construction, but it offered clerical services last year, and several professionals have asked to join. Its diversity doesn't seem to be a problem. "The management of these things is much more important than their structure," says Richard Long, Professor of Industrial Relations at the University of Saskatchewan. "If you have a management that is democratic and communicative, then you can make a number of different structures work."

Like many young, intelligent, and initiative-seeking workers today, Paul Martin gets his job satisfaction not just from the basic work he does — as he says himself, construction work is hard and dirty — but from developing the skills of an entrepreneur: organizational, management, administrative, marketing, interpersonal.

Paul Martin: We started it because we were all working in the construction field, but "under the table." We couldn't have Workmen's Compensation Board or UIC or any of those benefits, because we were all working individually, for ourselves. It was very messy. So we decided to pool our skills, basically, in home renovations. We started an advertising campaign using our business cards and advertising in the paper and wherever we could to drum up work. Now, a year later, we have a clientele which comes to us when work needs to be done.

We started off with just the five of us, the five directors that it takes to start a co-op in Newfoundland. Our treasurer for our first year was an accountant. That was super handy. You really need someone who knows how to set up the books. Then we had a secretary, a president, and myself as vice-president and general manager. There were really only two working members. The other people contributed on a voluntary basis, but they didn't bring work to the co-op or work as carpenters.

We hired people on, for example from the John Howard Society, or from Manpower to help us with the work load. I think we made a bit of a mistake there. If we had paid members who were committed, we would have had them still when the job was over.

Constance Mungall: Do you have much turnover now?

PM: No. The working members are there to stay; some of the volunteers may change a bit. In the beginning we needed people so desperately that the only qualification was being interested, but now we are reaching the point where we may have to restrict membership. However, our constitution does stipulate open membership and a fair dealing with anybody who wants to be a member.

We have 13 full members now — they are the ones with voting privileges at the annual or general meeting. And we have about 20 associate members working with us. They don't have the right to vote until they've paid the $50 membership and have fulfilled some of the criteria for membership.

We like to get some voluntary work from an associate member and we also have a minimum of at least a week's work, and then they can be voted in. The three-month waiting period can be waived if four out of the five board members agree. Some find the $50 fee expensive; some worker co-ops only charge $10 or $5, but we think that with $50, we get more commitment. They don't have to pay the $50 fee right away as long as they make a verbal commitment to make payments on it. Usually we take their vacation pay and put it towards the $50 until it is paid. And they pay $5 of share capital on each weekly pay cheque.

CM: Are you getting a lot of applicants to join your group?

PM: We are now that business has picked up. More people are interested, even though we can't find work for everybody. In April, we only did $471 in gross wages, but in June we made $4,000 gross wages, spread among five or six fellows. Again in September we paid out $4,000 in wages, but above that the co-op made a certain percentage.

The co-op takes 25 percent of the amount paid on a contract, after expenses for material. We hope to drop it down to about 18 percent once we get straightened away. From that we have to pay the employer's portion of Unemployment Insurance and Canada Pension Plan and Workmen's Compensation. That takes 11 percent, so we really get only 14 percent for our own overhead expenses, which are the telephone answering service, the business telephone, a part time secretary, ads, insurance, audits, etc. I am not getting paid for the office space, which is in my house at the moment.

CM: What does your pay work out to by the hour?

PM: After the 25 percent is taken off, what is left is divided between those who worked on the project. At times, I have made $25 an hour, and at other times I have made only $5 or $6. The average is around $10 an hour, but there's an awful lot involved in that because you have had to estimate the job, buy the materials and carry your overhead expenses as well. Every contract is different. Every week my wage is different; the best week I made this year was $448 gross, and the lowest was $235. In this fiscal year, I have worked 11 weeks in 6 months, which is better than last year when I got only 10 in the whole year. I expect to have 20 weeks by the end of this year, pretty good for construction, especially when we have to share the work with a lot of other members.

We have an advantage in that our workers get a higher proportion of the labour contract than the workers for private companies.

CM: When you bring in a new member, do you require him to find contracts?

PM: It isn't a requirement yet. We do want people with skills and practical experience in drumming up their own work, because we just can't find work for everybody. If a person can find *some* work for himself, it helps. As it stands now, the cost of estimating is basically the expense of the person who gets the opportunity to look at the job. When a call comes in, one of our members will go and see the job and hopefully will build the cost of the estimation into the price. If he doesn't get the job that is his expense. For example, another fellow and myself must have bid on close to $70,000 worth of contracts this year, and probably only got about $15,000 to $20,000 of them. So you can see the tremendous amount of effort we have to put in, for no money.

Usually the person who does the estimating does the job — if he gets it. When more than one co-op member work on the same job, they usually split the labour contract, but where one of them is a journeyman carpenter, say, and the other is unskilled, then you have to make some allowance for that. Sometimes a member will hire outside the co-op when he needs extra help, but this isn't done so much now.

CM: Where did you get your money from to get going?

PM: The five founding members each put in $50 for a total of $250, which was the registration fee. We didn't have adequate insurance in our first year, which is something that every co-op should really look at. We got away with it only because we were lucky. We need insurance on work performance, and liability insurance to cover accidents, for example to property. Our line of work is a bit dangerous.

Last year we incurred expenses that were too grandiose for the co-op. We had a car and a full time secretary for 10 weeks, and it was too much to handle. We ran into a little bit of a deficit — about $3,000. But we're in the black again now only six months later. Two weeks ago, we had our first $1,000 surplus. We have some loans that we have to pay back, but some of our directors would like to see a float in the bank at all times, so we will pay the loans back gradually.

The loans were for the expenses we made last year. For example, we had a full time secretary at $180 a week, but we could only afford to pay her $90, so she put the other $90 in as loan capital. We also owe share capital to last year's president and to myself. I have about $600 to $700 share capital in the company. Last year, because we were running expenses so high, I had to turn my pay cheque right over to the co-op, and that was considered to be my share capital. The members themselves are the people who made the loan to the co-op. That means they have a fair amount of commitment, but on the other hand, three or four members have a lot of share capital and the rest don't.

Some people think they should be repaid, and others think they should share the loss, since they were the ones who misjudged. I'm quite willing to let the co-op have $400 of the $700 I loaned, and if a couple of other members would do the same we would be in a lot better position and could open up a line of credit at the bank. But when the bank sees that we owe $3,000, we can't do business.

We would like to have a line of credit in order to pay our members before the job gets done. Now we have to take on smaller jobs. If we had $10,000 in the bank, we could take on bigger jobs, and pay wages as the work was done.

CM: Is there a credit union that's open to your kind of operation?

PM: The credit union here in Newfoundland hasn't been very responsive to us. We've applied for a line of credit several times. We couldn't even get $2,500. It seems to me against the constitution of every co-op — to help develop other co-ops — the credit union here is not doing that. They basically shipped us to Central Nova Scotia Credit Union and told us to ask them for a line of credit, so we are drafting up a request for a loan with them. Whether they will accept us or not, we don't know.

CM: How about the provincial or federal governments? Can you get help there?

PM: We are applying for funds for advertising and educational material for our members as well as promotion to the community of the concept of the worker co-op, and possibly a coordinator to do that. But that wouldn't help us in our line of credit for our work.

CM: How much of the construction work in St. John's do you do?

PM: Not very much. Some construction people have been around for a long time and have a good name, and it's hard to get it. Construction is very competitive and we are not operating under the table, and that puts our prices up. At times we have to take a lower salary than if we did the job ourselves under the table. If we do that, though, we are defeating our purpose.

CM: Does being a co-op make a difference in selling your services? Are people more open to hiring a co-op?

PM: The fact that we are a limited liability company is an advantage, people like to have that security. But are we getting work because we are a co-op? Interesting enough, we are. We are doing work for the women's institution here, Transition House, for Oxfam . . . . We did some work for the Newfoundland/Labrador Federation of Cooperatives. We haven't got much with the really big cooperative sector, because we haven't had much chance to advertise to them. But that seems to be a very good place to get in — to work with other co-ops and other institutions like the school board. I think they appreciate that there is someone out there who is not just taking all the bucks and putting them in their own pocket. They'd rather see their money going right to the worker.

It's good to have the whole cooperative movement behind you. I was at a meeting in Gander called "The Worker-Producer Co-op," and I found it really exhilarating. People involved in a co-op should get to know what is going on in the other sectors of the co-op movement, not only in worker co-ops. Co-ops have been around for hundreds of years, and when you start to realize the roots of it all and the movement that is happening right now world-wide, it makes you feel that you are doing something substantial. To know that there is the credit union behind you, and the Federation of Co-ops and the Registrar of Co-ops . . .

CM: Can some of these other agencies help you in the education of your members about co-ops? Are there workshops and programs already set up?

PM: The Federation has helped us considerably. They have given us rooms for our general meetings. They have an education specialist. We are just beginning to use them a little more.

Our secretary has learned to do our final ledgers from the Registrar of Co-ops manual. She goes there and gets instruction, and she's learning a very professional way to do it. She's on the board of directors. We give her $30 a week, and she doesn't have to pay 25 percent back to the co-op. She works about six hours a week, but there are other things like writing up the board minutes and preparing the agenda — that is her voluntary work. She probably works more like 10 to 15 hours a week. We are getting a good deal.

CM: How do you make decisions?

PM: We have a board of directors elected at every annual general meeting who make policy decisions. They meet on the 15th of every month. We call general meetings as they are needed. So far this year we have had two general meetings not including the annual meeting in March, and we'll probably have two more this year. They are called basically for information and awareness because we want to keep our members in tune with how their co-op is working.

The directors meet without problem, some workers are not very interested in coming to meetings.

The biggest downfall of co-ops is personality conflicts that arise because it is such a close-knit body, and having to tell somebody that he is not doing a good job can be a bit tricky. We haven't had too many problems. None of us are super professional at meetings, at decision-making or at administration and management. We're all just learning. Although there are a lot of social implications, a co-op has got to be run like a business — a viable business — and if you make decisions because a person is a friend, that can really hurt.

We have tried to open it up to others besides the men who work on contract. For example, we had an accounting division last year for a woman who does bookkeeping. Another idea was to make wreaths for Christmas. An economic consultant with $3,000 and $4,000 contracts is interested in joining the co-op. And a graphics person is interested. We would be very glad to have people like that, so we can get experience in different fields.

CM: So that is why you call it the Atlantic Employees' Co-op rather than a construction cooperative? If people want to resign, how do they get out? How do they get their share capital?

PM: Most people feel that because we are a non-profit society, they don't wish to withdraw their share capital. And usually there is not that much money involved. The founding members have a substantial amount of share capital, but as a member works, $5 a week is taken off his pay for share capital, so it takes awhile to build a substantial amount. The money in the share capital account just stays there.

CM: That would be what you could borrow on?

PM: Yes, but we don't have enough in there right now for that.

CM: Was it difficult to draw up by-laws or were you just able to adopt regulations that the co-op branch provided?

PM: No, we found that we couldn't use any existing formulas. There was only one other skilled trades co-op in town, and they have only been working as a co-op for about a year. We did not have anything to go by, being the first worker co-op in this city and being so far away from any other worker co-ops. Probably in places like Toronto or Montreal or Vancouver they are right up on it, but not here, you don't expect it. We had to make most of our own policies and by-laws, but we found that they came up naturally enough in the administration. We'd run across problems and we'd straighten them out at the time.

We record in our minutes whenever we pass a by-law. At the last annual general meeting a formal draft of our by-laws was made available for all our members. They really show how we work. They are much easier to understand than the constitution, which doesn't tell you how we work.

CM: What is your own background?

PM: I came here from Toronto about five years ago to go to Memorial University. I attended there for a couple of years, but never completed my degree. Then I bought a house in the country where I continued studying literature and reading. Then a buddy had this idea to start a worker co-op. I didn't know anything about worker co-ops, but he explained it to me. It sounded good, and since I had had some experience with construction in Toronto I got involved.

When we started, it was the farthest thing in my head. I don't even think construction is a good line of work to be in. It's hard and dirty, but it was a necessity. I'm hoping not only to learn the construction trade, but also to learn a lot about running meetings and administration and ironing out insurance policies and other policies and talking with businessmen, etc. What gives me the most satisfaction is that I'm doing it from scratch to finish. It's just like baking your own bread. Estimating, purchasing, selling yourself to the consumer, drawing up a binding contract, dealing with creditors, dealing with the general public — because most people don't know what a worker co-op is — and having to evaluate the situation around you at all times.

CM: What do you visualize for the future?

PM: I don't know. I think the directors would like to keep it open to other kinds of work besides just contracting. We could still use more members and they would probably help by bringing their own work.

If we could get about 10 more people involved we'd have enough money coming in to maybe eventually buy a building in town, put up a sign and maybe have a storefront and start selling things such as cabinet work or other things we can make. We need a central office. At present, it's moved from house to house, year to year, but I don't think that can continue.

It's a nice feeling that the co-op doesn't depend on any one man and our members are free to go. Because there are so many people that are getting to be interested, a person could leave and it would not have an adverse effect.

CM: Are you typical of the other members, not only in your commitment to the co-op but in your background?

PM: Our last year's president was from B.C. too. Most of the members are Newfoundlanders. We are all in our 20s and 30s. There are three or four female members who are full members and entitled to vote. One of them has done public relations for six years and has been a school teacher; this is the sort of person who could work as a coordinator if we get the educational funds we have applied for. We try to get a bit of diversity, especially among the voluntary members. I'm committed because I'm one of the founding members; I don't want to see it go down the chutes.

CM: You have read about the co-op movement?

PM: I'm only beginning to get information. Newfoundland has been a bit slow in some of those things. For example, I went down to the provincial government office of the education specialist for the co-op sector on the whole island. I asked for reading material on worker co-ops, and she had just received a box of information that she had not yet had time to look at. There hasn't been much of that sort of information on the island. We are hoping to promote that a bit.

CM: What is the educational level of the other members?

PM: Some have been working in the field since they were 15 years old, so they haven't had a chance to get a university education. I myself only have second year university, but you don't need to have a great level of education or even experience administering. You have time to work that out, I find, and learn from it, with some help from the Federation or the Registrar.

CM: Do administrative requirements, justifying your accounts and that sort of thing, become a burden?

PM: We have to have our audit at the end of the year; this will be the first time we've had to do a professional audit. In our first year, the Registrar did it for us and it was sort of unofficial. Manpower asks for additional information from time to time. Their concern is that we are a legitimate employer; is it really an employee-employer relationship?

CM: Can you estimate how many unpaid hours you have put in?

PM: Probably twice as much as I've been paid for, which is hard to get by on. I think in my case it is a little more because I have the office in my house, and as president this year I do have more responsibility than some of the other members and directors. I don't know if you can expect people to work for nothing, and that is a bit of a problem. There is dedication there, yes, but to what extent is it really benefitting me on a financial level? Not very much. I'm struggling and getting by just as much as any other worker in the co-op. Everybody is committing what they want to commit and no more, which is legitimate enough — we don't pressure anybody for voluntary work, and we don't want it.

I feel the strongest thing that any board of directors can convey to the rest of the membership is information on how it is . . . how it works, and not only to the members but to the community too. But firstly to the members. Let them know how to run it. If it is really going to be a co-op, make sure that everybody gets a vote that is entitled to it, and make sure that everybody knows how it's run. I think that's the only way you're going to get a commitment. If anybody hangs in there just because he thinks he might get the odd job, that's not good enough. They've got to know how it works because it's their business — they own it as much as I do. The biggest thing is to keep the educational material at their disposal, even send it off to them in the mail; keep them aware of it. We're going to do a lot more this year.

CHAPTER THIRTEEN
Evergreen Tree Planting Cooperative
Slocan Valley, British Columbia

"In our co-op it's basically up to the individual."

It was a golden day in September, at the end of the tree planting season, when I drove the 48 km from Nelson to the clearing in the woods where Glenda Patterson, her husband and two young children live. Glenda had been recently elected president of Evergreen Tree Planting co-op, and her husband was one of the founders in 1974. They had been immigrants from the States, settling in Slocan Valley in the Selkirk Mountains, carving a homestead out of the bush, looking for ways to make some cash. Like many of the co-founders of Evergreen Tree Planting, they were opting out of the rat race — and their attitude to authority, to limits, was reflected in the structure they set up for their worker co-op. It was minimal. In this group of individualists, authority tended to be assumed by the founders, those who had the largest capital investment — and those with the loudest voices.

Nevertheless, perhaps by an annual act of will, the co-op did good work, became established as the second largest tree planting co-op in B.C., a half-million dollar annual business hiring up to 100 planters for the four- or five-month season each year. And proud of their work. "Our trees live," Glenda says.

Since members are also founders and directors of the local credit union, Evergreen has no problem with financing — they're the credit union's biggest customer.

Evergreen is one of the four enterprises I went to that have a unionized membership — everyone who plants for MacMillan Bloedel on Vancouver Island must join the International Woodworkers of America. There are pros and cons, and the relationship between co-op and union is still evolving.

As Glenda spilled out Evergreen's story, talking fast and unrestrainedly, I had to wonder if the co-op structure really was appropriate for the individualists who make up Evergreen. From what she said, it seems that the new structure evolving is really a management co-op. In it, members will bid on jobs, do their own hiring and paying, and draw on the cooperatively owned equipment to fulfill the contracts. There will be more autonomy for each manager, and he will be responsible for his own job, while maintaining Evergreen standards. The managers will form the co-op, but as in the past the workers who do the actual planting will be hired for the job, and may or may not be co-op members.

I wrote to Evergreen Tree Planting Cooperative for an update on their progress. Glenda Patterson wrote back:

"We are still alive and working very smoothly under our new autonomy proposal. The new system allows some entrepreneurial and individual spirit but maintains a cooperative-run business. In '85 we grossed around $1 million; it was too busy as we planted eight million trees. So this year we are going to gross around $800,000 and do about five million trees. In '85 we had all seven managers out in the field and I was paid to stay home to work. This year was the same. You might note that we are only six members now . . . ."

Glenda Patterson: Tree planting was the only opportunity for work that we could see in this area. People had a vision. My husband was one of the original members and he still has a vision of how the co-op is going to be. It's definitely evolved, and now at the tenth year it's like — it's wonderful. We finally reached something that I think is going to be very beneficial, and we can move on to getting more work.

There were four original members. They got together and spent about a year planning the co-op. The original idea was to create work and jobs for themselves, but they wanted to be the workers and the boss as well. In 1974, there were well over 30 members and everybody put in $100, and they got their first job in the fall of '74 and from there it went on and of course it changed a lot; a lot of people left, and new people came in. There were no set policies and structure in the beginning that said this is how the co-op is going to act. It was open to anybody who wanted to put money in, but membership policy or where you were going to work or how the job was going to get done — your costs, your bidding, your overhead, how the money was going to be spent — was basically decided by the original three or four people. After a few years they were asked to share the power, but they couldn't make the change and hand it over to the group, so they left and from then on it was pretty confusing. For the last five or six years the co-op has never had a really good overall management. Our meetings were chaos — just really frustrating. You never knew if the job was going to get done. Year end reports, any kind of correspondence, committee coordination, just forget it. Our administrator for the last three years was terrible.

Constance Mungall: How did the administrator get appointed?

GP: Apathy. People not wanting to take responsibility. In our business, you go to work for five months, you go to a camp and you work five days and you have one day off. You are constantly with people — you get up in the morning at six and you are with people — the interaction with people is very intense and so by the end of five months people don't really have the energy to come back and say, "Let's get this co-op organized, this is what went wrong, this is what we should do." When the first really strong people left, the co-op sort of dispersed and nobody who had that vision — the original vision — came up. Everybody really just wanted to plant trees and nobody was concerned about the overall running of the co-op. We can do the in-field work 100 percent. Evergreen is one of the best companies in B.C. and I think one of the main reasons is because we are a co-op. We have very good standards and we pay our workers very fairly and we work with companies that appreciate that, and we do really good quality work, which is something that is very controversial right now in the tree planting business.

There are certain areas that private lumber companies are obligated to plant every year. They send out a sheet saying we have so many trees in this area, to be viewed at this date. Viewing, which is on-site inspection, is mandatory, so a person in our co-op would go there and estimate how much a person could plant a day. We are paid by how many trees you plant, a piece-work rate. And on that estimation we would add all our other costs plus a certain profit, which in a co-op is very small. They don't necessarily take the lowest bid, but if they do we usually get the work.

We don't work locally, we work all over the province. Most of us live here in Slocan Valley, so we can get to meetings together. The idea of the co-op was to only hire workers locally to go away on jobs, but I can see that's going to have to change because I myself get pretty outraged when people come in and take the tree planting jobs from Slocan. Most of our work is on Vancouver Island. We have a very good working relationship with MacMillan Bloedel on the division just outside Port Alberni, and we do a preferred bidding. We have worked there for 10 years, and that has been our saviour. If we didn't have that, we wouldn't be here. We get very good bids. But in that area there is a very militant division of the IWA — the woodworkers' union. We were forced to join, everyone who works for the co-op, members and employees. It's fine, we get a lot of benefits, better camp conditions — we have to stay in a logging camp — provide the best kind of boats. But in that area a lot of the sawmill workers have been laid off, and now since we are in the same union, they are demanding jobs tree planting, so we are starting to work out some kind of deal.

The union doesn't really know how to deal with tree planters yet. I believe we are one of the first to join the union. They've set up a special committee to investigate the role of tree planters in the IWA. Of course, if we have to adhere to union standards for working conditions, it costs, and we have to make MacMillan Bloedel pay more. We used to camp out there, now we have to pay $50 a day to stay in a logging camp. And in theory anybody else working in that area has to pay those costs. The IWA is supposed to protect us. But this year there was another company working for M.B. planting trees, and they didn't belong to the IWA and their costs are lower. So we now have to put the pressure on the IWA to enforce the standards across the board.

We didn't really want to get into the union, but I don't want to cause waves, and there are a lot of benefits. And there are disadvantages: bureaucracy, strikes, walkouts. They had a big walkout this year. Had they locked out the rest of the workers in that logging camp, we would have been directly affected because they wouldn't have kept that camp open for us. I don't really want to be attached to such a massive group. The dues are not a factor, because we get incredible benefits and dental and medical plans.

CM: You have employees as well as your own members. How many employees do you have?

GP: In our best year we had over 100 in five months. We like to keep our individual jobs under 20 people, because after that it gets pretty expensive and chaotic, but we may have three or four jobs going at the peak. There are two people paid: me as president, I get $2,000, and the treasurer is paid $2,000 a year. People who look after the equipment get $7 an hour. It's not worth the money, as far as I'm concerned, but there is no way to get around that now because we had a very bad year, and there's just not the money around. It used to be when you viewed, you got $75 a day plus your expenses and hopefully we will be able to stretch our budget so that we can view more and be more competitive.

CM: Can you distribute the unpaid work among the co-op members so everyone is sharing it? Can you make that a requirement?

GP: I know what you're trying to say; it doesn't work; we're not that kind of co-op. We don't divide things up and say, OK you have to do two hours a week here and there. That would never work with us. You have to work at least two weeks of the year, which is very minimum, and you have to attend all meetings; that's our basic thing and it's not enough. In our co-op, it's basically up to the individual and if somebody puts a lot of time in for two years, they take off a year or two, and if somebody wants to continue through, then they do. You acquire equity on the amount of work, and on the tree planting you do. People who don't do any work don't have any equity shares.

We've had huge profits in the past. We had profits last year, but nothing like we had before. But we don't pay dividends. We leave our money as equity in the co-op. The assets of the co-op belong to the members. We have a system of withdrawal if a member leaves. Any equity is paid within three years, but we have made deals with people when they left.

We were afraid that if four or five people with a lot of equity left at once it would break the co-op. Actually, we just found out that four or five people cannot leave the co-op and take their equity if it means that the co-op would be in a financially bad situation. That's up to the Director of Co-ops. You're lucky because I just read the whole Co-op Act and I know it inside out!

CM: So you are registered as a co-op under the provincial Act?

GP: Yes, and we have a whole string of policies, rules and regulations, as long as they are not in conflict with the Act. Every time you change them, you have to have an extraordinary resolution and submit it to the department in Victoria, which requires two weeks' notice. But that never happened in our co-op, which is what I found out this year when I took over as president. We were registered 10 years ago, but we have not registered the changes that we have made along the way. We didn't even do our year end reports for three years. It's a mess.

CM: Does the co-op office not send out inspectors or have people following up?

GP: There's nobody out there. There's a thousand small co-ops and I'm sure they can't keep them all under control. One thing members never realized was what registration as a co-op really meant. It means that everybody is equal. Just because you have more equity you don't have more power; you have a one dollar share, and one vote.

Last year we had a really bad season. We got underbid. I could see that some members were becoming very frustrated and by the end of the spring it just blew up. Four said they were leaving Evergreen and taking the name, and so much for the co-op. That's why I went through the whole Co-op Act and found out exactly what it meant, and that you cannot do that. You can't vote people out; you can't take your equity out. The co-op is very protected.

As a result, over the last two months we've had three proposals for autonomy for the managers. The co-op remains itself and does all the hiring, all the financial aid, but people who do the viewing, if they win that job, it's theirs. If there is a profit or a loss, they take that. The co-op takes a certain percentage of the contract, but the jobs are much more autonomous, so the manager doesn't have to hire certain people, he can run the job how he wants, no co-op members are telling him what to do. I think it is going to be a better system. If you can bid a really good job and make $10,000 profit then that's yours, but you're also taking the risk, too.

CM: If a manager makes a bad mistake and loses a lot of money, would the co-op give him some support?

GP: That is a very controversial point right now, because people don't trust each other; we've had two jobs where we lost a lot of money. We'd have to look at it. If they were paying themselves $300 a day, and lost $5,000, for example — it would have to be reviewed. That person would have to go to the bank and get a loan.

Under the new system, we have a code of ethics, and a schedule of standards and quality work. Anything that would deface the name of Evergreen would not be tolerated, everybody agrees on that. We're still bidding in the name of Evergreen, but the manager, if he wants to pay himself $300 a day, he can, as long as he maintains the minimum wage for his planters, and the standards. We don't have an hourly wage. We used to have a protected wage of $150 a day, which might seem like a lot, but it's not in the tree planting business. Now we've lowered it to $100, because last year the bids that won were $130 a day.

The board is elected by the whole membership at an annual meeting. We have about 50 meetings a year, but we're elected at the annual general meeting. We've got three other meetings coming up next week on Monday, Tuesday and Wednesday. I have to do it that way because we've got a job in Alberta right now, and then the viewing starts and I don't know when we'll be able to get a quorum. I try to schedule them all together so we can get all the business and have it all ready so it gets processed. The job as president, in the past, was very sketchy. I'm the only woman in the co-op, and I felt I could do the best job. I'm creating my own job based on what I think are my responsibilities. I set the agenda. I call the meetings. I meet with all the committees, and they review what they have to do and bring recommendations to the co-op. Last night the executive set up the whole agenda, how we're going to divide our viewing, all our priorities for the next three months, what we feel committees should be dealing with and what the executive should be dealing with.

We have a viewing committee responsible for getting all the work and making sure that people go look at it, an equipment committee which maintains the equipment, a food coordination committee which does all the shopping and finds the best prices and puts together the kitchens for each camp, and a truck committee which involves maintenance, leasing, continuity, where to put the money — into what truck — they're getting old, etc.

We spend a fortune. We spent $40,000 in the last three years on supplies, including all kinds of paper, some tools, log books, tree planting tape. We purchase food from CRS, which is a food workers co-op in Vancouver, although it's not always convenient for us to do that. We spend probably $100,000 on food in five months. We pay a cook, and an administrator, first aid, all the proper government deductions, Workmen's Compensation, hard hats, everything. Every committee has to have its budget approved by the co-op. In our new system, it's very organized. The managers submit what they need on a written form, with the dates they need it. The managers on each job have to pay for equipment on a daily rate for each item. We've just started doing that.

When we get that system going, then we're going to restructure the co-op and give each committee a lot more power. Then we won't have as many meetings and the committees will make more reports to the general membership.

CM: Can you see any conflict where there are overlapping requests for equipment?

GP: We'll see how much work we get; we'll know how much we have by the end of November. We can rent more trucks if we need them. The problem is the kitchen equipment, and the camp: the tables, the lights, the water line, the pump, the generator — it's the camp that costs a fortune. We only have two of them; we've skimped by for a few years. It's difficult to rent a kitchen that could go up in the bush. So you either have to provide it or pay the logging companies, and if the cost is not in your bid, you can't afford to do that.

CM: Where does the money come from for the capital equipment?

GP: When we do a job, we add overhead and profit. Last year our volume was half of the year before, so our profit was fairly small, below $20,000. Evergreen did $500,000 the year before last. We have a line of credit from the bank of $20,000 at the beginning of the season, and we have gone over that.

We haven't bought trucks in years. We have only four. They are cost-effective so far. We aren't going to replace them until necessary. There is no depreciation fund, but we don't owe anything either. We own a piece of land, our equipment, our trucks, and we owe no money. When we need to buy a new truck we'll get a loan to cover it. The value of all the equipment comes to around $80,000, but that doesn't include what Evergreen might be valued at. The bank account differs from one year to the next, like from $60,000 to $20,000. It is amazing what can happen in one year.

Evergreen has no problem with its credit. We bought our trucks originally through loans — about $100,000 — and they're paid off. The capital that we began with was just 30 people each putting in $100; they just rented trucks then. The camp equipment was scrounged. You could buy old army tents and make plywood tables, all that stuff didn't cost so much 10 years ago. Now, you have to have the best of everything so it will last.

CM: Who do you deal with for your financing?

GP: Our credit union. I think we're their biggest customer. They want our work. Basically credit unions are co-op oriented. Also, starting 10 years ago made a difference, because banks tended to loan money easier, and we didn't have the volume that we have now.

I don't do the bookkeeping. We have a treasurer and a secretary and president and a vice-president. We have a very good treasurer, who I am so thankful for. He's been doing it for six years, does all the payroll, and all the proper government deductions and all those things that are so vital, actually that we've been forced to do because their regulations are so strict. Ultimately, I'm responsible for what goes on, and I make sure that people do it. If something goes wrong, it comes back to me. When I take a job, I do it thoroughly.

CM: Is that kind of business skill valued in the co-op?

GP: No. Before, it was so lax that nobody really appreciated it, so I believe that in our new structure there's going to have to be an allowance for me to be paid more, and the treasurer and the vice-president, because the work we do keeps it all stuck together. The managers will be depending on us. Last night we allowed for more of that in our overhead.

CM: Have you had any kind of help with business administration or with interpersonal relations?

GP: We've realized what we don't want to talk about, and what are just personality conflicts. I figured everybody out after six months — certain people just avoid certain people; some work better together. In committees and meetings, what it basically is, eight people agree and four people don't, so they lose every time. It's pretty much the same four always. There is definitely a power structure, and always a few people who just don't agree, ever. They like to have controversy. I've been trying to figure that out all week — how am I going to deal with people who like controversy? It hurts the co-op. It causes bad feelings, talking behind people's back, resentment, and we don't need that.

CM: Is there any qualification for joining the co-op that has to do with getting along with people?

GP: Not within our structure. We don't want new members; we've only had one in the past four years. The basic feeling is we want to get rid of members. It took two years to get that new member OK'd by the rest of the group, and he's just wonderful to have, so energetic. Now that he's a member he has to have a two-year probation, with a review at the end of the first and the second year. That's how we set it up. There was never any requirement like that for the first people who came in. There should have been, though.

So far, co-op members have been allowed to go on any jobs they want, but they also have a say on who else they want to go on that job as employees, so all the girl-friends definitely get hired; all the wives get hired, and all the best friends, etc. I'm really happy now that on each job, the manager only has to hire a co-op member; he doesn't have to hire someone's girl-friend.

A co-op is different than a company. You have to work things out with people. You can't slough them off. It's not like a company where one person has the power. If I make a really radical decision as the president, it still has to go back to the membership to vote on it. And every policy has to be approved by the co-op. I can only make recommendations, and the same with the committees.

CM: How do you compare in size to other tree planting organizations?

GP: The giants are all private companies. Then there are the next in size, like us. We're not the largest co-op in membership, but we are the largest in volume of trees and work in the province. I can only think of Western as the other co-op, and they are more structured as a co-op; everyone is a member and everyone has to do their work share. We're not like that. And then there are the little guys who do $100,000 or $200,000 a year.

A worker who has worked for both a company and a co-op will tell you that there's a world of difference, because we have so much more appreciation of and consideration for our workers. We don't sit in a truck and watch them work in the rain. We're out there with them, and it's in our interest to get them the best situation, the best food, because they will produce and make money for us.

CM: Isn't it in the interests of ordinary corporations to do that?

GP: You would think so, but from what I've heard over the last two years it's so chaotic and they have such a high percentage of profit and overhead that they really don't care if their workers are comfortable or if they have the proper truck, or a first aid attendant. This will only work to our benefit; even over the last month people are phoning me wanting jobs because we are a co-op, and they've heard such good things about us. We have tremendous competition, and since there are no standards within this business, anything goes. A logging company doesn't have to get the best job done; they have to take the lowest bid. That is the big issue. We have trees that are 30 feet tall. We do really good quality work, because we care, but that costs. People have to slow down to plant better trees. You get fly-by-night companies or lowest bids and maybe they get 50 percent survival. The trees have to grow for about 80 years before they can be harvested, so a company that doesn't have a long-term view will accept a sloppy job.

It's the government's responsibility to start enforcing higher standards. Reforestation is a really big issue right now. Evergreen is becoming very politically involved, because I'm a fairly political person. I feel that we have that responsibility and I feel that both the provincial and federal governments have to put pressure on those companies. The way it's set up now, the provincial government forces them to take the lowest bid. So the provincial government is actually pushing poor reforestation. It's terrible. We have the Western Silviculture Contractors Association. It's a group of contractors that's been going for four or five years — and now that the media has really gotten into the forestry issue I think we're going to have a really good effect. I work very hard on that. We have a lobby for them to grow more trees and produce standards.

CM: How about organizations like the Department of Regional Industrial Expansion or provincial agencies that might have given you advice?

GP: The Federal Business Development Bank is all we have ever used. We don't get a loan from them because we're like a service industry. We provide jobs; we don't manufacture. But they send us their newsletter, information, etc. We can go and use their consultant but we haven't.

I don't know about government agencies; they actually look at a co-op as a hassle, I believe, although the B.C. co-op office has sent us lots of information, and each time I phone them they are very responsive and generally helpful.

I just went through registering us in Alberta as a co-op, and they just kept saying, "Why do you want to be a co-op? Why don't you become a company? You're going to be one of the only co-ops in this province!"

The name Evergreen is already taken in Alberta, so we have had to set up a separate company under the name ETCO Forestry Cooperative. Alberta is a whole different ball game. When you've practised business in B.C. for 10 years, you pretty well know what your costs are going to be, but in Alberta there will be unforeseen costs. Their requirements are so strict, and they don't have roads — they do things with helicopters — and the weather is so horrendous. The mud is three feet deep. That means you can be totally stopped for two days, and that costs you a fortune. But we plan to *make* a fortune there.

I would recommend that people who want to start a business don't start in Alberta. Start very very small and make sure you know the people who are going to be doing the work, and put pressure on the people you work for to give you references. We send out letters with references saying what we've been doing and why we're a co-op, and why that's better than a company.

We've just started to develop all that part of the business. Part of my mandate over the next two years is to make ourselves known, and do some advertising. I'm going to write to the forestry minister and tell him who we are and ask him what money is available to us, and why he's not promoting good tree planting.

CHAPTER FOURTEEN
Umbrella Co-operative Ltd.
New Glasgow, Nova Scotia

"To make a name for ourselves, instead of letting her go under."

Betty Crosby met me at the bus in New Glasgow, half way between Antigonish and Truro, on Nova Scotia's Northumberland Strait. She took me in her half-ton pick-up truck to Frenchy's Used Clothing, in a warehouse up the hill, where two other Umbrella co-op members, Betty MacDonald and Agnes Macumber, were waiting to talk to me. The fourth, Debbie Patton, was away at a funeral, and Arlene Smith who fills in when a worker is away, kept shop as we talked.

These gutsy women, used to back-breaking work in fish plants and cutting brush, were having a wonderful time. For the first time in their lives, they had some control over their working situation, and the skills they'd learned — purchasing, bookkeeping, financial management, organization — they'd won by trial and error. They had help at the beginning from Anne Bishop, a very able organizer who now works in Ottawa for CUSO. Periodically after that they called on the Extension Department at St. Francis Xavier University in Antigonish — historic base of the community-minded priests who helped establish housing co-ops and fishing and working man's co-ops in the dirty thirties.

It's hard to exaggerate the difference the Umbrella co-op makes in the lives of these women. Four years ago my chauffeur, Betty Crosby, didn't even know how to drive. Now they are operating a successful business, have overcome a deficit brought on by bad financial judgement, and solved some difficult personnel problems. They have a different status in their homes. More than that, they feel like part of a world-wide movement — in 1982, they attended an international conference of worker co-ops at the university in Antigonish, and discovered their problems were universal, and their solutions were valid.

Another evidence of their part in a larger trend — after our interview, Betty Crosby drove me out to Lismore, 30 km away, to visit yet another Betty, Betty Murdoch, a key figure in the Northumberland Job Creation Society. She was working to re-open the fish plant where the Umbrella co-op founders had laboured before they were laid off — this time as a cooperative owned and controlled by the fishermen. The Society gave moral support when the Umbrella co-op was formed — and according to Betty Crosby, would be involved again if the members ever wanted to pack it up. It is also the trustee of a $5,000 fund to help other worker co-ops form in the area.

The four of us talked and drank tea in the tiny office of the Umbrella co-op, wedged in between desk and refrigerator. Betty Crosby did most of the talking, but Agnes and Betty MacDonald put in their two cents' worth too. Since we met, business has flourished. They have doubled their display space, and brought in two good new workers.

Betty Crosby: The fish plant closed in '81. We were sick of sitting at home looking at our husbands. We were doing nothing and not getting paid for it. So we decided to do something for ourselves. We decided to get out and try to make a name for ourselves instead of letting her go under. It was quite a job to get it all organized; it took us about six months or more. Then it started growing and this is what it has come to now. It was my idea to start this used clothing business, but I didn't know where to go or what to do. Anne Bishop, she was the one that went out and did all the research and digging around and found out what to do. She was one of the workers in the fish plant. She had a lot of connections with different people. She was a college graduate from Ontario, from Oshawa. I can't really say where she got all·the information she needed.

The management said the union put them in the hole, but the trouble was that it was the manager himself that ran the company into the hole. He built a new home out of it and bought all these new clothes — blamed it on the women for not working hard enough. He went to jail over it for a little while, but not long enough. I don't really know what the charge was; it never really said in the paper. The time wasn't very long and he could spend it on week-ends.

Constance Mungall: So the plant was closed and you got together. How many of you in the beginning?

BC: There were about 10 who were interested until the word money came up — that the workers would have to borrow some money. That weeded quite a few out. We had to borrow money for this. Each individual borrowed so much money. We needed $4,200 and there were seven of us, so we borrowed $600 each. With that money we paid the rent and got our lumber for the tables and our stock. We didn't pay any wages for six months. In that period we paid off our loans with a little profit.

CM: And in that time you built all the bins that I see here and put up all the racks? It must have been fun getting together. And there were still seven of you?

Agnes Macumber: Yes. Anne Bishop had to quit because she was allergic to the dust. She just dropped out and was chairman. She had another job.

And we had another good help, too, Doug Roberts who was working for St. Francis Xavier Extension; he was a real good help. Between the both of them, they steered us clear of a lot of the pitfalls.

BC: We first got in touch with Frenchy's. Their head office is down in Meteghan down the valley, in Nova Scotia near Yarmouth.

Anne and I went down. There's a woman there who told us what we had to do, how many tables to have, how much space we'd need. We only paid half on our first order until we sold that and made enough to buy another order. So everybody all worked together, even the suppliers.

It was something that was really needed in the community. We knew that from our own experience. There is a Frenchy's in Truro, and when my kids were small I used to go there to shop, and I used to shop in a war surplus store here in New Glasgow, and watch how he was running things, and I think it all kind of rubbed off. Even before the fish plant closed, I said to Anne, let's start a Frenchy's.

For about three months, we met in each other's homes to get it organized, meeting a couple of times a week. When anything new came up, it was pounded out, any big proposal about what we were going to do and how we were going to find the building and how much rent we were willing to pay. That was quite a job, finding a suitable building.

AM: More or less everybody was in on it. We tried to keep it quiet what we were going to start up. Ten or 15 years ago there was a used clothing store here in New Glasgow, and the merchants, they didn't want it, so the rent went up from $200 to $900 in six months. So we were going to do it kind of undercover.

BC: We didn't tell anybody what we were going to start. But the landlord is really good. He has given us a lot of breaks and has been very considerate of us. He said he'd cope with anybody that tried to make any trouble for us.

But we ran into some other problems with some of the workers we had. We couldn't all agree.

AM: We get along now because we work at it, we cooperate with one another and if there's anything to discuss we bring it out and discuss it and see what's wrong and solve it. We holler at one another sometimes. Sometimes we feel like throwing something at one another, but we don't.

BC: We have been here so long now that pretty well everybody knows what the other person is going to do anyway. This is our third year. It will be three years in January. There are four of us now.

CM: What happened to the other three?

BC: The first two couldn't agree. They wanted to be boss; they couldn't be bossed by anyone else and whatever they wanted to do they wanted to do it, and not work it out together. We tried for three or four months to work it out. When we got enough money . . .

AM: We paid their two loans first, figuring that it would ease the tension because they were so worried about it. But they thought that we paid them first because we didn't want them. It wasn't that; it was because of them asking about money all the time, but they wouldn't believe anybody.

BC: That wasn t a very good meeting when we said they were out. They were going to take us to the Human Rights, but they couldn't do anything there because we didn't do anything that wasn't legal. And here this spring there was another one we relieved of the problems. We voted to let her go, completely unanimous. She wanted to stay in. In one way she wanted out, but she didn't want to admit it. She was sick for awhile, then she wouldn't come to the meetings, she didn't want to participate. So we gave her a little push to go the rest of the way. We can handle the place with four.

Betty MacDonald: Yes. We work about 30 hours a week — 29 to 31 hours. We have three weeks vacation during the year and two weeks off at Christmas. So it's pretty good. We can make our own rules, as long as we all agree on it, or at least three of us. We have meetings usually once a month. How long depends on the discussion and whether anyone comes in to talk to us. Since we're working together, we talk these things over in between. We have worked pretty much together ever since we opened. We work well together. Now we're paying Arlene as a back-up if one of us is sick or wants time off.

CM: Would you think of taking on Arlene as a member?

BM: Yes, if we needed her, that would depend on the business. We passed a by-law saying that someone would have to work here six months before they could become a member. After six months we can ask her to join if we want. It's like a probation period.

BC: We have a weekly wage — $180 gross. It's quite a bit higher than wages for work like that around here. But we have the whole responsibility of the business. Betty MacDonald here is our bookkeeper. She does it as part of her job, part of the hours that she puts in every week.

CM: You learned on the job. Did you get any help?

BM: Yes, from Doug Roberts, from St. Francis Xavier Extension, he showed me how to set up books; I never had a clue before, but I've been able to do it ever since. Debbie Patton is learning it too. And we have to keep things organized, keep stock coming when we need it, keep the place clean, make sure it's open the hours that it is supposed to be open.

BC: We make as much money as we did in the fish plant, and we don't work as hard for it. That was hard work down there and long hours. I'd go in sometimes at 7:00 in the morning and I'd still be there at 11:00 o'clock at night, and have to go in the next morning at the same time. It was hard and dirty; you were frozen or you were cooked to death.

AM: Betty worked killing crabs or killing lobsters and she worked outside. She worked in oilskins in the heat.

BC: You'd only work there from the first of May to the end of June when the lobsters were over. Then we did Queen crab; that would last from July to September. Some years we had haddock and one year we did frozen red fish — that had been frozen for about 10 years and we had to thaw it all out — and worked to about February. It was supposed to be sent to Bangladesh, but the cans all blew up before it got there. There was stuff that went into the cans that I wouldn't even think of feeding to my cat. It was rotten. We'd take it to our manager and say, "Here, the stuff is bad"; he'd take a mouthful of it and chew it up and say, "That's good, put it in the can." Then he probably walked out and spit it out.

About 75 or 80 women were laid off when the fish plant closed. The fishermen are meeting to try to buy the processing plant as a cooperative. Then they would hire the women to work in it. The women thought of buying it and running it themselves, but they would need $600,000 for equipment, never mind for running expenses. And the fishermen don't want to have women bossing them around.

CM: What did the other women that were laid off do?

BC: Four or five were working at that Sew and Sew Co-op. That was separate from Umbrella co-op. Anne Bishop helped to start that, too. Some of them worked on the highways till they got their stamps for UIC; some of them have worked on grants. Two of them have got a shop in Antigonish, another Frenchy's. It's not a co-op because there are only two women, and in order to have a co-op you have to have three or more.

CM: So you are registered as a co-op. Is that an advantage?

BC: I suppose so, but I don't know how.

CM: Is it easier to get money? Loans for instance?

AM: When we go to borrow money, we have to borrow it on a personal basis. We deal with the credit union, and they don't lend to businesses. If we needed a big loan, we'd go to the Federal Business Development Bank, but we've never needed it so far.

BC: If we came up with a good idea that we thought was going to take off, I would agree to borrow enough money.

BM: But the idea is to find people who will really work to make something go, that is what you need in it — people who will put themselves out. There should be something to give people who work in a thing like this the training and education about what they have to sacrifice in order to keep it going. There are a lot of people who think you can just have it handed over on a platter and there's nothing to it, when there's a lot of hard work to it.

AM: I didn't know how much before I came in, but I knew I was willing to work hard enough to get something going. Even though it is easier work than at the fish plant, it has in some ways been harder because of the responsibilities, the risk and taking leadership.

CM: If one of you leaves the co-op now, how would you handle that? How do you give back what the shares cover? The business itself must be worth something now?

AM: Well, the only thing we'd get if we left tomorrow would be just the share we paid into it. When you become a member you pay $5 a week until you have $2,500 in shares in the business. You can have as much as $2,500, but you have to have at least $1,000. But you each have one vote. You don't have the number of votes that your shares indicate. Then when you leave, you take your shares out.

BC: If a member wants to leave on her own accord, we could pay her shares back at, say, $10 a week; we wouldn't have to give all the money at once. But if we ask somebody to leave, we feel that we should give them all their money at that time. The first people who left only had their $600 loans. That was some problem to pay off, because we were struggling. But it still seemed worth it to clear the air and then when the last person left she had around $1,600 in, and we were able to give that back.

We each put in $5 a week for three years, so we've got some capital base, about $10,000 working capital. Enough to keep the business going and have a bit of a buffer.

CM: And you must be adding to that, too. Are you making profits as well as running the business?

AM: We just have whatever we bring in. At the end of the year it is added onto our pay. We give bonuses before Christmas.

CM: And that is like the extra profit that you make during the year. So you just keep enough working capital to keep this business going and give youself a bonus to cover any profit. Can you imagine having a bad year and coming out less — starting to eat into your working capital?

AM: Yes, we did. One year we borrowed and three people were laid off until the capital built up again so we could pay off the loan. We all had to borrow so much, each one of us. We borrowed $5,000, so it was $1,250 each. We slowly paid that off.

BC: Every month there is a financial statement. And we have an auditor every year, too. We haven't had to show our books to the government yet, but they can ask.

CM: Have the requirements of government agencies been complicated or difficult to handle?

BC: They really don't bother us.

CM: Do they give you any help?

BC: No, certainly not. Only we can go and ask the Extension Department of St. Francis for help at any time we need any assistance. When that one took us to the Human Rights we settled that and cleared that up. The time we had a deficit, we worked that out ourselves.

CM: Do you do any advertising?

AM: We did, but we haven't done too much lately. We had ads in the paper. Word of mouth is better, now that we are known. Some of our customers come all the way from P.E.I.; they don't have a Frenchy's there.

When we opened, the New Glasgow newspaper wrote about us. We got it here, a really nice article, good advertising.

CM: Tell me something about what you feel you have learned out of this experience.

BC: Well, it has given us a little more self-confidence to have accomplished this, more freedom; how to get along with our workers — and how to get along better with our husbands.

CM: How have the men acted about this — felt about it?

BM: Mine acted real good. And I have four kids and they don't mind.

BC: Well, mine is a little different; he is retired now and thinks I should be home with him holding his hand, where I feel there is a little more use in me working outside than staying home and growling with him all day. I feel that we are helping people that otherwise wouldn't have the help that we are giving them — the clothes at a cheap rate and a little moral support sometimes here and there.

CM: How about you Agnes, what does your husband think?

AM: He's retired, too, and hard to get along with.

CM: Were they afraid that you would lose financially?

BC: No, we signed ourselves. The men had nothing to do with this; it was the women alone. Now my man has gone on pension, and by me working, they have cut his pension, and Agnes's man, too, he don't get as much pension. So actually, what I'm earning in here, they took it off his pension.

CM: But you are still bringing the same amount of money in, only you have control over some of it.

AM: That's about it.

BC: I could put some more in shares, but once that is paid up I don't know what I'll do then unless I can put some into a retirement fund, although I don't know if that counts as earnings or not. I guess there are ways. Why should a woman have to sacrifice her money for what her husband is eligible to get in his army pension?

CM: Could you see yourselves helping other people learn some of what you have learned?

BC: I can't see why we couldn't. There was a meeting in Antigonish. There were co-ops from as far away as Holland and England and all over Canada. They had pretty much the same story as we had in our problems. This was two years ago. We were kind of green at that time. That was our first summer. To hear the other one's problems, we didn't feel as alone then. And we met other ones who seemed to be the same kind of people as we were.

CM: How can you see sharing what you have learned, getting it over to other people?

AM: I don't know, but different people come in and we talk to them about it. If they said they'd like to open a Frenchy's or something we'd tell them the problems they were going to have to face if it was going to be a co-op, and if it was just going to be an ordinary business, we have lots of the same kind of problems that they'd have, too. They'd have to be very determined to want to start it first, and then pick good people that they can work with, and the problems are pretty well solved. Then you just go and make your mistakes.

CM: It sounds as if money hasn't been a problem for you at any time. You somehow have managed to gather the capital that you needed.

AM: It was never that much of a problem. It must have been our honest face or something. But the fellow at St. F of X told us where to go to get the money. He told us the credit union would be the best place, but we'd have to each borrow so much. So we went down and talked to them and that is all there was to it.

I suppose if this business here hadn't of taken off the way it did, we would have been left holding the bag.

BC: One thing, if somebody wants to start a co-op like this, before starting out they should do a little research on whatever they are going to do. We didn't. There was nothing like that around here at that time, and we felt that there was a need for it. There was no work and people needed a break to buy clothes at a cheap rate. For a start I think they should start something that they know a little about. I think this was the greatest problem with the sewing co-op. None of the women ever did any sewing; they had no idea of what they were getting into. You have to work hard at doing it and want to do it.

CM: What made *you* want to do it so much?

AM: I guess I was tired of depending on other people for my livelihood; I figured it was time to be out and doing something for myself.

I'd say that the only way we're different from most of the people around here is that we did get out and do it on our own, plus when we started we were determined that we were going to make it go if there was any way possible.

BC: The reason we stuck . . . we had the spirit to borrow money and start out. I didn't care whether I gained on it or not, that was just the feeling I had. If this is not going to work, well the hell with it. But we made it work. But you got to have a gut feeling, too, to do something like this. As long as we are getting a little money out of it; I think there has to be something in the person in order to like to do it themselves.

CM: Are you getting something else out of it besides money?

AM: Yes. We meet all kinds of people, really lovely people that come in here . . . .

BC: All walks of life — and most of the ones who shop in here are not poor people. They are the ones who go away on cruises or to Florida. They know what kind of clothes they are shopping for — the brand names and the values. We very seldom ever get anyone here that would, say, be on welfare, and those are the people that we figured we were going to help, but they don't come. When we went to see the one in Meteghan, before we started, she said don't expect the ones that are on welfare to come and shop in your store — they are too proud; they don't have to, the government pays for their clothes anyway.

CM: What is the most fun about working at your store?

AM: Meeting the people coming in, and opening the bails, putting the stuff out, how excited people get when they get the brand they want. They will come in some days and get four or five things that they really want, and other days they will not be so lucky, but the majority of the time they get what they want. It's really fun. It's all the more fun because it is our business. It's almost another home for us, because you have to keep your office clean; we have a fridge that has everything here for meals. This whole place is scrubbed constantly.

CM: What is this business worth now?

AM: I don't know. It should be worth quite a bit.

CM: What would you do if someone came and offered to buy you out?

AM: I wouldn't sell.

CM: But what if you did decide to disband as a co-op, what would you do with the value of the business?

BC: If we decided to sell, four other people would come in. There is another thing that is set up, the Northumberland Job Creation Society. They would be the ones that would step in and take it over. The only way we would close it down is if it wasn't viable to run anymore.

CM: And that would mean that the business itself had run down so it wouldn't be worth so much. You are determined ladies. Supposing all this flack you get from time to time from families got too much and you said . . .

BC: Never. It couldn't get any worse.

CM: So you haven't really planned for a way of getting out, because you don't think you ever will.

AM: I don't think any of us wants to get out. We want to see the business . . . .

BC: There might come a time that we will want to get out. We might want to retire. But before any of us do get out, we want to see someone else who is ready to step in our prints to do the things that we are doing.

AM: We'd really have to put some effort into it not only to educate them, but to pick the right parties, to see that they had the same attitude about a business like this.

CM: If somebody came along like that, would you make room for them anyway?

AM: We would if we could afford it. We'd keep them in mind when an opening would turn up.

CHAPTER FIFTEEN
Canadian Sealers Association
St. John's, Newfoundland

"Threatened economically . . . threatened psychologically."

Kirk Smith's involvement with the Newfoundland fishermen began with a film he made in 1977, designed as an educational message from the Department of Fisheries, telling fishermen how they could improve their economic returns. Smith was using his media skills to stimulate social change. He was a journalist, a film-maker, a community worker within both government and university settings, who later worked for Memorial University in St. John's, Newfoundland, teaching communications. The film was called "A-1", the top grade for seal pelts, and the film-making process included a reflection back and forth between different fishermen, and industrial and government leaders, both politicians and bureaucrats. Changes were made as a result — a grading inspector in the plant, a feeling that the fishermen could have some influence, and more meetings followed the film.

In 1982 the process culminated in the formation of a worker co-op. The men asked Smith to step from behind the camera to speak with and for them, and to help them respond to the battering they were taking, economically and psychologically, as a result of the decline of the centuries-old sealing industry, and the bad press they got.

The Canadian Sealers Association was incorporated as a worker cooperative in 1983, but it was left inactive while the men found markets and ways to process the pelts. I talked to Smith when the sealers' cooperative was still in formation, two years after the first major meeting. The Association had 2,000 members embracing a whole industry spread over several provinces, and three languages: Inuktituk, Newfoundlandese and Québecois. The group, although basically fishermen, visualized incorporating all the economic activities dependent on the seal hunt and selling of pelts: processing, tanning, fabrication of articles, use of by-products like blubber and seal meat and marketing. What has happened since?

About 30,000 pelts were taken in 1985, and about 5,000 were tanned and stored for sale by the Association. Ottawa withdrew its earlier support for the five-year plan to rebuild the industry. However, the CSA completed feasibility studies predicting annual sales of 15-20,000 pelts a year, submitted a comprehensive operating plan, and was granted Local Employment Assistance and Development (LEAD) and Newfoundland Fisheries Department financing of $280,000. Kirk Smith left the Association and went to work for the Canada Fur Council, leaving others to carry out their program.

Early in 1986, the CSA started a membership drive for a cooperative to serve Newfoundland's northeast coast. Within a few weeks, it had 400 members, the maximum decided on. Each member had agreed to pay $300 in share capital, $100 cash and the rest in seal pelts at $20 each. The cooperative, renamed the Northeast Coast Sealers Co-operative, works out of Fleur de Lys, on the Baie Verte Peninsula. It will buy skins and carcasses from members, mechanically deblubber the skins, and sell them to tanneries and furriers in other parts of Canada. Long-term plans call for the construction of a tannery in Newfoundland. The processing operation will employ eight to ten people. The co-op hasn't decided yet if they will be full-fledged members, or employees.

This is the only co-op I found with a hired, professional organizer. Articulate and persuasive, Smith obviously had a lot of commitment and identification with the fishermen — he reduced his salary to about a third of what it was as a university teacher to work with them — but there was no way he could be taken for one. His office on the fourth floor of the Fishermen's Union Building at the end of the St. John's harbour, except for a display of sealskin products, looked like any bureaucrat's office. Of course that was part of his effectiveness. He was contributing his knowledge of how to analyse, plan, organize, raise funds, and his contacts in government and industry as well as his enthusiasm and idealism. Talking with me, he did more theorizing than did the workers in the other groups, who also were organizing a structure from which to operate, but at the same time themselves producing a product or a service.

Kirk Smith: We had a sealers' conference in November of 1982, and it resulted in the formation of an organization with very deep community roots. We had taken our time and done it properly, and as a result the organization just sky-rocketed; it just took off. They passed the hat and collected $400 and they said to me, "Well Kirk, why don't you leave the university and join us?"

We had about 150 people there, 100 sealers — it was the largest gathering of sealers in the century. It is a fantastic example in several respects because these people were not only threatened economically, but were threatened psychologically. So much had been done to rob them of both their dignity and their livelihood that it was absolutely necessary that they step forward.

The fishermen took some time to come to the realization that they had it within themselves to form an organization and then to put that in place and to see it active and working. Fishermen have been in the position of workers on an assembly line making a car. Not only did they not have enough money to buy the end product, they didn't even see it! To be out there under these terribly harsh conditions in small boats, shooting seals with rifles, living well below the poverty line, and that's it. So we decided that if we could show the economic benefits of getting together, perhaps some moves could be made. So as an organization, we have put in place a whole range of studies.

The fishermen hired outside experts to conduct a study of what it would cost to set up their own pelt processing plant in the community convenient to them, close to them. They have looked at the national market situation. They have developed new sealskin products that are in sync with consumer attitudes today. You know, if you wear seal fur, it must be for a good reason. It is a practical, waterproof garment, not a fashion item, and they have thought about and accepted the whole environmental awareness movement and seen their lifestyle in relation to that. So they are really gearing up both for the marketing and advertising and the economic infrastructure for setting up their own small scale industry, where in the past it has been completely dominated by one foreign-owned company, the G.C. Reiber Co. of Norway.

First they formed the organization, next they got people that could find government grants.

Constance Mungall: How did they pay those people?

KS: In several ways. One, the sealers decided to put a certain percentage of their own pelts into the organization, so every time they sold a pelt to the company money was deducted for their organization. It was really tough last year, so they put in 25 cents a pelt. That would total approximately $10,000. Then there were memberships; people signed up and gave $5 for a membership. And then there is a certain amount of fundraising, selling articles and so on, and they have done all this plus we have established enough of a relationship with the Fisheries Department to get fairly continuous funding there.

In the first year we went from passing around the hat for $400 to raising over $250,000 in various ways. Government grants are for specific projects; we would find ways to get funding for work we needed to do anyway. I am a full time worker; there was never enough money to pay me initially, of course, but . . .

CM: So you had to moonlight.

KS: Well, we made a go of it, and now we're very stable. For two years in a row now, we've had $200,000 a year in grants from various government agencies. I think that illustrates a few things. One, government had just about given up and yet they all wanted to do something; it was a psychological battle that everybody was losing. Suddenly there was this group dealing as a legitimate industry.

We could completely turn this thing around from unemployment to a source of employment, from frustration, concern and anger to something that people take pride in. We are proud of what we do, and the Association would have its own store as a way to raise significant non-governmental funds for its operation and would play a lead role in the marketing of these products. These goods would be marketed across the province, on the east coast and other selected places in the rest of Canada.

CM: What proportion of the market are you aiming at?

KS: We know that there is a small local market in Newfoundland-Labrador. We will have some hard data on the size of the eastern Canada market. I think we will just have to wait and see how things work out. You start small and work your way up. You set a goal that you know can be accomplished because you are building social infrastructure at the same time that you are getting the machinery to do something, and that is even more important. The whole fishing business gets people working against each other rather than with each other. The people are very scattered over wide areas, and so to build an organization that can work cooperatively is as big a challenge as to get a government grant to put some machinery in a shed and get work done.

We are talking about 5,000 pelts for our first year. The total take last year was about 30,000 pelts. The total allowable catch, which is determined by biological study of what the seal herd can sustain, is about 180,000 to 200,000 animals. In those terms, our take is a small percentage. In terms of market conditions, it's fairly substantial, but in a sense it's irrelevant, whether it is 500 or 5,000 pelts. The point is that *if* those pelts can be bought by the fisherman themselves, and if they can be processed here in their own country, and if people can make something they have not made before and sell it and provide employment — as long as that procedure is put in place and is successful, then it can grow. The initial size of it from a developmental standpoint is irrelevant, and it should be lower rather than higher just for purposes of having a success story that can be built on.

CM: So your main costs are going to be transportation, distribution, organization — you are not going to have big capital investment.

KS: A few hundred thousand dollars of equipment to automatically take the blubber off the pelts. The previous system was one of centralization; the fishermen had to ship both the pelts and meat from outport locations to one central spot. This was good for the company because they maintained control over everything. It was bad for the fishermen because there was a loss of quality in transportation, and they can't be there when the pelts are graded.

The deblubbering operation would be central to the heart of the sealing area. Most of the meat is used locally. Last year it was selling for a dollar a pound in St. John's, if you could get it. It's bottled, it's pickled, it's a form of currency in the spring, it's as popular in outport communities as flipper, or lobster dinners in P.E.I. This is a resource which is a model of marine resource management. All of the fat and the meat and the pelt is used; it provides significant employment for people who are living well below the poverty line; the products that are produced are wonderful. Seal fur happens to be one of the most weatherproof and waterproof furs on the go.

CM: These other products, the meat, blubber, fat, etc., can they be processed locally? Can the villages where the sealing goes on do that?
KS: Yes. At the moment there is a private company canning 500,000 pounds of seal meat a year. It is quite expensive at the moment. The transportation system is not as effective as it could be to get fresh seal meat to market, and we're going to work on that. There is the possibility of canning and bottling more locally.

Now this is only part of the fishermen's income, of course, because they are only on the seal hunt for a matter of weeks, a month, sometimes two months. But on the other hand, if we extend it, if we do some of the processing and the working up of the articles and the use of the by-products, then it will be a larger proportion. Certainly a larger proportion of the total income of the province as a whole, the community as a whole.

CM: So you foresee some people who are not fishermen being involved in this?
KS: Yes. The women who fabricate these items would be connected to the primary producers themselves in a business relationship. The way you can make money at this is by putting your own labour into it — a form of investment, lots of sweat equity and then when the product is sold everybody gets their money.

CM: Would there be other money investment required from the members of the co-op?
KS: They will also have to put in some of their own cash and sell their pelts at reduced rates or for nothing at all, or take a certain percentage of their pelts and give them to the co-op and sell the rest to the company. These options will be laid out very clearly with professional advice, discussed at community meetings and decisions will be made by the fishermen. That takes time, but it's got to be done. We have a board of directors which is elected each year, and an executive elected at large from that board of directors. We're in the process of forming chapters across the country, an Inuit chapter and a Quebec chapter, so we are working on a national as well as a provincial basis.

It's a national problem. As long as Newfoundland sealers were isolated on their own iceflow, they could be attacked and destroyed, but if we are national, if the Inuit are alongside of us, and the sealers from Quebec, if we are saying the same things and understand the same things, then we have a chance for larger funding as well; it adds a great deal more political clout.

CM: How are you going to look after this diversity?

KS: That doesn't seem to be any problem. When the crisis is great enough, when your back is up against the wall, then you get the greatest cooperation.

We have a very good working relationship with the Inuit Tapirisat of Canada, who have three representatives on the board. We have very good representation with the Quebec sealers through the Magdalen Island Sealers Association. We have formed sub-chapters. There are four from Newfoundland-Labrador, three from the Inuit and two from Quebec who form the national executive.

CM: So far the directors and the executive are all sealers, all fishermen. You don't have any fabricators on your board.

KS: That will be up to each chapter. Certainly we would leave our structure open to it. Again, the thing to do is to keep going back to your roots, and make sure you are doing what your membership wants you to do.

CM: To be a devil's advocate, I can visualize a set-up where the fishermen run the co-op, make the rules, and the people who do the fabricating — who are mostly women — being again in the colonized position.

KS: It's easy to come in from the outside, but you have to look at that in relationship to the day-to-day living patterns. A man goes away for several weeks at a time fishing, and the woman has to look after the household. He comes back and he has a completely different relationship to her than if he were in a nine to five job or in a more affluent society. The relationship between men and women, although it may seem to be much more traditional than it is in mainland Canada or in urban centres, makes sense in terms of their own day-to-day situation.

CM: I can visualize the fishermen operating the cooperative, but the fabricators being employees, not worker co-op members.

KS: Whatever they decide and agree on would be what would be done and what would be best.

CM: How will the fishermen pay themselves for this enterprise?

KS: The more affluent fishermen, who have been more involved in the organization and can see a little further down the road, will be in a position to take the lead and probably not take anything back, or very little at first. There will be a decreasing need for that kind of investment.

CM: So some people will put more in and have more equity in the business.

KS: The principle of co-ops is one vote per person, and that has to be maintained, but you have hit on something that is a basic and continuing difficulty in the community development process. It's usually only a few people who get involved, and those people have every right to, at times, get upset that their brethren are not standing up and being counted — that they are doing all the work. And usually, what they get for all this work is a lot of hassle. Their job is to turn that same strength around and give it to others. If you can start a process like that then you have got something that is a living entity, almost a biological organism that will keep moving on its own.

The only qualification will be that you are a fisherman — that you hold a sealer's license. Those that step forward will have an interest in cooperation. The formula for entry has to be worked out. Not everybody has to invest the same. It could take a number of forms. One would be a straight amount of money that you would put in to be a member, and that would be the same for everybody. Membership in the organization is $5; membership in the co-op might be $100 or $1,000 or $10,000; the fishermen will decide that themselves.

But then when you're selling pelts to your own organization, if the group decided that the first years' pelts will be donated or sold at half the market price, or that you have to wait six months for your money — whatever it is — then you have a second level of contribution that is completely voluntary. It's like paying so much to join the co-op bank and then you can put as much in your account as you like. You get back a return based on how much you put in the co-op.

The co-op members live in the outports and are in contact on a fairly regular basis by radio when they are fishing; sometimes they fish together for the same species. There are about 200 longliners — 30- to 60-foot boats. Then there are another several thousand small boats — 15-foot outboard boats.

The area in which fishing and sealing occurs is very widespread. It would take you eight hours to drive from St. John's to Wild Cove, which is the home of our president and our treasurer, and is a fairly central sealing location. It would take you twelve hours to get up to St. Anthony, where a lot of sealing occurs. Great, great distances between places — very small communities of two, three hundred, up to 1,000 people sometimes — and people who are not well connected.

These facts pose great barriers not only to formation of organization and business on a day-to-day level, but also on making sure that the product can get to market.

In age the men range from the early 20s to the late 50s — a good range of ages. The average income is about $10,000, well below the poverty line. The fishermen in the organization tend to be the leaders; they have expressed leadership qualities in many other ways, so they would tend to have the larger incomes. The investment in boats would vary greatly. Some people in our group would have up to $1 million of boat and nets; other people are very simple fishermen with small boats and maybe $20,000 to $40,000 in equipment.

CM: And they would have been educated in their villages probably, and quit school at a very early age in order to get out there fishing.

KS: Yes. These people deserve tremendous respect because your average fisherman has to know so many different skills to survive, and the system is working very much against him. He's educated about the biology of the fishery, about where each species is at what time of year, how to make nets, where to put them, how to work his books, how to fix his boat, how to take a motor out and put it back in again; it's incredible. They haven't been treated as businessmen; they haven't been given the respect that businessmen . . .

CM: They don't think of themselves as businessmen.

KS: True, and the media doesn't reflect that back to them either. They're not equivalent in the public mind to the farmers of central Canada, for example, who are more and more appreciated as businessmen. We have this quaint image of the outport fisherman, and it's just not true. We have people in our group who have held very responsible positions and have had university education. One man who has been a high school vice-principal has a degree and left his high school to go back to the fishery, and is now an eloquent spokesman for the sealing industry.

CM: Will you register as a co-op under the provincial legislation?

KS: We already have. We could operate as a corporation, not as a cooperative, but you come back to what is the ultimate end. It would be very easy to have a successful business. Anybody could come along with the right amount of capital and set this thing up, but that's not what we're talking about; we're talking about human development. We're talking about people getting actively involved and achieving aims that they understand in their own way and at their own speed, people changing their own destiny and controlling the reins, and the cooperative way is one of the best ways of doing that.

CM: Are there advantages as far as financing, getting grants, etc.?

KS: Some of that depends on the present government, but I think more and more, government is seeing cooperatives not as a threat, not as something opposed to the union system, but as something that lets them off the hook in a way.

CM: You are getting funding from the Department of Regional Industrial Expansion for instance?

KS: We expect to get assistance with the marketing plan, the product development plan, etc. We've felt that the best way to achieve our ends is to lobby from the inside. This approach has got us great results to date and will get us even greater results as we show that the sealing industry is going to be able to provide jobs.

PART V
. . . and Production

CHAPTER SIXTEEN
Richmond Plywood Corporation, Ltd. (Richply)
Richmond, British Columbia

"You're buying a job and you're buying a dream."

Richmond Plywood Corporation was the biggest worker co-op I visited — and the oldest, founded in 1956. It has 283 worker-shareholders, and at the time I visited in March 1986, another 150 full and part time workers who are not shareholders.

Compared to the giant wood processors, Richply is small. They put out 16.5 million board feet of ⅜″ plywood a month, compared to MacMillan Bloedel, which produced 20 million board feet as only part of their operations. But smallness can mean flexibility, and be an advantage, according to Employee Relations Coordinator Brian Williams, part of the management team.

"We can switch from market to market," he says. "Some mills are strictly sanding and some are sheeting, and we can go either way." In 1985, MacMillan Bloedel closed their plywood plant, and the Canadian Forest Products plywood sector closed down, too. Whereas Richply has $48 to $50 million sales predicted for next year.

Richmond Plywood Corporation Limited was incorporated in 1956, under the Companies Act. It is incorporated as a limited company, not as a cooperative, and it calls itself an employee-owned, or a worker-owned company. Its worker ownership is protected by its Articles of Association, which specify that each worker has only one share, and that share carries one vote. At the annual general meeting the shareholder-workers elect seven directors, five new ones a year and two with a two-year term to maintain consistency. The chief executive officer, who is the general manager as well as the sales manager of the company, is a shareholder, and his position is confirmed each year at the annual meeting. Except for the sales manager and the mill superintendent, the other members of the management team are not shareholders, and they report continuously to the board of directors.

The Articles of Association specify that each shareholder must be a worker, but they do not specify that every worker must be a shareholder. This has led to a rather anomalous situation in which as much as two-fifths of the work force may be in effect hired by the other three-fifths. They are doing the same jobs, but at almost half the rate of pay, and with none of the extra benefits, including a right to have say in the control of the company. These workers can theoretically join the anointed, and become workers-owners, too. But they have to buy a share first — and the current rate is $65,000, increased from the $5,000 original input when the company began 20 years ago. The purchase is not as unlikely as it may sound, because if a worker is accepted as a shareholder, and some are every year, he gets the higher rate of $15 an hour, compared to $8, and he can use some of that to buy the share on time. The company being in good shape — its assets are worth millions of dollars, and it paid prime plus ½ percent for loans to purchase new equipment last year — he can usually get a bank loan. And he can claim the investment-related interest as an expense on his income tax return. As a shareholder, he will also receive annual dividends. In 1985, which was a good year, 25 percent of the million dollar profit was returned to the workers, at a rate of 37 cents for each hour worked.

I felt an exhilarating spirit of cooperation throughout the plant and the office. The ages of the workers range from 18 to 69, education from high school dropouts to university graduates, all working on the same level at the same wage rates. Shareholders and non-shareholders seem to work well together, despite the differences in their benefits — perhaps because many are relatives and friends, perhaps because, in these times, each group is equally glad to have a job at all. Plant committees similar to a union grievance structure are accessible to both groups.

The shareholder/non-shareholder situation arose partly because of fluctuations in the industry itself. In times of high production, they have needed up to 550 men. But in times of low production and low employment, the 300 shareholders themselves have not had enough work to share full time. And in order to remain competitive with other plywood plants, they are modernizing and automating their equipment, thereby reducing the man hours needed. The workers are trying to deal with this trend by actually reducing the number of shareholders — they have given themselves the right to buy up to 10 shares a year, foreseeing a time when they would need only 200 to 250 workers to maintain full production.

Richply is not unionized, and there has been no move to organize. The powerful International Woodworkers of America appears to be just now adjusting to the idea of worker co-ops. At around the time I visited Richply, the IWA was instrumental in the purchase by workers of another plywood company, Lamford Cedar Products, with plants at New Westminster and Sooke on Vancouver Island. The union had earlier refused to support the employee take-over of Victoria Plywood, a former Canadian Pacific Industries subsidiary.

I went to Richmond Plywood in March 1986 to interview Brian Williams, the Coordinator of Employee Relations. After our interview, I was lucky to bump into Charlie Spriggs, the current president of the company, who was in the office to help prepare for a sales trip to Europe by Bill Jones, the chief executive officer, general manager and sales manager. I'm letting Charlie Spriggs speak first, because he knew more of the history of the company, and could give an overview, while Brian Williams filled in with the details about the operation.

"How would you define the dream?"
— Charlie Spriggs, President

Charlie Spriggs: I've been here since 1958, since 1960 as a shareholder. When I was first president, in 1968, I went right through the books, and having worked here with most of the fellows, I'm familiar with the history of it. Worker-owned wood processing plants started in 1921 in Olympia, Washington. Many of the loggers in the area were Scandinavian; they knew about co-ops and had cultural ties. Some of the co-ops weren't as successful as they should be, but some were fortunate because they owned timber and sold out for high dollars before 1956. During the war they were doing quite well.

The shareholders here at first were people familiar with the worker-owned concept, some plywood workers from Washington State, the Anacortes area. But they sold shares right down into California, you know. When it first started up, the shares were just sold to anyone for $5,000. They advertised 300 shares and it was oversubscribed; I think there were 306 people who wanted to buy. The value of the shares went down in the first year or so, because the promoters, of course, were using up some of the money for their own expenses, fees, etc., but nothing was being done. The promoters weren't interested that much in making plywood, more in making a profit. They were turfed out at a meeting with the superintendent of brokers. Some people sold out their shares for about $3,000. This was I guess '57, somewhere in there. One of the things that's been our salvation is that they did decide to buy this property in

Richmond at that time, so we do have our own land. They started building here in 1957 and they had the lathe running and peeling veneer in March of '58. They had the dryer going when I came in July of '58 and I think about August they were just hooking the press up.

I would say in 1958 the company was running into difficulties. There was a threefold effort to pull it out. The investor of the development bank put in some money, I forget the amount. Anacortes Veneer put in some money. And the shareholders took a 15¢ an hour wage reduction. The outcome of that was that Anacortes had the sales contract, the contract to sell the production of this plant.

Constance Mungall: And were *they* a worker-owned company?

CS: Yes, they were. Anacortes Veneer started up in 1939 and they sold out in about 1970, I guess, or in the late 60s. The plant wasn't as modern as what we had here. We had the modern manufacturing facility but we were short in the timber end. We're finally getting into the timber end now.

The reason that Anacortes came in of course was that a lot of their shareholders also had shares in Richmond Plywood, and the first president of this company, Paul Levera, was from Anacortes. When they had the sales contract they formed a subsidiary, Transamerican Plywood, with an office on Broadway, I believe, to handle our sales, with a small commission. By 1958 we were shipping veneer down to them and they were processing it. But then over the years as we got more people employed here we'd buy back the shares from the American shareholders. There may be three or four shareholders down there yet, I'm not sure.

I would say we had, oh maybe only 100 regular shareholder-workers in 1958 because there were still about 100 down in the States and there were people back in the Prairies that had shares.

CM: What was the advantage of having shares if they weren't working in the company?

CS: Well, first of all the people in the United States were buying in other worker-owned plants for investment purposes, thinking that they would have a good return. On the Prairies some of them were shopkeepers, some of them were people in their late 40s, early 50s who thought they would come out here and work in the summertime and go back there in the wintertime. Or if they retired to B.C., they had a job.

I bought my share in 1960 from a postmaster in Croll, Manitoba. He was a guy that was then in his fifties and he just bought it because he thought it was something worthwhile to buy.

In 1959 there was an IWA strike on the coast, July and August of that year, maybe longer. And the wages went up here. They were about $2, and we took a 15¢ cut. But, that summer, because the other plywood

RICHPLY / 179

plants were down, we started making profits and were paying $3.27½; part of that I think in the form of a hold-back. In the spring of '60 shares were going for up to $12,000 because people were interested. It looked like a good thing. In the fall of 1960 the wages went down to $1.50 an hour for a two-month period. And of course the shares dropped back to $6,000, $7,000 again. They fluctuated.

CM: Have they risen roughly at the same rate as inflation?

CS: Some people seem to think so. But I paid about $7,000 for mine in 1960 and at that time for $7,000 I could buy two fairly nice lots. Now the shares today go for $65,000 and I'd have to pay more than that for one lot. So if you look in terms of real estate, perhaps not. In terms of inflation I'd say yes. In terms of working here and the benefits — I've had steady employment, good wages, had the opportunity to put in lots of hours. In a good market time, employment is more available and our shares would probably go down. But when a person has exhausted Unemployment Insurance benefits, well then it's attractive for him to come in at our wage rates. And the interest on our shares is deductible for tax purposes. So that way they can come in and work and meet high payments. Right now our casual rate is $8 an hour for non-shareholders, compared to $15 for shareholders. So some of the guys say, "Hey, we get $7 more an hour, we can work extra hours and gradually pay off the shares . . . ."

CM: That must seem like a lot of money to some.

CS: Yes, it is a lot of money. The bank will finance up to about $50,000, and some families get together and some sons end up with their dad's shares. But the price has always been in relation to the ability to pay it back in terms of earning dollars. One guy said, "When you buy a share in Richmond Plywood you're buying a job and you're buying a dream." The job is very real, as is the dream.

CM: How would you define the dream?

CS: The dream is an opportunity to have freedom in the workplace, to take part and be a part of the owning of a company. To be an owner, be a worker, be involved in the politics of it, be involved in the destiny, which direction the company wants to go. As shareholders, they can all be directors of the company, and we've had quite a turnover there.

It's an opportunity to do very well. We made $1 million profit last year, and we paid 25 percent in bonuses, about 37 cents an hour. The biggest asset we have is the shareholders. Mind you it could be our biggest disadvantage, we could self-destruct for very petty issues if we let internal politics get in the way. There's a real danger. The U.S. plants have sold out.

If a person wishes to work a little harder, take some responsibility, he's not thwarted in any way. We do have a seniority system, you have to go through the channels. But in some other plants, production is geared to the slower workers and the men try to protect them because they're in effect protecting themselves. In our company it works just about the opposite. If a person can produce more he gears things up, sometimes physically speeding up a machine, taking a heavier work load. And the rest of the people are usually drawn into it; not always, sometimes they drag their heels too. But there is opportunity for them here.

Directors of course, they're the policy makers and they're the ones that have the legal responsibilities. Our chief executive officer is responsible for the management team and reports to the directors. So you have a conflict there; when a guy comes in the boardroom he's a director and when he goes back in the plant he's a worker. People always try to take the easiest route and if there's a complaint out there, real or imaginary, they'll go through a director quite often, because they'll want to go right up to the top. Sometimes that causes a little friction, but usually it gets results. And the directors recognize that the superintendent, foreman, other supervisors have responsibility and they have to have authority to carry it out. I would say the word for Richmond Plywood would be 'flexible'. We can do things other companies can't do, in terms of how we treat ourselves. If we want to work for straight time then we can work for straight time. If we want to take a wage cut, then we do. The net result is that we do whatever is necessary to make sure this company goes.

CM: Have there ever, for instance, been recommendations that the wage be increased when because of market conditions the company couldn't handle it?

CS: Yes, there have. There's always pressure for more wages and more benefits. Some boards have given an increase and a few of the more conservative people have questioned the wisdom of it. Of course we all accepted it! But usually there's not the push for wage increase unless there's good economic sense to it. When times are tough, the guys out there know they're tough.

Until 1982, we had a professional manager and a professional salesman, costing us a lot of money in terms of their salaries and benefits. Then we began to think something was lacking in professional managers. They seemed to want to operate by the textbooks, not according to the work force we have. We're the people — the shareholders point out "Hey, this is costing us dollars," when things aren't working right.

So we suffered in the plant. We didn't cut the wages, but we cut the hours. That year we didn't work 20 weeks. That's the first year in the history of Richmond Plywood that we didn't work, but in 1982 interest rates were so high back in eastern Canada that there was just no market. If a guy's got a warehouse full and he's paying 18 or 20 percent on his inventory, you couldn't *give* him any more plywood.

At that time there was a change. The professional manager was let go. There was a young guy, Bill, in the plant, really bright, he had started here when he was 18, come up through, ended up as a foreman, ended up president and chairman of the board for a couple of years. He took over in sales and he took over the manager's job. He ended up with both jobs, sales and management. He was holding down the fort. Bill was astute enough to learn . . . it was on-the-job training. He learned the sales end, and he took to it very well, exceptionally well. And he's good in production; he was a foreman, so he knew the manufacturing part of it. And at the same time, the directors got more involved, took a more active part, because Bill is just spread so thin.

We don't want the alternative and that is to hire somebody for a big salary, secretary, expense account, car, all this. In other words we're trying to run a pretty tight ship here.

The Companies Act requires every company to have a president, so I'm president and chairman of the board, but Bill is chief executive officer and sales manager. He heads the management team. He has terms of reference which are loosely those that a normal chief executive officer would have.

CM: And is his salary comparable too?

CS: We don't have different pay categories. Bill gets two hours a day extra. For a 40-hour week, he gets paid for 50 hours at $15 an hour. Members get straight time for overtime. That was agreed to by all the shareholders some years ago. The non-shareholders are paid time-and-a-half because they're covered by the Employment Standards Act.

In plywood the jobs are semi-skilled, except for the tradesmen, and there isn't a big discrepancy in the skills, so we don't mind the same wage. We do have skilled workers; we have qualified electricians here, we have steam engineers, we have millwrights, we have lathe operators. And if you start giving one person higher pay, then where do you draw the line? It's pretty hard to separate them.

CM: And so far all the employees have accepted the across-the-board rate?

CS: Yes. The superintendent also gets two hours a day extra, because sometimes these guys do put in long hours. Some foremen get an extra hour a day and some get a half hour, because they are required to come in earlier on the shift or stay a few minutes after the shift. Other than that no, the person that's feeding a dryer or sweeping a floor as the case may be, is getting $15 an hour if he's a shareholder, same as I'm getting and same as Bill's getting.

CM: Is there a fair amount of mobility between jobs?

CS: Yes. Dryers to some people are a little bit monotonous. We have a spreader area where it is a young man's job, he's moving back and forth,

travelling at a high rate of speed and you know you have to be in fairly
good shape to do it. We need good people there so a new shareholder
applicant is put there and if he can't do that well then, unless he's a trades-
man, he probably isn't accepted as a shareholder. If a young fellow wants
to change jobs, like to get up on the lathe, they put his name in and they go
pretty well on seniority and when there's a vacancy up there, if a person is
sick or on vacation, the lathe deck trains him. Now I've been here long
enough that probably any of these jobs I could bid on and seniority-wise I
could get them.

CM: And you still work on the floor?
CS: All of the directors work in the plant. I work in the finishing end.
Right now the directors, they instruct me to spend more time over here, in
the office, especially with Bill going away for two weeks to Europe on
business. But normally what happens is we'd have a meeting on a Thurs-
day, I'd come in on a Wednesday and spend the full day in the mill — I
enjoy that — keeping in touch. I'll be in the office while the CEO is away,
but I'll be working in the plant Saturday and Sunday because I want some
production work.

I like Richply, it's more progressive, we emphasize the manufacturing
part of it. Instead of confrontation, we work with the government and
with employees. The old shop steward type was often a bully, making a
demonstration, pounding a desk. We need people to risk concessions, to
make changes; it's not a unilateral thing. It's more flexible here. In general it doesn't mean we're anti-union. A working person needs an organization. Seeing how we work — I'm hoping there'll be a day when instead of
a union shutting a company down, they take a look at Richply.

Some shareholders make a point of pointing out things to casual workers,
training them. Fathers take a role in teaching their sons good work habits.
Sons have preference working here. Boys in their teens, it can be a god-
send. One father was a shareholder; he had six boys, and they all worked
here. Today, one is an accountant, one an engineer.

We don't have any women working in the mill. One applied to be a shareholder. She worked her 20 days probation OK but she missed one weekend and she said to hell with it. The other plywood plants do have women.
We are very much production-oriented; the lunchroom and washroom
facilities are not what they should be. We're trying to improve them. In
some companies the women are better than the men, they have a better
touch with the wood.

"To sell your shares means you're quitting."
— Brian Williams, Employee Relations Coordinator

Brian Williams: Originally there were 300 shareholders. Our labour force in the mid-1970s was around 550, with 300 shareholders and approximately 250 non-shareholders. When times were tough, all the non-shareholders were let go, even as far back as 1979. They were all gone by the end of 1981. We ended up in 1982 with the shareholders having to work one week on and one week off. They'd collect Unemployment Insurance for that alternate week. And that happened for most of 1982. The company, realizing we didn't ever want to have this kind of a problem again, said, "We're going to buy some shares back, reduce the number of shareholders, so that if this problem ever happens again, we'll lay all the non-shareholders off and help maintain full employment for all the shareholders."

The management made the proposal to the board of directors who in turn brought the matter up at the annual meeting. The shareholders annually authorize the board to buy back up to 10 each year, if the money is there. Now that doesn't mean to say that we are going to purchase 10 shares back each year. We may decide that we don't want to purchase any back because the market is really good and we'd rather invest our money in a new expansion or something else. So a lot of factors come into play, including price. We know what the market price is, what shares are selling for.

We don't know what the ultimate number of shareholders is going to be. We didn't have non-shareholders in production for several years, and only since about '83 we've hired some and we're getting more and more all the time now. But they're told, "When times are good you're here, but when times are bad you're gone."

At this point we've purchased 17 shares back. So there's 283 shareholders out there now, and about 150 non-shareholders, in total, working in the plant either full time or part time. That includes part-timers working on the weekends.

CM: Does the fact that a worker-shareholder can sell his share to anyone he chooses mean that he has control over the training and background of the worker?

BW: The board has ultimate control, because they have the initial interview. The prospective buyer goes before the board of directors, seven people elected from inside the mill. They've worked on all these jobs; they know. If the person's interview is passed, approved, then he goes for a medical. If the medical is approved he starts a 20-working-day trial period inside the mill at $8 per hour. If the trial period is satisfactory, then we approve the share to be transferred between the buyer and the seller.

CM: So the worker-shareholder has to sell to somebody that meets the qualifications? In a way it's buying a job, isn't it?

BW: Yes, it is. Basically when you have a share you have a job, as long as you perform satisfactorily. So to sell your share that means you're basically giving up your job, you're quitting. But we don't control the sale of the share as such. A shareholder can sell it for whatever price they can get on the market, and that's none of our concern. A worker borrows from his bank or credit union or trust company or relative or wherever. And the interest they pay on this money is deductible from their income tax because it's interest on investment money. We also don't want to get involved in any kind of financial arrangements with shareholders at all. It just gets too messy.

CM: Do they have any trouble getting the loan?

BW: Some places don't even recognize a Richmond Plywood share as being worth anything. Other places, like the Toronto Dominion Bank, the bank we've dealt with for over 30 years, they've seen the operation, seen financial statements, so they know what Richmond Plywood is all about. So they would lend money. But the share's worth quite a bit, so some non-shareholders may want to buy a share but can't afford it.

There's no different set of rules for shareholders and non-shareholders with respect to attendance, absenteeism and work performance, they're all the same. As long as they perform they'll have steady employment. The person that sells a share is deemed to have quit. But we may, depending on the job and his performance, offer him work at the non-shareholder's rate of pay. That is $8 an hour at the present time. A shareholder gets $15 an hour, and medical, extended health, life insurance, dental plan, long-term disability. The non-shareholder working in the mill gets none of these at present.

CM: What's the turn-out like for meetings?

BW: It's quite good, usually over 230 people. Now I have to say that we use a bit of an incentive to get more people out. We want to avoid someone getting all the proxies and then controlling a meeting, so as an incentive we pay a $50 participation bonus. The meeting is usually on a Saturday and we usually close the operation down, except for minor maintenance work.

There's also a plant committee, which is like a union grievance committee. There's two members elected from each of the three shifts and the seventh member represents maintenance. They are like shop stewards. The chairman of that plant committee is also the chairman of the board of directors. And management participates in that process. And there's a safety committee with two members also elected from each shift, as well as one other for day shift. The chairman is one of the elected members of the committee. It's easy to get people to participate on the plant committee, but not on the safety committee. I guess everyone likes to be involved in grievances!

CM: You don't have a union here, even the non-shareholder people are not unionized. Have there been any attempts to unionize?

BW: No there haven't. We don't even know what kind of luck they would have to try to unionize the non-shareholders. Especially with the nature of the company; we don't think it would go very far. Usually if a non-shareholder has a problem he has the same recourse — all employees have the same recourse — they go to the supervisor and try to resolve it. They can go to the plant committee representative, and the superintendent and there's a board of arbitration.

CM: Do the committees function differently for non-shareholders and shareholders?

BW: No. Except for termination. For a non-shareholder we would have to follow the Employment Standards Act. A shareholder would also basically follow those guidelines, except that a superintendent cannot terminate a shareholder but can only recommend termination to the board of directors. He's got a vested interest, so depending on the problem, they'll give him one more kick at the cat.

CM: So really job security is only in terms of the market and employment situation. You know you're not going to get completely laid off if employment is low, you'll get a share of the work. But you can still lose your job for other reasons?

BW: For cause — for absenteeism or poor performance, fighting, any other reasons that anybody else would be terminated for. It doesn't come up that frequently, a couple in recent years. Basically this is just like any other company and all the rules are for everybody.

CM: How do wages compare with other companies?

BW: Some years ago we used to keep the same as or higher than unionized operations but over the last few years, since around 1981 or 1982, we've basically stayed at $15 an hour. The rate is probably higher, $17 or $18 an hour, in many operations. But then again, *we're* still working! The basic rate of pay is reasonable, an equitable rate, and when times are good then we give the shareholders a larger bonus.

CM: So if you work 40 hours a week you get more than somebody who works 30 hours a week? And the non-shareholders don't get the bonus?

BW: This was the first year the non-shareholders received some bonus. Not as large as the shareholders because there's no investment . . . .

CM: What do board members get out of it?

BW: Nothing really. They get one dollar honorarium a year, and that's basically it. There's a directors' meeting every two weeks. It's a day meeting, and so they'll get paid their wages for that particular day and if they go out for lunch they'll have their lunch paid for, that kind of thing. I guess they like to be leaders. Some do it for the good of the company. We have seen people run for, I'd say, the ego trip. Hopefully those people don't get elected.

CM: And is there a real feeling of 'this is my company'?

BW: For the shareholders it certainly is, yes.

CM: I get that feeling from you, too.

BW: That's right. I've been here a long time and we've put a lot of years in this place and it's just like ours as well. There's about 13 office staff for the whole operation, marketing, sales, receptionist, secretary, account- ant, not very many.

The salaries are a little behind the times. That is being reviewed by man- agement because we've got a good group and we don't want to lose them.

CM: Does the office staff have a chance to become shareholders too?

BW: No, they don't. When I started here, in 1971, there were three or four office people in shareholder positions. Actually, the job that I'm doing was a shareholder position, so I could have bought a share at that time. In 1974 there was a change in board policy so that now no office staff person shall be a shareholder.

CM: I noticed in the 1956 prospectus it was predicted that produc- tion would be higher per employee. Figures showed that in other worker-owned companies, production was 10 to 15 percent higher than in conventionally owned companies. Has that been the case?

BW: Yes, our productivity is higher than other organizations. The share- holders work hard because they want to make sure they're working.

CM: And the fact that they have some say in the matter?

BW: Yes. We're doing some expansion right now with a synthetic patch line and we had a meeting of all the forklift drivers that would be driving in that area and the people that would work on that particular line and who worked on the old line. They had a meeting to talk about, "What do you think about having it here, here and here and here; what do you think about this?" So you get the input from people and when you finally put the thing into place — there's always obviously going to be bugs, but they'll be more receptive to helping work out those bugs. That kind of meeting's pretty common.

CM: So you can sell at a better price because of your higher producti- vity?

BW: Well, that's definitely one of the reasons, yes. Raw material costs are the main thing. We don't have the timber holdings some of the bigger places do. But we're definitely making changes to make sure we're a little more competitive. We have timber now. And we just finished obtaining two new lathes from another plywood mill that was closed down. That means we can purchase or trade logs more than in the past. We're getting more into the raw material end of it, trying to become more and more self-sufficient all the time. That's always the goal, to upgrade production, find the weakest link and if we can afford to, upgrade that particular area.

The market is good for us right now. Unfortunately we can't see into next year or the year after. The management team looks at all the pros and cons and sees what the market's going to be, what's going on with other competition: there's some place closing down, another mill opening up. We try to look at all these factors, and weather and everything, to try to determine what our market's going to be in six months. We have to be competitive in order to stay in the business. We're continually looking at ways to become competitive. It's said that there's only going to be one, maybe two, plywood companies left on the coast and we intend to be the one. To that end we have to look at purchasing shares back, at modernization. In the short term there may be more non-shareholders here, but in the long term there will be a lot less. Let's say if you bought enough shares back to modernize a particular piece of equipment, say that piece of equipment takes ten people, now it might only take two people.

Maybe we'll end up with 200 shareholders, maybe 250, I don't know; the more modernization you do, the more you can buy these shares back, then the better off you are, purchasing more shares.

CHAPTER SEVENTEEN
Ventair Industries Co-Op Ltd.
Winnipeg, Manitoba

"It was either go co-op or lose everything."

When the Manitoba Department of Co-operative Development first told me about VentAir, the spokesman described it as complicated — a takeover involving a sequence of four companies and crisis financing. Stability was reached when the co-op was incorporated in December 1985, eight months before I visited the plant in the northwest of Winnipeg.

The two founders of the new co-op, Don Roy and Ralph Kubic, met me in their new boardroom, around a 12-foot-long table they had spent a weekend making and had copied from one in the Co-op Development offices. With them was Wayne Wiebe, office manager and purchaser, who had been with the company before and was invited to return to the co-op. He is not yet a member-owner, but expects to become one when his six-month probation is up.

The three tossed my questions back and forth, looking to each other for verification. They also looked to Ken Bourquin, the Manitoba Co-operative Development consultant who, as with Winnipeg's Accu-Graphics, helped them untangle their affairs and learn the potential and implications of going co-op. He sat in on the interview, and added his own summation: "They've spent six months putting out fires and trying to survive. Six months scrambling . . . "

The scrambling included solving financial and legal problems, and I often had to turn the tape recorder off as the three managers decided how much they wanted to reveal. "Ask us again in two years," they would say. "Then we can tell you the whole story." The details had nothing to do with the cooperative nature of their new organization, but much to do with taking over a bankrupt business.

Adjusting to the idea of a cooperative seemed to be easy, once the principals understood what it meant. They had after all worked for years with the men who became their fellow owners. The clincher was the help the Manitoba Co-operative Development Department was able to give — in guaranteeing bank loans, and in advice and support in the year of travail. One major burden remained when we talked. In their industry, constructing and installing ventilation systems, each contract is covered by a bond that work will be completed. The bonding company accepted the two founders' personal guarantee, because their reputation was established, but they would not accept the cooperative's. Don and Ralph had in effect personal responsibility for the $3 million worth of business the co-op could do in a year. As Ralph said, "If it's your own it's OK but when it's a one-vote-one-share-type deal with the co-op it's scary, it is, 'cause you're signing your life for everybody." During our visit, Don and Ralph took the opportunity to bring the problem up. Ken Bourquin promised to discuss it with them, and with the bonding company if necessary.

So far, relations with the Sheet Metal Workers Union have not been a problem. All 45 employees at VentAir — save the office staff and one of the founders — are members of the union local. Essential in the construction industry in Manitoba, continued certification was taken for granted. Bourquin continued his summing up. "From where I see it, after six months scrambling, in the last month they've. been able to sit back and say, 'We've got a business now. Where do we go with it'?"

Don Roy: We started out when Air Flow Industries went into receivership. Myself and Ralph talked about the possibility of taking over the company from the receivers. We knew the company was in trouble for a couple of years so we had talked about it before. I was a construction supervisor at the time and working mostly out of the office. Ralph was a construction supervisor as well but in the field. We've worked together for many years so he was one of the first people I approached. We bunched up our monies together and made an offer to the receiver.

Ralph Kubic: We operated as a numbered company I guess maybe about two months. At the time of receivership, there was many contracts that were still being worked on, and to save our — to start the new company — we had to obtain all these jobs that were on the go, so we started off with a numbered company, to keep going while we're still negotiating. So that's where Don and I came in first. Then we needed more financing. Right from day one we thought that we would be able to at least get the same amount of monies that we personally put in from any lending institution but we soon found out differently. We were still a numbered company when we approached the employees to get more financing.

DR: It was too late for Ralph and I to turn back . . . we had our bucks in it . . . and we felt strong about being able to make a go of it . . . .

RK: Don and I were personally on the hook for quite a bit of wages, in the numbered company as we were going.

Constance Mungall: And did you keep all the employees?

DR: Not all of them. As the receiver was giving them their walking papers, Ralph and I would be rehiring them. The key people. I think of all the people that we asked we didn't get one rejection.

RK: You'd have to go back like with Don and I. We've worked with them for years, they've respected us, and they knew what was going on, and I guess they had good faith in Don and myself.

DR: And trust, yeah.

RK: We've invested so much in that they'll take the gamble and invest with us . . . .

Wayne Wiebe: We took over all of the work . . . some of the jobs that the receiver wanted to have finished. Over and above that we approached the contractors so there were other jobs that we had on the go as well. We changed the office staff around of course.

CM: The management of the original company went?

WW: No, we retained the previous owner of Air Flow Industries, as a general manager, but as it turned out that didn't work out for us.

DR: Myself, I mortgaged everything to the hilt in order to be able to get the money I needed and Ralph's pretty well done the same. The other people didn't put in as much money but they all had to get mortgages in order to be able to do it.

CM: And yet to be a co-op you only have the one vote for your one share. You don't have the influence that the money you put in would indicate.

DR: That's correct. Ralph and I were the goats!

RK: Don and I have put in pretty well four times the other guys, you might as well say.

WW: In effect these two fellows have got half as much money put up as the other nine fellows combined have. And it's unfortunate but it's one share one vote. But they recognize it, at least they recognize it, I've never heard anybody complain about it or hold it over their heads, just — we work together, we look after things.

CM: And how do you two feel about the fact that you've got more of a stake financially in the company?

RK: Personally, it doesn't really bother me that much, I hope someday of course to be able to recapture some of it, no getting away from that.

DR: It will eventually all come back to us.

RK: It's broken down into shares and into loans, right?

DR: That's right. I think it's ten and five right now . . . $5,000 into shares and $10,000 into investment, it's a loan-investment-type deal. You would have to come up with a total of $15,000 to join. The total capitalization is close to $200,000.

RK: It was only $10,000 at the beginning — five shareholders loaned five investments. But right now through our by-laws and policies it's gone up to $15,000 for a new member.

CM: And do the old members have to find that other five too?

RK: No. We just made that one of our by-laws as part of the co-op.

CM: And the sort of "sweat equity" that they put in in the beginning covered that. And you guys went out on a limb originally to get that financing.

RK: We went to all of the lending institutions, and we were unsuccessful until a gentleman with Venture Capital, that's a provincial small business encouragement agency . . . . They considered us for a while and then they told us to approach the Manitoba Co-operative Development people.

WW: So it was Air Flow Industries, and then it was a numbered company, then it was VentAir Industries Limited, then VentAir Industries Co-op.

CM: And this was about a year ago. So you decided to incorporate as a cooperative.

DR: We hadn't thought about it as such until we spoke with Ken and Ed at Co-op Development, and still we didn't know what really a co-op was. Ralph and I weren't aware of the fact at the beginning that of course we were going to lose our investment to an equal share with everybody else.

CM: You thought that you would have an amount of influence in the company related to the investment you've put in.

DR: Until we found out the ways of the co-op, yes. By this time again we were to the point where we would have lost everything, it was either go co-op or lose everything and we would do anything for money (laughter).

RK: That's right because we operated on just our investment of $189,000 for about six months . . . on a C.O.D. basis until we realized that we had to have financing to keep us going.

CM: And how did the Co-op Development people help you with that? They guaranteed your line of credit so if you go out of business the province backs it?

DR: Yeah but that won't happen.

RK: We started out by . . . before all the dealings were complete . . . we gave out a personal guarantee for what was it, $100,000? All of the shareholders gave out personal guarantees for a loan of $100,000. That was only to see us through until the co-op was able to finalize everything.

CM: But now your line of credit that you operate on is backed by the province?

RK: That's correct. The personal guarantees are all off, except we have personal guarantees of course on our own personal investment.

CM: That's like your capital. And the line of credit — how much is it?

WW: But that reduces every year by one-third.

RK: Which is just about due now (laughter).

WW: No, December.

CM: And are you going to make it OK?

DR: Things are starting to look well.

CM: Good. You recognized it as an economic proposition. Did you

have any business plans, or business advice at that time?
DR: Next time we will (laughter) . . . . I had previous business experience. Ralph, I think it's the first business he's been in, and while Air Flow Industries was in business, about two years ago, Wayne was the manager then.
WW: I worked here for 13 years. Then the owner and I split. Then I came back when these fellows asked me to.
CM: What are your orders like? Do you have a sales manager?
WW: Everything we do, being in the construction business, is called bid-spec work. Every project that comes out we bid on, and of course low tender takes the job. Sometimes we have an edge, sometimes we don't, it just depends on the type of work. Some people prefer to deal with us, and we'll get that job without going through a tender stage, but 90 percent of our work is bid-spec.
CM: And you're bidding for ventilation systems?
WW: We'll look at anything from a few thousand dollars up to a couple of million. Mostly industrial and commercial, no residential.
CM: What kind of turnover do you have? What would your business be in a year?
WW: I'm not sure at this stage but when it was Air Flow Industries it was $3½ to $4 million a year. I don't know if we want to quite get that big but . . . we've thrown some numbers around, $2½ maybe $3 million a year.
CM: For the next year you're predicting that amount of business?
WW: Trying. We're quoting everything that's coming out right now and we've got a good success rate and we're pleased with it, and money seems to be reasonable.
CM: You're paying your salaries and you're paying your suppliers?
RK: On time.
WW: When I got here there was an awful lot of credit problems still and I've got everybody on our side with the exception of one supplier. We're establishing credit. We must deal with probably 150 suppliers I would think and it's a real challenge, getting these people into line and getting the backing, and their support, and they're coming, they've given us an awful lot of help. And again to re-establish our credibility with the contractors. It was a few tough ones, but I think we've got them under control now.
CM: What's your big expense in terms of supplies?
WW: Well steel for one is probably one of our biggest . . . and of course supplies. I do the purchasing. Because of the type of trade we're in we have to buy . . . things like you see up here, diffusers, air-distribution equipment. Well, when you get into boxes, and sophisticated control valves, they get very expensive. They can cost as much as one-third of

our total bid. The projects that we tender on, the process of bid-spec, is an engineer's drawing. So everything we have has been engineer-designed, and we're quoting on supplying and installing that portion of the contract.

CM: So you don't have to have your own engineer.

WW: Don't need it, no. Besides we've got enough people on staff we probably know more than the engineers do anyway. Well Don's got, what, 40 years' experience, Ralph's got 30, I've got 20 . . . .

DR: Thirty-five. Don't make me older than I am!

WW: Just trying to help you along!

CM: And there were 40 employees before when the company went bankrupt so you've taken on more people.

WW: Forty-five at present. You have to remember this is construction season, this is prime time. We will probably not have as many January-February, which is typical.

RK: We'll drop down to about 15 to 20 I think at low peak.

The way we picked up our shareholders or partners into the co-op is Don and I are the office area, we've got three in the shop area that manufacture the stuff and then there's five in the outside field for installation. So at a low period of construction time if we have to go right down it would be just the members of the co-op that are still working, we can operate with that core of people, 11 people.

CM: How big is the office staff?

DR: Six with our secretary-accountant. And that includes Wayne.

CM: And is Wayne a member?

WW: No I'm on probation for six months.

CM: And are there other requirements?

WW: Money!

CM: Do you take anyone who applies? If somebody that you hire on wants to be a member will you accept that application?

DR: We'll accept it and look at it, yeah. But we'll have to see if we've got enough work to keep him because in construction you never know what you're down to, you might be working for three months or maybe working a year, so we'd have to look into the future amount of work we've got and if he's a guy that's going to be a good asset to us then we will consider him. We want to get the co-op worked out, how it operates and everything, before we do any more expanding.

WW: So I'll have the honour of being the first.

CM: Are you still feeling your way about what being a co-op means?

DR: We've got an idea of what it means, it's just a matter of operating under a co-op, and the guidelines and everything you go by . . .

CM: Have you had to do some studying about that?

DR: Well Ken and Ed were pretty good to us, explaining things to us in a few meeting sessions on this and that.

WW: Even when I came aboard you fellows came down and gave me a hand and explained what a co-op was and went through the flow charts and the organization and everything else and it was most helpful. Because what I had thought it was, was not right.

CM: In what way?

WW: Well, I'm coming in as an employee, and I see there's 11 members of the co-op, and esentially, they're the boss. To come in in the morning and say "Good morning boss" 11 times is totally ridiculous. So from eight to five everybody's job function is a little bit different. And it depends where we're meeting, when we're meeting and why we're meeting that changes the hats, right? The first month was confusing, but after that session with Co-op Development it's helped me. I've got no problem at all dealing with it. It's been easy.

RK: We've pretty well . . . all of the members have pretty well adjusted. At first they . . . enjoyed maybe a little bit of a swelled head thinking that they were owners but then they had to accept the fact that they're plain working people just like they were before. It's the only way you can operate . . . .

DR: Now Wayne pretty well organizes everything, and Ralph and I see to it that it's done.

WW: But we still treat it as a team effort, which we did before when we were all working together . . . and it's working. Once a week we have a regular staff meeting. Myself, Ralph, Don, we try to get a mix between the outside and the inside and of course you have to have administration in there, or purchasing, so the shop foreman comes in, to get that input, and then our estimator. The five of us meet once a week.

RK: That's the management team. Then there's a board of directors, we meet every two weeks.

DR: There are five on the board, by election from the members, a different five from the management team. Wayne attends as advisory only.

RK: Any time any of the other shareholders requests any information we make it free to them.

CM: What's the union role in all of this — did they help in the original switch-over?

WW: I don't think they know what's going on. They don't have a clue.

RK: I'm not sure if they understand totally . . . "co-op" . . . it doesn't really make any difference to us. We abide by the union rules.

WW: I don't know if the union fully recognizes who all the shareholders are.

DR: All of the members except myself are members of the union. Wages are all controlled by union agreements, except for mine, and the office staff. When I was working for the prior owner I was a construction supervisor working mostly out of the office, same as I'm doing now. It wasn't required for me to be in the union. At that time Ralph was on the job site — he had to be in the union. And there was no need to really change it. We haven't seen any need anyways.

CM: And you still have the same set-up as far as grievance procedures and shop stewards?

RK: Well our union, Local 511 Sheet Metals, is not that sticky about anything like that. They're very flexible.

CM: At the time you were approaching other workers for their involvement, was the union involved at all?

RK: No, since then, they've approached us to sign a contract with the union that we'd be a union shop.

WW: In other words we had to be signatory to the agreement as signed by the Labour Relations Council of Manitoba.

CM: And did you take over the agreement that had been made with the previous employer? So there wasn't a re-negotiation. Have you met for negotiation yet?

DR: It will be two years down the road before negotiations are on the table. We don't foresee any problems.

WW: There'll be a minimal increase I'm sure.

CM: Will the union representative who will be doing the negotiating be one of your co-op people?

DR: Could be. One of our members was on the last negotiating team.

RK: You can't predict that because besides us there's about five or six other union shops in the city, so everybody negotiates at the same time. There'd be three or four guys representing the companies' side and then three or four on the union side, negotiating for all the shops.

WW: I can't speak for the other two guys but to tell you the truth, myself I'm not really big on unions. I've been on the other side of the negotiating table, and through all that nonsense and the strikes and I'm not terribly enthused with unions.

CM: But you're working with . . .

WW: I don't have a choice.

CM: Does it make a difference to you to have the union in here or would you just as soon have it out?

WW: Oh I can live with it . . . I just don't like all the policies and . . . well, there's some personality conflicts there with the people.

DR: Local 511 is pretty lenient compared to any other union.

WW: Yeah, when you look at it in that light . . . this local is not near what you'd call militant as opposed to some. They can be atrocious. Of course, I'm going back 10 years.

CM: Do you see any value in educating the union about worker co-ops?

WW: I don't know how to answer that, because it's so new. We're the first construction co-op in Manitoba and we're not sure what's going to happen.

RK: The role of our union was never discussed in much detail because the shop has to be unionized to work on the sites . . . so there was never any discussion in the interim stage about it.

WW: I don't think the union was ever considered, whether you're taking an employee who's a union member or not.

CM: But people who come in to work with you have to be union members. It is a union shop.

RK: Yes. Every man we hire has to come through the union hall.

DR: If you want a journeyman or an apprentice dispatched to the job they'll just take the first one on top of the list and go down the list. That's how it works, but you can have a guy at the bottom of the list if you know he's unemployed. You can phone the union hall and if you want him dispatched, they'll dispatch him . . . . When we hire a journeyman he's had to serve an apprenticeship for four years. He's got a certified ticket that he's gone through his apprenticeship, he wrote his exam, to be a certified journeyman.

CM: And the work that you do is standard, so you don't have to have a long training period. How would you describe the workers in terms of age and education and background — what's the range?

RK: I guess about 17-18 to . . . what's Hank?

WW: He's going to retire in a couple of years so he's about 62-63.

CM: And you have to retire at 65?

RK: No. We won't insist on it. As long as he's producing. When you're older, you've got the experience, you can teach the youngsters what to do.

CM: Have you had any grievances since you took over? . . . Nothing? Does that imply that things are going pretty well?

RK: Yeah, pretty well. Whatever there is we can handle it, whenever there's a problem it's been looked after.

DR: There's never been anything serious at any time.

CM: Has the feeling around the place changed since you took over as the co-op?

DR: Yeah, it's getting better, the morale is getting better day by day, let's put it that way. We went through growing pains . . . probably more than average.

RK: Don mentioned an owner-type feeling and members had to go back to being workers; from the start some of them've given the impression to the workers beside them that they're boss-type owners. But now they've settled down and everybody's pretty well accepted that they're all working together. If you've got a guy that's on an owner-type deal and he's in the field, well he puts more pressure on the workers because he's got an investment, so he's pushing a little bit — sometimes a little bit too hard, so they resent it. Some we've talked to and some just managed to control themselves, see it themselves that it's not working the way they were. So now this is straightened out, the morale's better.

DR: It wasn't all of them that created problems.

CM: Well it's understandable, if you've got money in a place as well as your sweat you figure . . .

RK: Some of the members are quite young. As a matter of fact one of our members has just finished his first-year apprenticeship . . . . I'm not pointing the finger that he's the one that was causing the problem but the younger members are the ones that maybe had a little bit of a swelled head at first.

CM: Do the members all meet together periodically? You've described the directors' meeting every two weeks and the management meeting.

RK: Up until a month or so the board was meeting quite regular, like once a week. Now we've kind of settled down a bit.

DR: Yeah and then the whole membership group at least once a month.

RK: We're still even trying to keep that fairly regular as well. We're trying to have a board meeting and call the shareholders in so they can sit back and . . . if they want any questions it's more or less open. Right now the board meets on company time. At the start we were meeting on our own time; we figured we can meet after hours, on-our-own-goodwill-type deal, to keep everything going. 'Cause you've got a few that are on the board, they're in the field, so if you pull them off the job, then you've got workers there unsupervised. We're getting things to a point where we can say we're organized again.

CM: What are you dealing with now? What are those meetings about now?

WW: Well we're still trying to get all our policies sorted out. They're not completely sorted out, and we're still dealing with our legal matters. We were incorporated December 16th, as a co-op.

CM: And did that involve a lot of legal nitty-gritty?

DR: A fair amount. Ken and Ed assisted us with it.

CM: What are your plans for the future?

RK: Make this thing work and have a good long holiday.

DR: I took a week's holiday just a couple of weeks ago.

CM: That's a good sign! It's safe to go away!

DR: Well we didn't go too far.

CM: You left your phone number, eh? And what do you foresee in terms of expansion?

DR: That's too far down the road.

RK: There've been so many other new problems . . . .

DR: We are looking into . . . at least in the future we will look into maybe getting into a production line of some kind, supplying pre-constructed units.

RK: We do quite a bit of high velocity systems, dust-collection systems, which is sort of a specialized type of materials and workmanship, and we do it quite well, so it would be one of the things that we would probably go into.

WW: The thing is we've got the men and the machinery to do it, so . . .

DR: One of our pieces of equipment that's kind of unique in the city is our spiral vent machine . . . and there's other things that we can look into — access doors, and . . .

CM: But you haven't had time.

DR: At first, all the suppliers and everybody figured we were a spin-off of Air Flow, just a change of a name. It took us time to convince them that it's a new company altogether.

CM: And is part of that explaining that it's a co-op or do you go into that?

WW: That's never come up. In all my dealings with suppliers it's never been mentioned.

CM: And you don't mention it.

WW: I don't know if I like the connotation . . . workers' co-op. It sounds like I'm in China or Russia or somewhere. I just don't like those two words together. It's definitely true but . . . I just call it the co-op.

CM: I notice in fact on your sign that you are VentAir Industries Co-op. Is that any problem?

RK: We've had no problems. If anything, anybody that we've been associated with has always been more than helpful to us. They realize the problems we had to go through to make this thing happen. They've helped us a lot.

CM: Of course in this part of the country co-op is known . . . the wheat pools, retail co-ops, credit unions . . . and they have a good name . . . they're not fly-by-night operations.

DR: Before the help that we received from the Co-op Development people we had a lot of help from the majority of mechanical contractors that we dealt with. They saved us going under a few times. When we couldn't make the payroll they would advance us the money, pay on a job before it was finished. They showed a lot of trust in us.

RK: All the people that are involved in here, they've been in the trade for a long time . . . . Air Flow was known to be one of the better companies in the city for manufacturing and installation and doing good workmanship so it's the guys that are still involved, it's a spin-off, they know that workmanship, everything is still there. It's the people that make the company's name, the people working for it . . . the contractors we worked with, they recognize that.

CM: Are you guys happy about what you've done? You're feeling really good?

RK: We didn't have time to think about it yet.

CM: Take a minute and a half.

DR: Well we're going to feel good about it, at least I am.

CM: It's been a pretty tense time for you.

RK: What Don and I went through from day one till now — I wouldn't want to wish it on anybody, to go into business that way, but . . . we've held our hand together and we've made it through.

CM: And you don't have conflict between the two of you, you haven't had problems . . .

RK: We've worked before, I guess I started off the trade under Don and that's 20 years ago, so I've worked with him for years. We pretty well knew each other pretty good, right from day one.

CM: Wayne do you foresee any difference in your attitude to the whole thing when you became one of the owners?

WW: No, nothing. As far as I'm concerned it's still a team effort, and that's the most important part.

PART VI
Working Together

CHAPTER EIGHTEEN
Models We Can Use

Where to look for models? What experience to follow in setting up a co-op? First, let's look at varying needs, depending on how groups begin. Raymond Donnelly, director of the Cooperative Education, Research and Training Unit of a university in Derry, Ireland, defines four different ways worker co-ops can grow. Being Irish, he calls them fairy queen, lifeboat, conversion, and ME TOO cooperatives.

He amplifies: "Fairy queen co-ops . . . someone bestows lots of money on them and then waves a magic wand in the false hope that by changing the structure of the enterprise a failed capitalist business will become a successful cooperative." However, "A failed business is a failed business . . . . Cooperation is not a magic wand," and jobs created this way won't last.

Donnelly mentions as one example the Scottish Daily News which closed down in 1975 six months after a major push for conversion, and libations of both government and private money. I haven't heard of any Canadian experience like this.

The lifeboat co-op is more likely to succeed. In a typical example, a branch factory is being closed down by a large company — as when Northern Breweries was put up for sale by Carling O'Keefe, or Epton Industries taken over by senior employees at Goodrich Tire in Kitchener. Another label for lifeboats is phoenix co-ops, because they rise from the ashes. VentAir and Accu-Graphics, the two Winnipeg co-ops presented here, could be seen in this light: one had gone bankrupt, and the other would have folded if the former employees hadn't taken it over.

"Initially, these take-overs are very much job saving moves," writes the Irish historian of cooperatives, "but there is enough evidence, mainly from England and Scotland, to show that it is possible to create a viable worker cooperative . . . . It may well be that the branch factory was already making a small profit, and was being closed down due to adverse results elsewhere in the group; or it might be due to the energy of workers who now have a stake in the firm; whatever the reason — it can work."

The U.S. experience substantiates this conclusion. In Canada Northern Breweries and Epton Industries seem stable and successful — but their worker-owners vote according to value of shares held rather than one-person/one-vote. Baseline Type and Graphics of Vancouver, a "true" co-op taken over from a shaky management, has done well for four years. And the Winnipeg companies, although new, have high and realistic hopes.

In Donnelly's definition of conversion, a successful private enterprise is converted to a worker co-op by its owners. There are not many conversions of this sort. The best known example is the Scott Bader Commonwealth in England, a large chemical and plastic company which was given to its 300 workers in 1951 by its former owner, a Quaker with strong ideas about worker ownership and democracy. A Canadian example of conversion could be the attempted turnover of the liquor stores in Quebec.

Conversions are likely to provide secure, long-term jobs, especially when the transition is accompanied by worker education, so that the new worker-owners are aware of what they're getting into, and can assume responsibility once a benevolent ex-owner has left. Regulation by government or union may also help avoid some potential abuses.

In North America, conversions are more likely to come about because of the need for capital rather than because of benevolence. The boss, or management,recognizes the assets held by the workers, either in pension funds or in private savings, as a source of financing. There have been bad experiences as well as good in this kind of conversion. A more recent motivation for conversions is the trend to privatization by both federal and some provincial governments in Canada. If a government responsibility — like alcohol distribution — can be loaded onto employees, the former employer, as well as the new worker-owners, may all benefit, the theory goes. Conversions are really job preservation, not creation.

The last area of worker co-op formation is genuine enterprise, where a group comes up with an idea for producing goods or services together and decides to pursue it within a cooperative structure. The Irish writer calls these worker co-ops "ME TOO" because usually the group chooses a task or service that is already being done, but they think they can do better. Most small businesses, cooperative or not, begin this way. I prefer to call this type YES WE CAN co-ops. They've also been called bottom-up, whereas most conversions are top-down.

This is the area of greatest potential for new job creation. "Whether they will be long-term jobs will depend largely on the ability of the co-op to solve the problems associated with infant businesses."

How true. The experiences in this book substantiate this dictum. Most Canadian co-ops so far are versions of YES WE CAN. Most of their stories began as visions. The people involved may be a group of disgruntled minority owners in a health food store; idealistic would-be publishers in Vancouver, Toronto or Waterloo; friends and co-workers laid off when a Maritime fish plant closed; or unemployed construction workers in Vancouver and in St. John's, Newfoundland. They shared their dreams and their sweat and ingenuity and a minimum of cash, and created a job for themselves. But as the worker co-op movement thrives here as it has done in other countries and more workers and more managers become aware of employment co-ops as an option, more conversions and more lifeboats are likely to come about.

I would like to look at four models that may give us some direction for our cooperatives in Canada. The first is Mondragon, the by-now legendary worker cooperative in Spain. Mondragon is visited by every group of self-educating cooperators in pursuit of support and of ideas, and is the subject of a laudatory BBC film which has been shown on videotape as a come-on at just about every worker co-op formation meeting. Mondragon itself is in the YES WE CAN category, and is most valuable to groups who visualize their work activity in a cooperative structure, and to resource groups hoping to increase their effectiveness.

The O & O (Owned and Operated) experience would be especially useful for both lifeboats and conversions. In it, the employees' union local took the initiative to save 2,000 jobs when the Great Atlantic and Pacific Tea Company (A & P) planned to fold most of their stores in the core of Philadelphia.

The Industrial Common Ownership Movement in Great Britain receives most of its enquiries from YES WE CAN cooperatives, and has developed a system for shepherding them through to operation.

And finally, it would be useful to look at a typically Canadian model, used by the cooperative housing movement in Canada. Many observers have pointed out that worker co-ops are at about the same stage — conceptually, in terms of actual experience, and in the public mind — that co-op housing was 20 years ago. There have been two key elements in the successful development of cooperative housing in Canada since then. One is that mortgage loans have been guaranteed by the federal government for housing development and construction. The other is a well organized network of volunteers and resource groups across the country. This model could benefit all three of the worker co-op types we're likely to see in Canada: YES WE CANs, conversions and lifeboats.

Mondragon

Mondragon is a whole community of worker/consumer/credit/educational/social service/research cooperatives in an area of the Spanish Basque country around the small town of Mondragon. There are 160 co-ops in the Mondragon system, 100 of them industrial enterprises, and they employ 20,000 people. This represents over 10 percent of the workers in the area and half the work force in the town of Mondragon. In 1983, they had sales of about $1 billion.

Mondragon developed in the 1950s and 60s under the stimulus and philosophy of a remarkable local curate, Don Jose Maria Arismendi. In 1943, Arismendi, charged with unifying the town's 10,000 people, divided and wounded by the Spanish Civil War, set up a professional technical school to fill a gap in the educational system in the area. Workers from the town's large metal-working industry became night students. In 1956, five of the graduates, following Arismendi's ideals, tried to democratize their work place. Their employer wasn't interested, and when they talked with the curate, he advised a cooperative. With his advice and encouragement, they borrowed $5,000 from friends and bought the workshop of an electric stove manufacturing company in a town nearby. They founded ULGOR, the first industrial co-op in the Mondragon group.

The enterprise flourished and grew. It changed the stoves to butane gas burning and extended the market. As the co-op grew, it budded off other cooperatives, to do parts of the manufacturing and feed into the parent. It started a small consumer co-op.

In 1960, it founded a credit union called the Caja Laboral Popular (Bank of the Peoples' Labour) to mobilize local savings as capital for the co-ops. The Caja became the focal point for the movement and the reason for its phenomenal success since.

Greg MacLeod, an economics teacher at the University College of Cape Breton, is one of the many students of the cooperative movement who has visited Mondragon in the last five years. In a book, *New Age Business: Community Corporations That Work,* he relates the story of one of the most recently established enterprises at Mondragon, Ikus. It gives us a context in which to see how Mondragon works.

Ikus started with a group of 10 unemployed people from a nearby town who got together to look for a way to find work. They went to the Entrepreneurial Division of the credit union and began a process that would last five years. With a development officer of the Caja, they discussed and studied what they might do. Together, they chose a manager, and each put up an amount equivalent to a third of a year's salary for an unskilled worker, about $6,000. Those who did not have the cash borrowed it from the credit union, to be repaid over two years in installments from their salary when the business got underway. They purposely chose a manager who had no experience with the product, so that he would be open to new ways. He took a one-year training program in the Entrepreneurial Division of the Caja, and with their technical advisors and the group he looked at different possible products like furniture and bicycles. They settled finally on eyeglass frames, which previously had been imported into Spain at high prices. As part of the product investigation, they visited eyeglass factories in Europe, the U.S. and Japan. They picked a French firm to work with, obtained a licence to produce and contracted for the technology and assistance they needed.

At the same time, the group made market surveys, feasibility studies and business plans. For these, it could buy the services of the Centro de Investigaciones Technologicas, a cooperative with about 50 members which provides research and development for the system. The reports were turned over to the Financial Division of the credit union, and after its approval, the group was incorporated as Ikus XXI. The start-up capital was made up by the original shares of the member-workers, a small start-up loan from the Spanish government at 3 percent interest for 10 years, and a loan of about $30,000 from the Caja at 8 percent (compared to the market rate of about 18 percent).

All the expenses, including the salary of the apprentice manager, were costed to the project. If the project had not gone on, the credit union would have made them a grant of up to $50,000 to cover the expenses. Anything over that amount would have been paid by the group itself. Since it was incorporated, the expenses were costed as a loan. The development and technical help given by the credit union was donated, and in return the new co-op agreed to give 10 percent of its profits to the credit union during its first five years. This donation would be used by the Caja to support the next group asking for help.

About one in ten of the projects suggested to the Caja are chosen for development, and four or five a year are incorporated. The average size of an established industrial cooperative is 200, with a maximum of 500 set because of the emphasis on friendly relations between the workers, although ULGOR has over 3,000 workers.

The new co-op set its own wage rates, equal to or a little higher than rates for comparable jobs in the area. The minimum is set by the Caja, and the highest paid worker usually only makes three times that of the lowest. (In Canada the ratio is over 100 to 1.)

After all this preparation, Ikus began operations on as small a scale as possible, in rented space, with low operating expenses. With time, they increased their scale of operations and their costs, and the Entrepreneurial

Division continued to advise, providing a "godfather," a management expert to advise during the first few years.

In the future, the Caja would audit their books every three years, and they would submit a yearly budget and monthly financial statements. These would become part of the financial planning of the central funding agency, the Caja, and if serious deviations from the annual budget should come up on the computer, the credit union would request permission from the Ikus board to intervene.

The unemployment rate for the Basque region is 20 percent, but as members of a Mondragon co-op, Ikus workers can count on secure lifetime employment. If, because of technological or market changes, their work is not needed, they can transfer to another co-op or go back to the cooperative school for retraining. If the enterprise should become shaky — unlikely after the careful study at the beginning — the Caja would reinvest in a new product line. Only one co-op has ceased operations in Mondragon's 30 years.

When Ikus begins to make a profit, the surplus will be distributed as follows: 10 percent for educational and social services; 50 percent to Mondragon reserves; 40 percent to the members' accounts in the cooperative. This last 40 percent cannot be taken out until retirement or death. With the initial share contribution made by each member, it represents the member's financial investment in the cooperative, and it grows according to the success of the member's own group.

On retirement, each member receives an annual pension equal to 60 percent of his wages in the last 60 months of work. He also receives back his original share plus his annual share in profits, with interest of six percent. This usually comes to between $30,000 and $60,000. If he leaves Mondragon before retirement, he receives his accumulated share plus interest over a period of time which does not jeopardise the co-op's financial stability.

Every Mondragon member has a vote in the General Assembly, which normally meets only once a year. Sixty-five to 70 percent of the workers turn out to elect a Board of Directors of six to twelve members, who meet once a month to supervise the business and to appoint a general manager. There are no trade unions in the Mondragon system. Each department, consisting of about 20 workers, elects a member to the Social Council. This group is responsible for workers' concerns, and interacts with both the general manager and the Board of Directors.

The story of Ikus illustrates the importance of the Caja as the basic development and financing agent at Mondragon. Nearly 400,000 families make deposits in its banking outlets in four Basque provinces. Today, the Caja invests 35 percent of its funds in Mondragon co-op; the rest it invests on the market at higher rates, thereby subsidizing the co-op movement. It

is the Caja's management section which is pivotal to Mondragon's success and stability. Every cooperative in the system forms a contract of association with the Caja, agreeing to eight provisions:
— democratic self-government
— efficient management
— management-worker solidarity in each enterprise
— capital contribution by all worker-members, with limited return on capital and regulated profit distribution
— job security, and standards of work behaviour and discipline
— solidarity and coordination between co-op groups
— solidarity with local communities and with non-co-op workers and enterprises in the neighbourhood
— open-door policies to encourage maximum job creation rather than concentrate on internal development.

A recent Canadian visitor, Chris Axworthy, director of the Centre for the Study of Co-operatives at the University of Saskatchewan, has made some criticisms of Mondragon. The most important seem to me that in the emphasis on economic efficiency by the Caja, the co-op spirit is flickering, and that Caja representatives are paternalistic and look down on the "peasant" work force. He sees an analogy with the head office of a large multi-unit corporation. I look forward to a visit myself, to check out these impressions. Visitor Greg MacLeod has another conclusion:

> One element striking me personally is that there was a handful of dedicated people who *assumed* leadership. This small group moved from one management position to another in the complex. They were and remain extremely dedicated and have a system of values which they owe to their teacher, Don Jose Maria. Through such actions as accepting low salaries they proved to their community they were dedicated. The community responded with tremendous support . . . .

Canadian resource groups like Co-operative Work in Toronto and Common Ownership Development Association (CODA) in Vancouver could be envious of the research and development co-op alone. Likewise, Canadian credit unions which are serious about encouraging new initiatives could look seriously at the Caja operation. But of course we must remember that Mondragon is rooted in the culture and history of the Basque country. It is not exportable holus bolus. Even so, the spirit and some of the wisdom gained from the practical experience, as well as some of the organizational features, could be exportable.

O & Os and PACE

Philadelphia's O & O (Owned and Operated) was a lifeboat take-over, organized from the bottom up. O & O has become as significant to the Canadian worker co-op movement as Mondragon. Representatives of PACE, the Philadelphia Association for Cooperative Enterprise, instrumental in the take-over, participated at two symposiums organized in Saskatoon in 1985 by the Centre for the Study of Co-operatives and Co-op College, and were called in to advise during the evolution of the Manitoba Co-operative Development program. They have also talked to Canadian Labour Congress leaders. The A & P supermarket chain made a surprise announcement at the end of February 1982 that it was shutting down almost the entire Philadelphia division. This would have put nearly 2,000 people out of work. The United Food and Commercial Workers Union local was not unprepared, but it had to act faster than it had contemplated.

The UFCW had already explored employee ownership as a response to increasing job loss, and to a threat to privatize the state liquor store system. It had contacted PACE, which has provided public education about worker ownership in the area since 1977, and technical help to worker-owned businesses since 1980. The union had commissioned feasibility studies on some A & P stores, and had considered the best ownership form. It had rejected Employee Stock Ownership Plans (ESOPs), despite their popularity since U.S. tax law changes beginning in 1974.

In a typical deal, an ESOP trust fund buys the stock of a company and allocates shares among employees, usually on the basis of salary and/or seniority. The stock and the dividends are tax-free until the employee leaves or retires, when the shares are handed over. Until then, the trust fund owns the stock, and the trustees cast the stockholders' votes.

In most cases the trustees are chosen by the financiers who lent the money to buy the shares. They therefore tend to be dominated by management, bankers, and their lawyers. Only about 30 percent of all ESOPs give voting rights to the workers. The UFCW union was worried about the lack of worker control in voting their stock, lack of worker representation on the board of directors, disproportionate distribution of stock to management, and pension and wage concessions.

ESOPs *can* be more than a tax dodge and a cheap way to raise capital, and they can be used by worker co-ops and to bring about more worker participation in private corporation management. But the union chose to go for one-worker/one-vote in a worker cooperative. Under U.S. tax laws, the co-op would also have a tax break, since corporate profits distributed to the workers on the basis of labour participation are tax-deductible.

When the company announced that it was closing within 20 days, the union made a block bid for 21 of the best stores. It commissioned PACE to educate the workers in the fundamentals of worker co-op operation, and asked for $5,000 each as worker equity towards purchasing the stores. Six hundred people attended the classes and made the pledge. PACE also held a regional employee ownership conference to educate local government officials and lending institutions.

More than a month after the offer, A & P countered with another suggestion. They would reopen the closed supermarkets, re-employing the laid off workers, who would take a 20 percent reduction in pay, but with some concessions to employee participation. If any of the new stores, called Super Fresh Food Centres, were to close, the employees would have an option to buy them at a fair market price. And finally, PACE would open two of the closed stores as fully worker-owned.

A core group of about 50 workers participated in the foundation of the two worker cooperative stores. They continued their training with PACE for another seven months, meeting three times a week in large store committees and in eight smaller working committees dealing with by-laws and legal structure, governance, union role and personnel policies, worker and management selection, financing and business planning, and worker education.

One worker-owned grocery store opened in October 1982 with 25 worker-owners, the other in November with 20. They paid themselves $8 an hour, the same as their colleagues at the Super Fresh stores. Each worker contributed $5,000 towards the initial financing, some of them borrowing their stake from the union's credit union. Additional financing was arranged by PACE.

Within a year, a third O & O was opened, this time built from the ground up in a densely populated and under-serviced part of the city. Again the 58 workers each made a $5,000 capital contribution. Part time workers contributed $2,500 and other financing came from the Philadelphia National Bank. After the first four years of operation, they qualify for a 12 percent return on their capital share, plus a share of any profits. They decided to have as many full time employees as possible. The ratio of full time to part time employees is double the grocery industry average.

Although separately incorporated, the three O & Os are linked through an umbrella association which provides common services. The corporate HQ is a back room of one of the stores. The O & O chain plans to expand — a PACE director predicts ten more supermarkets within five years; two of them may be opened this year. The umbrella concept was borrowed from the Mondragon system — the local union had seen the BBC film too.

The experiment wasn't all pie. The O & O worker-owners had to learn how to order goods and to avoid overstocking. They sometimes quarrelled among themselves about authority. But eventually they adjusted, and productivity and work satisfaction went up.

Cooperative Development Agencies

Worker cooperatives increased three-fold in Britain in four years, from 305 in 1980 to 911 in 1984. Now there are well over 1,000. The reasons? The Industrial Common Ownership Movement (ICOM) and the associated Cooperative Development Agencies.

ICOM is the umbrella organization for worker cooperatives. It received some statutory recognition with the Industrial Common Ownership Act, passed in 1976, which provided £250,000 a year to promote cooperatives and establish a revolving loan fund. ICOM produced model by-laws and encouraged worker co-op formation and development with education and advice and by lobbying national and local governments for supportive legislation.

ICOM's financial arm, Industrial Common Ownership Finance, administers the loan fund including, on contract, funds from local governments. Its role is not as pervasive as that of the Caja in Mondragon, but it does work with new cooperatives during formation and monitors progress after incorporation.

In 1978, the government set up the Cooperative Development Agency (CDA) to act as a national body to promote and help worker cooperatives, and there are now about 100 local CDAs, about half of them employing full time development officers. A few have staff of up to seven, but most are smaller. Applying ICOM principles, they are the major support available to the worker co-op sector in the U.K. It was the CDAs that put teeth into the Industrial Common Ownership Act, according to Chris Axworthy, director of the University of Saskatchewan Centre for the Study of Co-operatives, after a European study tour in 1984.

British worker cooperatives tend to be labour intensive and small (under ten members) although some have hundreds of workers. Almost all of them have organized from the bottom up, with a group of workers initiating their own enterprise, and meeting with CDA officers to plan, assess the market, develop a business plan, arrange finances, find space, and register as a cooperative. If the group needs a lot of guidance, the CDA worker may act as a manager at the beginning, training members to take over.

In a small study done by the Cooperatives Research Unit at the Open University at Milton Keynes, the percentage of groups that eventually did set up a cooperative after starting development with a CDA varied from 17 percent to a third. Almost all the CDAs in the pilot study provided formal courses on how to start and run a cooperative, but the researchers concluded that the courses were not very important in the development process. ICOM rules require a nominal investment of one pound from each member, rather than the substantial share required at Mondragon (although recently workers have been encouraged to make voluntary loans to their enterprises). The rule expresses the belief that workers should hire capital to work for them, not let capital dominate them. In other words, the emphasis of worker co-ops should be on the job and the working environment, not on return on money investment, and membership should be open to anyone, whether they have money to invest or not. This means that the money for local CDAs comes almost entirely from public funds, and that for capitalization, cooperatives depend on loans from different government levels. Since there is no individual equity, an advantage is that worker shares are collectively held and cannot be withdrawn.

Rejecting the use of share capital from its workers may also result in low pay at the start. Some ICOM enterprises are experimenting with considering as a loan to the co-op the difference between wages received and the market rate of pay.

Dependence on local governments for funding is dicey because of the Thatcher government policy of closing them down, which would, according to Axworthy, have a devastating effect on the worker co-op movement in Britain's inner cities. There are moves to set up funds separate from the county and city councils that could survive the demise of the super councils.

Loans to worker co-ops are heavily subsidized. Normally there is a one-year interest-and-principle holiday, and then interest is charged at 5 percent, usually for five years.

For instance, the London Cooperative Enterprise Board (LCEB) was set up to be the worker co-op bank in London. Its function is to lend up to $40,000 and make grants of up to $3,500. In a monograph after his 1984 study tour, Axworthy listed the requirements of the LCEB for funding. They include:

— the group must be registered as a co-op
— 75 percent of the work force and all the non-probationary workers must be members
— the entrance fee for membership must be no more than 10 percent of the co-op member's average annual wage
— probationary conditions for new employees should be reasonable
— if the co-op dissolves, the assets must go to another co-op or to a central fund

— it must follow ICOM guidelines
— it must be an equal opportunity employer
— trade union access must be guaranteed to all members.

There are worker cooperatives in Britain outside the Industrial Common Ownership Movement, but the vast majority come under its umbrella. Its value is indicated by statistics for two years, from 1980 to 1982. In areas without Cooperative Development Agencies, the number of cooperatives increased 24 percent, and the number of jobs in cooperatives increased 7 percent. In areas that did have the support of CDAs, the increase was much more: 131 percent for cooperatives and 56 percent for jobs in them. The Open University pilot study suggests that many co-ops would not have been set up without CDA help. Moreover, the cost to a local council for staff salaries and expenses comes to about $4,000 per job created, compared to $80,000 per job created by other British programs!

Canadian Cooperative Housing Movement

We can look closer to home than Europe, Britain or across the border for a useful model. We can look to the cooperative housing movement in Canada. Enormously successful on several levels, providing top-quality affordable housing for 150,000 Canadians in over 35,000 units, almost all this cooperatively held housing was built within the last 20 years. It was done, after the first few courageous pilot projects, through effective local development offices, a nation-wide network of volunteers and resource groups, and a close and fruitful if sometimes uneasy link with the federal government.

This is a movement that worker co-ops might envy and emulate for its success in reaching its basic goal. It is also one which even within its bureaucracy has retained the spirit of cooperation and has provided at least a base for the formation of worker cooperative and resource groups in the newer movement. It organized study tours in 1981 and 1984 to British and European worker cooperatives, including Mondragon and the Industrial Common Ownership Movement. Many of the people in Canada who are now playing an active role in worker co-op resource groups took these tours. CODA in Vancouver, Communitas in Edmonton, and Communityworks in Ottawa all either operate out of provincial or city co-op housing offices, or gain support in some way, with loan of personnel or money or advice. The growing worker co-op movement in the Maritimes is being nourished from the same Continuing Education offices at St. Francis Xavier University in Antigonish which helped get people together to build their own houses in the 1930s.

These building co-ops in the Maritimes, and others in Saskatchewan, Ontario and Quebec were the forerunners of the cooperative housing network we have today. Once each house was built, it reverted to the private owner/builder and the cooperative was dissolved. The first "continuing" house co-ops were the Campus Co-op Residences, houses renovated for students at the University of Toronto. They were followed in 1965 by Willow Park, a complex of family homes built and held cooperatively in Winnipeg.

In 1968 the Canadian Labour Congress, the Co-operative Union of Canada, and the Canadian Union of Students joined to form the Co-operative Housing Foundation of Canada (CHF). This was the beginning of the network that was to organize, educate, nurture and lobby. It was joined by regional groups who could do the job on a local level. These resource groups were partly funded by a federal government agency, Canada Mortgage and Housing Corporation (CMHC), for their first three years, until they were able to survive on fees for service from the housing sector. Now, their fees are built into the mortgages.

There are now 60 local non-profit federations, associations and resource groups which have had federal government grants to springboard their work. Most of them belong to the CHF. Other members of the national body include individual housing co-ops, sponsoring organizations like the CLC, the United Church of Canada, the Co-operators, Credit Union Central of Ontario, and a number of large trade unions. The regional organizations and the CHF are still figuring out how they can work together more effectively.

In 1973, mostly as a result of CHF lobbying, the National Housing Act was amended to provide financing for non-profit continuing co-ops. At that time, there were 10 family housing co-ops across Canada. Within four years there were 60. The movement continued to increase, helped by a new federal financing program, until the last few years, when government input slowed to a trickle. CHF and the resource groups looked at ways to reduce government costs in the program. Their proposal, for "index-linked mortgages" is now being put into practice. With these modifications, CMHC has agreed to approve up to 5,000 new units a year.

Now, when a group decides they want to initiate a co-op housing project, they usually approach one of the local resource groups or associations. The initial core group may be sponsored by a service club, a credit union or an ethnic group, or they may just be friends. They present their ideas in an interview with a development coordinator, who will talk to them about cooperatives and what is involved in a project: it must be non-profit, 15 percent of the units must be rent supplemented for low-income households, and certain technical guidelines must be followed. At this stage the group is eligible for some preliminary risk financing from CMHC: up to $10,000 for a feasibility study and to learn how to produce and manage the project. During Phase II, they may have an additional $65,000 to bring the project to the stage of CMHC commitment.

These funds are capitalized in the mortgage when the project goes ahead. At this stage, the group has what may seem like endless discussions. They have to make decisions about site, name, policies about occupancy guidelines, pets, parking, and find more people to participate in the building and then the maintenance of the cooperative. They have to decide if they will hire staff, including a coordinator, and who that will be.

The ownership of the project rests with the co-op corporation. Members of the co-op, who develop and who eventually live in it, have no financial equity in it. To join the developing group, they pay a nominal fee, usually around $10, which covers no more than the cost of periodic bulletins and notices of meetings. When they sign their contract before moving in, they buy a share roughly equal to one month's housing charge, which is refunded when they move out. And they pay monthly housing charges to cover the cost of mortgage payments, municipal taxes, maintenance, replacement reserves and administration. Since it is a cooperative, there is no profit margin.

The co-op is financed under the federal government program administered by CMHC, which insures the mortgage for 100 percent of the capital cost. CMHC also provides assistance to allow the co-op to charge market rents and may provide rent supplements for low-income households. The CMHC backing has been vital to the growth of the cooperative housing movement, but nevertheless it is no more than has been provided for other types of private and public housing in other federal programs.

The absence of equity in housing cooperatives was deliberate. It is what makes this form of housing tenure different from individual ownership and condominiums. It makes the housing affordable for low- and moderate-income earners. And it eliminates the factor of return on investment. Housing charges only go up as actual costs go up; they can be kept down by volunteer activity. And the members collect nothing but their small original share when they move out; there is no capital increase.

CHF, the national body, maintains a Co-operative Assistance Fund, a Risk Underwriting Fund and other special-purpose funds to ensure the sector's continued growth and health. And an important component is their education program, which includes courses on co-op housing management and member services.

The default rate on cooperative housing mortgages is practically nil. CHF research coordinator Nick Van Dyke could only think of two in the whole country, one which had been developed by CMHC with no co-op sector involvement, and one in an isolated community which itself lost its economic base and closed up.

Why did I choose to look at these four models? Because each one of them takes care of two elements that have been stumbling blocks in the development of worker cooperatives in most parts of Canada. These are start-up financing, and management advice and support. There are differences in the way these needs are answered, but they are addressed in each model.

At Mondragon, the Caja collects the savings of the thrifty peasants in the area and, with shrewd investment of two-thirds of the money and worker equity supplemented by re-invested profits, can independently finance new co-ops at much less than market rates. The O & Os in Philadelphia also depend on worker equity, with union backing for financing from the conventional banking system. Both the British Industrial Common Ownership Movement and the Canadian co-op housing movement have discouraged member equity, and have depended on government funding and guarantees to back conventional loans. In Britain, grants and subsidies and interest-free loans are all available to worker cooperatives.

The other big need, voiced again and again in my interviews, is for advice and support. At Mondragon it is again the Caja, along with the research co-op, that responds. In Britain, it is ICOM and the government-funded Cooperative Development Agencies. For the O & O's, the Philadelphia Association for Cooperative Enterprise along with private consultants serve this purpose. And in the Canadian cooperative housing movement, the Co-operative Housing Foundation and the local groups provide support.

In Canada, worker co-ops in most provinces struggle from credit union to bank, looking for start-up funding. The luxury of deciding whether or not they should count on worker equity is never offered to them — their own pockets and those of relatives and friends are turned inside out. In Quebec and in Manitoba they are lucky — they can, if accepted, count on government-guaranteed loans. They can also count on the government departments for developmental advice and support, which in other provinces they have to squeeze out of underpaid or voluntary resource groups or worker co-ops who have made it. The next chapter looks at the developing network of resource groups in Canada. These associations are attempts to support the burgeoning worker co-op movement.

CHAPTER NINETEEN
Looking for Support

Worker co-ops in Canada have been local self help with a vengeance — begun by workers to create jobs for themselves, and with little or no outside support. There is no federal agency which does more than collect statistics on the trend — the federal Minister responsible for liaison with the cooperative sector had not, as of September 1986, replied to the Report of the National Task Force on Co-operative Development. This was submitted to him in May 1984 by the Co-operative Union of Canada (CUC) and the Conseil canadien de la coopération, the English- and French-language associations of national cooperatives.

That report was modest enough. In three recommendations related to worker co-ops, it asked for:

— a support system to help worker cooperatives, created under the direction of the co-op system in partnership with federal and provincial governments

— an implementation steering committee with representatives from the established co-op movement and worker cooperatives to develop models and guidelines for worker co-op development, to examine the legislative environment, and to formulate a plan for the creation of regionally based worker co-op development assistance agencies

— the government of Canada to endorse worker co-ops as a priority vehicle for employment generation. This would involve joint funding assistance to the co-op movement for the steering committee, for regional development assistance agencies, and for a pool of start-up funds or guarantees for individual employee-owned co-ops.

These three recommendations were among a total of 32 dealing with the co-op movement in general. The CUC itself has made tentative moves in the first two directions. As for the third, asking for federal support, Charles Mayer, the federal Minister with responsibility for co-ops, said at a 1985 conference in Saskatoon ". . . governments should not be a major supplier of financial resources. It will be my job . . . to see that the cooperative movement and employment cooperatives get the same kind of consideration and understanding and breaks from government that other sectors do."

So far, that hasn't happened. It would mean an overhaul of employment and tax legislation to make business development assistance and regional development programs accessible to worker co-ops, and to treat co-ops the same as other common corporate entities.

At present, under existing tax legislation, employment cooperatives are not treated like other small business. Some tax deductions are denied employee-owners. Moreover, co-ops are not necessarily treated as Canadian-controlled private corporations for tax purposes.

Co-ops trying to fit themselves into the established system have met more frustration than success so far. Most have received no help at all, neither funding nor advice. Federal government counsellors from the Department of Regional Industrial Expansion, used to dealing with one boss and many subordinates, have usually been confused and retreated with the advice that the co-op reorganize as a private business.

"Not worth the trouble," says Elizabeth Abraham, Dreadnaught Publishing Company's general manager. The Big Carrot health food store, on the other hand, has benefitted from Federal Business Development Bank seminars. The Bank lent them $50,000 for eight years at one percent above the prime rate for start-up, and it also lent Dumont Press about $12,000 for funding. However, most of the other worker co-ops I talked with have either been refused a loan by FBDB, or have been able to get the money at the same or better interest elsewhere.

"A guarantee on a larger bank loan would really have helped us out," says Mary Lou Morgan, The Big Carrot manager at the time it got under way. "That would have relieved the stress on those of us who had to take out personal loans."

The Canadian Sealers Association had more than $300,000 of federal government money for planning and organizing, but that was to save an industry and the livelihood of the fishermen; the formation of the worker cooperative was incidental.

Two co-ops I went to depended on Local Economic Assistance Program (LEAP) grants administered by Employment and Immigration Canada for their original funding. CRS, the Vancouver natural food wholesaler, had $100,000 and Fiddlehead Restaurant in Thunder Bay had $623,000, both over three years. The capital was vital to their start, but the contact left both groups seething with indignation, frustration, and battered self-esteem. The LEAP administration was erratic, autocratic and unrealistically and wastefully demanding. The last thing they seemed to consider was the eventual successful independence of the co-op.

The CRS crew was strong enough to stand up to the local representative, to use the grant and then make it on their own. Fiddlehead was saddled with too many goals, some of them imposed by LEAP, and the conflicting and wasteful demands helped speed the collapse of the co-op.

As for help from the provinces, only four Canadian provinces — Quebec, Saskatchewan, Manitoba and Newfoundland — actively encourage co-op development. The first three have specific programs to promote worker co-ops.

A major reason for the incredible growth of worker co-ops in Quebec — the provincial Ministry of Industry and Commerce supports their development with technical assistance, financing and legislation. While they were in power, the Parti Quebecois government set up government-sponsored consultant groups in 10 regions throughout the province, and the Liberals have not so far curtailed the program. They have nearly doubled the number of worker co-ops during their first few years, with an emphasis on jobs for young entrepreneurs 18 to 30 years of age.

Another government agency, the Société de développement des coop-ératives (SDC) has designed a financial assistance program for new worker cooperatives. It offers low interest rates, and guarantees workers' investment in the business for 5 or even 10 years. In addition, Quebec began in 1985 to grant tax benefits for investment in worker co-ops. Shareholders qualify for a tax advantage equal to 10 percent of their investment. Under the program, most co-ops can issue preferred shares bearing interest to a fixed, maximum, non-cumulative rate payable at a time set by the administrators of the program.

Quebec legislation was changed in 1983 and 1984 to encourage worker co-ops and it has become a model for other provinces. The Quebec Cooperatives Act now includes a separate chapter on worker co-ops, sets the minimum number of founders required to form a worker co-op at three, and makes it easy for a company to convert to a co-op while remaining a private corporation, and without capital gains taxation. It also promotes the sale of companies to workers by small business owners who are preparing to retire by permitting workers to form a cooperative to acquire and hold the shares, and to buy it out over a period of years.

In Quebec, there are a number of separate private resource groups, as well as the government-sponsored SDC and 10 regional councils. And the province's Desjardins caisse populaire federation is promoting the formation of peoples' councils in several communities. In them, retired people will use their expertise to help the unemployed start and operate their own small businesses, including cooperatives.

The English-speaking province that offers the most practical help in worker cooperative formation is Manitoba. Last year, the province cleaned up their legislation to make worker co-op establishment easier, and the Department of Co-operative Development took on staff who nurture — sometimes nurse — new groups through worker education, incorporation, initial financing, and any other problems they may face. Since the changes, 11 "employment cooperatives," as the Manitoba government calls them, have been incorporated. Fifteen more are in stages of incorporation.

Two worker co-ops that I added to my initial list, VentAir Industries Co-op Ltd., and Accu-Graphics, were both protegees of Co-operative Development, and without its input it's unlikely they would be operating today. Both were "phoenix-type" organizations, revived by the employees from the ashes of threatened closure. In fact, VentAir was purchased from the receivers after a bankruptcy, although the plant was never shut down. Both were and still are unionized, but the union did not play any part in the take-overs.

Ken Bourquin, a cooperative development consultant with the Manitoba department, took me to both places. He had incorporated both businesses, and he was obviously trusted and relied on.

Bourquin's job begins the minute a group contacts the department. Often they have little sense of what worker co-ops are all about. Usually they are looking for funding and have heard that the department guarantees start-up loans arranged through banks or credit unions — a tremendous boost for any small business. Bourquin uses a set of standard by-laws developed by the department as a teaching tool. He meets with the group and "walks" them through each section, defining terms, clarifying principles, and stimulating discussion as they proceed. Some groups decide early in the game that a cooperative is not the way they want to go — a partnership or an individual business is more appropriate for them.

The charter by-laws developed by the group must be approved by the Co-operative Act Registrar and some requirements must be met. For instance, 50 percent of the workers must be members, and 50 percent of the members must be workers. The department recommends that two-thirds of the workers be members, but they allow flexibility in case seasonal help is needed. The one-member/one-vote rule is basic, but in a few cases a member who can make a special contribution may not be a worker.

Across Canada, banks and trust companies tend to treat worker cooperatives with the same wariness they treat any small business — and sometimes with added reluctance if they learn early that no one individual actually *owns* the enterprise. Toronto's Big Carrot is an example. It is phenomenally successful, doubling money intake from one to two million dollars in the second year of operation, filling a timely, growing and well surveyed need, with a practised and cohesive staff of 25, good management, foresightful planning, and a professionally developed business plan. Nevertheless, The Big Carrot was still having trouble raising the money for its next expansion. The reason? "Not enough equity."

Credit unions and caisses populaires are theoretically more receptive. The Big Carrot has in fact received funding from Bread and Roses Credit Union in Toronto, one financial institution with a policy and a practice of backing grass roots cooperative ventures. But its resources are themselves limited, and it could not put up the $300,000 needed for a venture that would house not only The Big Carrot, but other complementary enterprises.

Vancouver City Savings Credit Union has established a community ventures office with access to a small amount of seed capital — half a million dollars — and will give some development assistance to fledgling entrepreneurs. VanCity hopes to shepherd ten projects through the program this year, two of them worker co-ops.

The question of who develops the developing agents — who cares for the caregiver — was raised at the forum where VanCity announced its new Local Economic Development Centre. Cooperative- and community-based economic development needs organizational and technical help as well as money, and VanCity is not prepared to offer these. The question was not answered.

Despite these bright lights, credit unions and caisses populaires are usually as conservative as the banks they were organized to supplant. But saddest of all, the established cooperatives have so far failed to recognize that the worker co-op movement is at a stage where they were 50 years ago. They could be the same people, with the same preoccupation with how to survive with integrity and at the same time help others in the same plight. But the big producer cooperatives like the wheat pools, and the consumer cooperatives like United Cooperatives of Ontario and The Co-operators insurance company, have not offered support. They have not yet given financial backing, nor business advice, nor purchased goods and services from the worker co-ops.

There are signs of awakening — Co-operative Union of Canada members, including the biggies mentioned above, re-endorsed their own earlier recommendations to support worker co-ops at the 1986 annual general meeting.

What is true is that the worker co-ops themselves, while struggling to solve their problems and find a firm footing, have lent each other a hand. Big, well established co-ops like CRS in Vancouver have answered questions like the ones I asked in our interview countless times. Sometimes they've visited developing groups to give advice. They've put out a brochure, "What is a Worker Co-op Anyway?" And they make their boardroom available to new groups in the discussion stages. But they have their own committees to attend, and their daily bread to make. As a result of the vacuum, what we have is a loose network of support groups across Canada. Each group has a different flavour, depending on local conditions, and operates in a different way.

My own group in Ottawa, which for three years has met as Cooperative Enterprises, has functioned as a support group in that time. Six to nine of us have met at intervals varying from once a week to once a month, to talk about what we ourselves wanted to do as a worker cooperative, and how we could contribute to the movement. Our membership included an economist, a social worker, a computer consultant, a bookkeeper, myself as a writer and editor, and at times, an inventor, an accountant, an urban planner, and a biochemist.

We wrote a business plan for the inventor, who was developing a device to convert apartment balconies into sunrooms. We did a market study to see if we should develop the taped interviews this book is based on into teaching tools for other co-op groups. And we did a lot of listening and handed out a lot of free advice to other groups in eastern Ontario who were thinking about similar developing worker co-ops, and to non-governmental organizations like Oxfam, who are already working to stimulate cooperative development internationally, and want to keep in touch with the Canadian scene. At the same time, we supported each other. At times, several of us were unemployed. Others were over-employed, too much used up in daily or contract jobs and trying to contin-ue community work at the same time. In either case, we lent emotional support and assurance that there *were* alternative ways to work.

We have developed the concept of a core cooperative organization, which would encourage the formation of daughter co-ops in the fields we were interested in: writing and editing, social research, organization develop-ment, housing co-op management, etc. We are in the process of incorpo-rating under the title "Bespoke Cooperative Enterprises," taking the word "bespoke" from the English meaning of custom-made. Our first paid-for job was a brochure for Peacefund Canada, an offshoot of the International Council for Adult Education.

Toronto's Co-operative Work Ltd. and the Worker Ownership Develop-ment Foundation (WODF) evolved differently. These two groups were incorporated separately in 1985 with an overlapping membership of 20 to 25 and the same goal: to push, shove and stimulate worker co-op develop-ment. Many of the members are academics, but they include lawyers and economists and accountants and some actual members of worker co-ops. WODF now has a staff of four- or five-plus volunteers. It is a charitable, non-profit educational foundation. Its goal is to educate Canadians about the economic and social benefits of worker co-ops, and to provide educa-tional tools to members of existing worker co-ops and people interested in start-ups and conversions.

In 1986, WODF has three basic projects underway, all government-oriented. It is preparing a proposal to the Ontario government for detailed amendments to the Co-operative Corporations Act. Those proposed changes should, according to WODF coordinator Ethan Phillips, be passed within six months. They have the backing of the co-op movement in general, and even the provincial government itself recognizes that the present legislation is obsolete. Second, it is proposing an Ontario finan-cial assistance program which would incorporate elements of the British, Quebec and Manitoba programs with some suggestions of their own. The 20-page submission is going the rounds of church groups for review. It will be submitted to the Ontario Ministry of Consumer and Commercial

Relations, which administers the Co-operative Corporations Act and may take an advocacy role in promoting the program. The submission suggests tax credits for worker co-ops, loan guarantees, funding for up-front feasibility studies, and core funding for resource groups.

Finally, WODF is writing a detailed brief in response to the proposal in the 1986 Ontario budget for an Employee Share Ownership Plan to give a 15 percent rebate to employees who buy $2,000 a year of their company shares. Their research will be made available to unions and churches who are expected to respond to the Ontario government invitation for feed-back.

WODF also produced, in 1986, two publications to help worker cooperatives organize, plan, get themselves financed, and incorporate. The first, *Starting a Worker Co-operative, An Introduction,* a 40-page summary, sells for $7.50. The second, *The Handbook,* amplifies in 332 pages selling for $50. The coordinator and editor of both publications is Jack Quarter, a professor at the Ontario Institute for Studies in Education in Toronto. Jack is also the editor of a lively quarterly magazine called *Worker Co-ops,* which is published by the Centre for the Study of Co-operatives at the University of Saskatchewan in Saskatoon. This publication does a good job of keeping the worker co-op network informed about what brother co-ops and resource groups are doing, and looks at issues like co-ops and unions, and co-ops and government. It has been the source of many references in this book to worker cooperatives I was not able to visit.

WODF has been funded by church, government and other organizations. The sister organization, Co-operative Work Ltd., at the same address and with some of the same members, is the money-making arm. For a fee, it offers a broad range of services to worker cooperatives and community groups across Canada: organizational development, legal advice, member education, accounting, bookkeeping, financing, business planning, marketing, and referrals to outside sources of business help.

Co-operative Work answers several calls a week from groups seeking advice. It is also looking at potential foreign markets for distinctively Canadian food products, and may help set up a new worker co-op to export them wholesale.

In the last few years, it did financial projections for CRS in Vancouver, and drafted the business plan for the proposed expansion of The Big Carrot, and for several community organizations. When Canadian Porcelain in Hamilton was shut down, its 72 unionized workers formed Canadian Porcelain Co-operative Ltd., put down a $25,000 deposit and bid $1.1 million to buy the plant. Badly served by a major chartered accountancy, it called on Co-operative Work to write a business plan, but too late. The company, a manufacturer of high-voltage ceramic insulators used in electric power transmission, had been forced out of business by dumping of inferior products and by mismanagement. The receiver sold to the American competitor which had helped put the company out of business.

Another resource group, Hamilton's Christians for a Co-operative Society (CCS), was involved in the workers' attempt to save their jobs and control their work environment. Originally CCS was founded by church and community representatives as a think-tank on social affairs. They saw the Canadian Porcelain project as a way to help combat unemployment in industrial Hamilton, an active expression of their belief. It was CCS which met with the unionized workers to explain the worker cooperative option, and which launched a Fund for Workers' Enterprise to raise capital from business, labour, church and other community groups to help the worker buy-out and to provide the initial $25,000 deposit on the bid. They coordinated credit union and Ontario, municipal and regional government support. (The lender of choice was to be a syndicate including the Credit Union Central of Ontario, The Cooperators, Cumis (the credit unions' insurance company), with Hamilton-Wentworth Credit Union as the lead lender — a model of cooperation in the co-op movement, and a model for funding of future employee take-overs.)

CCS was as disappointed as the 72 workers at their failure. "You could cut the anger with a knife around here," says John Munster, a Hamilton management consultant who became the chief fund-raiser and full time unpaid volunteer during the campaign. "Especially when Flora MacDonald (then Minister of Employment) came to town to present a $200,000 cheque to the American owner to stabilize their operations," he added. The support group went underground after its failure with Canadian Porcelain, but is reviving its efforts now to launch a public education campaign, and is looking for another group to back as a pilot project.

B.C.'s Common Ownership Development Association (CODA) began in June 1983 as a volunteer steering committee representing 30 cooperative, church, community and labour groups. Near the beginning of 1984, CODA received a $50,000 Canada Works grant to cover the salaries of three people who had been active in consumer and housing co-ops. They expected to pay their overhead costs with supplementary funds from the co-op sector and other foundations.

CODA incorporated as a society rather than as a cooperative, since the members saw themselves as an educational resource rather than as a consulting firm, and as a non-profit society they were eligible for charitable tax status.

By fall 1984, nine months after they received funding, they had advised a number of groups about the worker co-op structure and ways it might apply to their particular circumstances. Kootenay West Wood Design obtained a LEAD grant (successor to LEAP) to help start a business building rustic furniture in Nelson. National Tradesmen was incorporated in Vancouver, as was M.O.M.s, a moving service. A women's support group was exploring the idea of a tour-guide company to give their members an economic base. In addition, CODA had helped to restructure and develop a training program for Isadora's restaurant, owned by its patrons in Vancouver's trendy False Creek area. And CODA staff had had long talks with the forward-looking branch manager of the credit union at 100 Mile House, in B.C.'s Cariboo country, where a mill closing left 150 unemployed. They had provided a package of material about worker co-ops and their role in community economic development, a guide for developing a community resource profile, and a business plan. The 100 Mile House Co-operative Association, with 68 members, was considering businesses including a tannery, a slaughterhouse and a silviculture venture. Later, it received LEAD money to establish a chopstick factory, using alder wood, which has few if any other commercial uses, and hoping to supply Asian markets. CODA members had developed pamphlets and newsletters and attended conferences in Edmonton and Seattle.

"We are just breaking up the rock, and trying to create the soil before we can plant anything in it, let alone harvest," said CODA's Dana Weber in Vancouver. "The need is there but the market isn't because the people with the need don't have the money," he added grimly.

CODA's Canada Works grant was not extended, and since February 1985 it has operated without funding or paid staff. Nevertheless, it has continued to advise developing groups in B.C.

When workers were locked out from their jobs at Loomis Armored Car, CODA helped them form a worker cooperative called Pacific Armoured Car to service credit union branches.

"Not a month goes by when CODA . . . isn't asked to speak or conduct workshops on worker ownership somewhere in the province," reported Dana Weber recently. "Many of these initiatives are coming from the province's community colleges which are acting as development catalysts in many of B.C.'s smaller centres."

He credits the innovative direction some Vancouver credit unions are taking to "a process of education and promotion which has been going on within the credit union system for the last two years."

Despite their success, Weber and the rest of the CODA board are losing enthusiasm for "continuing to flog it on a volunteer basis." He and another board member are now working for the Vancouver Inner City Housing Society. The society is considering putting some of its resources at CODA's disposal. According to Weber, this would help refloat the worker co-op initiative in B.C., and give Inner City more diversified activities outside the co-op housing sector. If the merger fails, CODA is likely to fold.

The WomenSkills Development Society is another new information, research and development group in B.C. It has had Canada Works and Labour Canada grants for a project called Economic Options for Women. Its goal is to encourage women to take part in planning and operating co-op businesses, and to provide some funding.

In Edmonton, Communitas, Inc., is the central office for cooperative housing development in the area. Its staff and volunteers also conduct social research on a consulting basis for community groups. In 1983, it spun off an advisory committee on worker co-ops to develop reference materials, including a bibliography, and put together a network of advisors. The group of six included community-oriented planners and organizers, among them Laird Hunter, the nationally known expert on cooperative law and manager of the Co-operative Union of Canada's Worker Co-operatives Program in 1985.

As with other resource groups, the Communitas committee has had problems getting funding, but nevertheless it has sponsored a conference on worker co-ops, and put together a resource package. This spring, it was helping develop a worker co-op to manufacture and install prefabricated construction components.

The C.F. Employment Resource Group in Winnipeg was only incorporated in July 1986. Its three members plan, like Co-operative Work in Toronto and CODA in Vancouver, to offer their services for a fee to developing worker cooperatives. They will supplement the support offered for free by the new Co-operative Development Department of the Manitoba government.

"There is a limit to what the province can offer," says branch representative Ken Bourquin. And groups planning a take-over or a new start can ask for provincial money to fund feasibility studies, perhaps by C.F. Employment.

This resource group is part of a complex of organizations founded by Dave Wetherow, director of Winnipeg's Association for Community Living, to help people with mental handicaps integrate as part of everyday society. Among the organizations is P.R.T. Manufacturing Co-op Ltd., the first worker co-op incorporated under the new Manitoba legislation. Eight workers make electric harnesses for boats and tractors, and one of the member-workers is mentally retarded. Like the other members of the co-op, he has one vote, which he exercises with the help of a family member or a friend/advocate.

Arctic Cooperatives Ltd. (ACL), the federation of 34 co-ops in the north, also now operates out of Winnipeg. Worker co-ops are still relatively unfamiliar to the north, although marketing and producer co-ops have been long established in most settlements. ACL is looking at worker co-ops seriously, and studying the feasibility of converting the Inuvik Parka company. They would give guidance to new starts as well as to conversions.

In the Maritimes, priests working out of St. Francis Xavier University in Antigonish, Nova Scotia, have traditionally encouraged cooperative action on all levels: education, housing, consumer and fishing co-ops, and worker co-ops. The support from St. F of X continues today. Duncan MacIntyre, a community organizer with the university's extension department, travels throughout the three Maritime provinces — speaking to a meeting about the general growth and development of co-ops in Montague, P.E.I., training the members of Umbrella Co-operative in New Glasgow, N.S. to do their own bookkeeping, organizing a conference in Antigonish . . . .

As a result, there are eight worker co-ops within consulting distance of Antigonish, including baking, woodcrafting, tree growing and marketing, musical instrument making, a theatre artists' co-op and a new group processing fish, as well as the gutsy Umbrella Co-op women who run a second-hand clothing store in New Glasgow, and contributed their adventures to this book.

As back-up, the provincial registrar in Nova Scotia, Fred Pierce, has managed to extend his mandate to help new groups as well as to register them. The Nova Scotia Department of Agriculture and Marketing puts out a whole range of practical publications to help worker co-ops, and most of them have been either written or edited by Fred.

The Maritimes movement got a boost at the end of 1985 when the St. F of X rep. gathered 35 participants from all the major cooperative associations, including Co-op Atlantic, credit unions, The Co-operators insurance, Nova Scotia Federation of Labour, government, and several existing worker co-ops. They agreed that government agencies could help, but often not in a way that was "timely, cheap, close-by, understanding and caring."

They hope, by establishing three provincial community development cooperatives, to help worker co-ops with their main problems: start-up, marketing, production, management and financial.

The Director of the Centre for the Study of Co-operatives at the University of Saskatchewan, professor Chris Axworthy, participated in a study tour to European and British worker cooperatives organized by the Co-operative Housing Foundation of Canada in 1984. At the end of his report on the tour, he draws some conclusions. Most important: "What are needed for the widespread development of worker cooperatives are initiatives which encourage small business and local control of those businesses, which provide all the necessary support services small busi-

ness needs and which encourage economic democracy and local control
of the economy . . . ."

Until the worker co-op sector is strong enough in numbers and in
resources to look after its own problems, it will need help, he points out,
either from government or the co-op sector or both.

Where to Get Help

Government

Alain Roy
Food Production and Distribution Division
Department of Agriculture
Government of Canada
Carling Building
930 Carling Ave.
Ottawa, Ont.
K1A 0C5   (613) 995-5880

Department of Co-operative Development
Government of Manitoba
700-215 Garry St.
Winnipeg, Man.
R3C 3P3   (204) 945-5796

Fred Pierce, Registrar
Cooperative Section
Department of Agriculture and Marketing
Government of Nova Scotia
Box 550
Truro, N.S.
B2N 5E3   (902) 895-1571

Direction des coopératives
Ministère de l'industrie et du commerce
710 Place d'Youville, 7e étage
Québec, P.Q.
G1R 4Y4   (418) 643-5232

Société de développement des coopératives
430 chemin Sainte-Foy
Québec, P.Q.
G1S 2J5   (418) 687-9221

Cooperation and Cooperative Development Department
Government of Saskatchewan
2055 Albert St.
Regina, Sask.
S4P 3V7   (306) 565-5786

Local Resource Groups

Communitas, Inc.
10551-123 St.
Edmonton, Alta.
T5N 1N9   (403) 482-5467

Dr. Phillip Newell
Christians for a Co-operative Society
116 Sterling Ave.
Hamilton, Ont.
L8J 4J5   (416) 527-6050, (416) 525-9140, ext. 4207

Groupe conseil des coopératives de travail de Montréal
3535 chemin Queen Mary, bureau 222
Montréal, P.Q.
H3V 1H8   (514) 340-6023

Richard Priestman
Cooperative Enterprises
100 Argyle St.
Ottawa, Ont.
K2P 1B6   (613) 233-6689

Amanda Shaughnessy/Peter Trotscha
Communityworks (financial and educational support)
200 Isabella St., 2nd floor
Ottawa, Ont.
K1S 1V7   (613) 238-5141

Worker Ownership Development Foundation
357 College St.
Toronto, Ont.
M5T 1S5   (416) 928-9568

Co-operative Work Ltd. (fee for service)
357 College St.
Toronto, Ont.
M5T 1S5   (416) 928-9568

Dana Weber
Common Ownership Development Association (CODA)
c/o Inner City Housing Society
1646 West Seventh Ave.
Vancouver, B.C.
V6J 1S5   (604) 734-8282

Melanie Conn
WomenSkills
No. 9, 4443 Irwin St.
Burnaby, B.C.
V5J 1X8   (604) 872-1128

Vancouver City Savings Credit Union
4205 Main St.
Vancouver, B.C.
V5V 3P8   (604) 879-5136

Dave Wetherow
C.F. Employment Resource Group
c/o 809-259 Portage Ave.
Winnipeg, Man.
R3B 2A9   (204) 947-1249

Other Non-governmental Agencies

Guy Adam
National Coordinator
Social and Educational Services
Canadian Labour Congress
2841 Riverside Dr.
Ottawa, Ont.
K1V 8X7   (613) 521-3400

Roy LaBerge
Co-operative Union of Canada
237 Metcalfe St.
Ottawa, Ont.
K2P 1R2   (613) 238-6711

Conseil canadien de la coopération
150 Avenue des Commandeurs
Lévis, P.Q.
G6V 6P8   (418) 835-1516

Fedération des coopératives de travailleurs et travailleuses
3424 rue Ontario Est
Montréal. P.Q.
H1W 1P9

Division développement coopératif et communautaire
Fedération des caisses populaires Desjardins de Québec
95 Avenue des Commandeurs
Lévis, P.Q.
G6V 6P6   (418) 835-2581

Duncan MacIntyre
Extension Dept.
St. Francis Xavier University
Antigonish, N.S.
B2G 1C0   (902) 863-3300

Newfoundland/Labrador Federation of Cooperatives
P.O. Box 13369, Station A
St. John's, Nfld.
A1B 4B7   (709) 726-9431

Education

Co-operative College of Canada
Library Services
141-105 St. W.
Saskatoon, Sask.
S7N 1N3   (306) 373-0474

Haut d'étude commerciale
Université de Montréal
2900 Edouard-Montpetit
Montréal, P.Q.
H3C 3J7   (514) 343-6111

Centre for the Study of Co-operatives
University of Saskatchewan
Saskatoon, Sask.
S7N 0W0   (306) 966-8503

Administration des coopératives
Laurentian University
Ramsey Lake Road
Sudbury, Ont.
P3E 2C6   (705) 675-1151

Institute for Research and Training for Co-operatives
University of Sherbrooke
2500 blvd. de l'Université
Sherbrooke, P.Q.
J1K 2R1   (819) 821-7000

Bibliography

Co-operative Housing Foundation of Canada, Ottawa, *Annual Report 1985*

Co-operative Union of Canada and Conseil canadien de la coopération, *A Co-operative Development Strategy for Canada,* Report of the National Task Force on Co-operative Development, Toronto, May 1984

Eva Hoare and Fred A Pierce, *Employment Co-operatives,* Nova Scotia Department of Agriculture and Marketing, Truro, N.S., 1983

Greg MacLeod, *New Age Business, Community Corporations That Work,* Canadian Council on Social Development, Ottawa, 1986

Ian MacPherson, *Each for All: A History of the Co-operative Movement in English Canada,* MacMillan, Toronto, 1979

Skip McCarthy, ed., *Employment Co-operatives: An Investment in Innovation,* Conference Proceedings, Centre for the Study of Co-operatives, University of Saskatchewan, Saskatoon

George Melnyk, *The Search for Community,* Black Rose, Montreal, 1985

David P. Ross and Peter J. Usher, *From the Roots Up, Economic Development as if Community Mattered,* Canadian Council on Social Development, Ottawa, 1986

Kris Schnack and Ted Jackson, *Worker Co-operatives: An Introduction,* Communityworks Inc., Ottawa, 1985

Joan Swain and Jack Smugler, *European Worker Co-operatives Study Tour, September 18 to October 7, 1983,* Communitas Inc., Edmonton

The Worker Ownership Development Foundation, *Starting a Worker Co-operative, An Introduction,* Toronto, 1986

-----*Starting a Worker Co-operative, A Handbook,* Toronto, 1986

Papers

Chris Axworthy, *Worker Co-operatives in Mondragon, the U.K. and France: Some Reflections,* Occasional Paper of the Centre for the Study of Co-operatives, University of Saskatchewan, Saskatoon

Chris Conforth, *The Role of Local Co-operative Development Agencies in Promoting Worker Co-operatives,* Co-operatives Research Unit, Open University, Milton Keynes, Great Britain, September 1984

David P. Ellerman, *What is a Worker Co-operative?* Industrial Cooperative Association, Somerville, MA, 1984

Raymond Donnelly, *Job Creation Through Worker Co-operatives, an Irish Perspective,* New University of Ulster, Derry, Ireland

John Jordan, *Developing Worker Cooperatives,* Working Paper #12, Co-op College of Canada, Saskatoon, April 1981

Terry Mollner, *Mondragon: A Third Way,* Trusteeship Institute Inc., Shutesbury, MA 1984

Robert F. Nixon, Treasurer of Ontario, *Employee Share Ownership Plans in Ontario,* Statement to the Legislature, June 17, 1986

Periodicals

Worker Co-ops, quarterly, c/o Centre for the Study of Co-operatives, University of Saskatchewan, Saskatoon

CUC News Services, monthly, Co-operative Union of Canada, Ottawa

Clippings

Paul A. Angelmayer, "Worker Owned and Operated Supermarket Yields Financial Success, Personal Rewards," *The Wall Street Journal,* New York, August 18, 1983

Jeff Faux, "Does Worker Ownership Work?" *Mother Jones,* San Francisco, July 1985

Lucinda Fleeson, "An Experiment by owner-workers celebrates year 1," *Philadelphia Inquirer,* October 16, 1983

Sherman Kreiner and Andrew Lamas, "Worker Ownership: Keeping APACE," *Win* magazine, New York, May 1983

Tamar Lewin, "Worker-Held Enterprises," *The New York Times,* April 17, 1984

Steve Schildroth, "How the Big Carrot Sprouted, The Story Behind Worker Co-ops in Ontario," *Catholic New Times,* June 3, 1984